Translation Theory and Practice in the Middle Ages

Edited by
Jeanette Beer

Studies in Medieval Culture, XXXVIII
Medieval Institute Publications

WESTERN MICHIGAN UNIVERSITY

Kalamazoo, Michigan—1997

Library of Congress Cataloging-in-Publication Data

Translation theory and practice in the Middle Ages / edited by
  Jeanette Beer)
      p.   cm. -- (Studies in medieval culture ; 38)
    "Held at the twenty-eighth International Congress on Medieval
Studies at Kalamazoo, Michigan, May 6–9, 1993"--Introduction.
    ISBN 1-879288-81-8 (casebound : alk. paper). -- ISBN 1-879288-82-6
(paperbound : alk. paper)
    1. Translating and interpreting--History.   I. Beer, Jeanettte.
II. International Congress on Medieval Studies (28th : 1993 :
Kalamazoo, Mich.)   III. Series.
P306.T7437 1997
418'.02--dc21   97-12898
                                                                    CIP

ISBN 1-879288-81-8 (casebound)
ISBN 1-879288-82-6 (paperbound)

Printed in the United States of America

Cover design by Stephen Beer

Translation Theory and Practice
in the Middle Ages

Contents

Introduction

The present volume arises out of a Translation Symposium on the "Theory and Practice of Translation in the Middle Ages" at the twenty-eighth International Congress on Medieval Studies at Kalamazoo, Michigan, May 6–9, 1993. With the sponsorship and enouragement of the Director of the Medieval Institute, Otto Gründler, I organized a series of sessions under such rubrics as "Translation Theory and Practice in the Middle Ages," "Translation and Authority," "Translation and Gender," "Translation and Literality," "Translation in Contexts of Bilingualism," and "Modern Translation of Medieval Texts." The Symposium was provocative by the multi-faceted nature of the papers and by the diversity and, sometimes, real divergence of the participants' points of view. And as editor, now, of that provocative set of papers, I make no attempt to disguise the diversity which was the *raison d'être* of the symposium.

Mention should be made here also of the student participants who were selected, on the recommendation of their graduate advisors, to attend the Translation Symposium. They were Elizabeth Claman, Catherine Conybeare, Tracy Crouch, Kevin Gustafson, Antonina Harbus, Marie Harker, Carol Martin, Helene Scheck, John Jay Thompson, and Ken Tiller. We were grateful for their presence and for the generosity of Otto Gründler that made it possible. I should like to take the opportunity here to thank also Deborah Starewich of Purdue University, who helped me to put together the manuscript of this volume.

Roger Wright's "Translation between Latin and Romance in the Early Middle Ages" argues controversially that translation between Latin and the Romance languages did not occur until the twelfth-century Renaissance because Latin and the Romance languages were not independent entities before that time. Several ninth- and tenth-century French texts that might suggest the contrary were, in Wright's view, "not translations so far as we can tell," and he (paradoxically?) refuses to talk of an "emerging" Romance between the tenth and thirteenth centuries, since "Romance had existed for centuries in everybody's mind and on everyone's lips, not least in a flourishing tradition of oral literature." The "conundrum," as he sees it, is the existence in the later Middle Ages of medieval Latin. He therefore reformulates the question "When did French/Spanish/Romance begin?" as "When did Medieval Latin begin?"

In England in the late ninth century, Alfred the Great instituted an ambitious program that encouraged the translation of important religious works (for example, Bede's *Historia ecclesiastica* and Boethius's *Consolatio philosophiae*) from Latin into Old English. In "The (M)other Tongue: Translation Theory and Old English," Robert Stanton discusses Louis Kelly's suggested components for a complete theory of translation (specification of function and goal; description and analysis of operations; and critical comment on relationships between goal and operations), notes the need in the Old English field for the first component, that is, specification of function and goal, then outlines various recent approaches that could in the future prove useful to fill the lacuna.

Douglas Kelly's "The *Fidus interpres*: Aid or Impediment to Medieval Translation and *Translatio*?" examines Horace's celebrated injunction "nec verbo verbum curabis reddere fidus interpres" and shows how the broad range of meanings of *interpretatio* gave rise to a broad notion of "translation." Horace had encouraged writers to take up subjects that had already been treated rather than something new. The new version was *not* to be a faithful translation or paraphrase of the old work, however, and, following that directive, medieval translation often involved literary invention. When translators aimed to render well-known sources with originality and "proprie communia dicere" [to treat in their own way what is common], they demonstrated the degree to which *translatio* and *interpretatio* were, in fact, strategies of medieval composition.

Ann W. Astell's "Translating Job as Female" also examines interpretation, that special form of invention by which an original was reworked and its inherent meaning glossed for a contemporary context. In a culture that saw heroic poetry as a masculine genre, St. Gregory the Great's

conception of the *Book of Job* as a *heroicum carmen* necessitated resolution
of the contradiction between the "feminine" text of the *Book of Job*'s central
Dialogue and the "masculine text" of the frame story (chapters 1, 2, and
the end of 42). Presenting Job allegorically as the champion of God's cause
versus Satan's attacks and, also, exploiting the figure of Job's wife whom the
(here) strong hero chastised for her temptress's invitation to curse God and
die, Gregory was able to reconcile Job, the "masculine" warrior, and Job,
the "feminine" sufferer. When Gregory's interpretive *translatio* was itself
translated into Griselda of Chaucer's The Clerk's Tale, the discontinuous
levels of interpretation, literal and allegorical, were now forced into a single
narrative line. Chaucer saw analogies between Job and Griselda as she was
trapped in a conflict between pacific suffering and a premarital vow never
to oppose Walter's wishes. The Chaucerian rereading overturned the misogynist Gregorian model of woman as weakness, however. Folly became
wisdom, weakness became strength, and the new female Job was greater
than Job.

In Madeline H. Caviness's "Gender Symbolism and Text Image Relationships: Hildegard of Bingen's *Scivias*," gender issues are again treated,
this time as they pertain to the pictorial illustration of a female visionary's
text. The Rupertsberg manuscript (formerly designated Wiesbaden, Hessisches Landesbibliothek, MS 1, but now lost) was made under Hildegard's
direction (ca. 1165). Because of this, Caviness argues, text and image in it
were inseparably linked, reflecting Hildegard's cognitive processes more
clearly than subsequent, more conventional illustrations. Some of the more
unusual pictorial representations (androgynous images, Life Giver Goddesses, women capable of procreating without men, and subverted patriarchal figures) even went beyond the text, exemplifying the Rupertsberg
manuscript's privileging of the feminine.

In "Scientific Translation and Translator's Glossing in Four Medieval
French Translators," Peter F. Dembowski analyzes various types of explanatory glosses that were used by medieval translators to improve the
accessibility of scientific texts in the vernacular. He begins with prefatory
statements, as exemplified in Jean de Meun's prologue to his Boethius, and
Oresme's *Proheme* to his *Livre de Ethiques d'Aristote*. He then examines, in

turn, redactorial interventions in which translators editorialized with section/chapter headings or rubrics; cross-referencing; and explanation.

Chapter seven moves from the practices of scientific glossators to those of two encyclopaedia translators; Claude Buridant compares the different approaches of two translators from the late thirteenth/early fourteenth century in his "La traduction du latin au français dans les encyclopédies médiévales . . . la traduction des *Otia imperialia* de Gervais de Tilbury par Jean de Vignay et Jean d'Antioche." The *Otia imperialia*, compiled for Emperor Otto IV ca. 1210, combined scientific didacticism with exotic travelogue material, thus posing syntactic, lexical, and stylistic problems for its translators. Buridant examines, through examples, Jean de Vignay's more rigorous literal style, calqued upon the Latin to produce functional and semantic equivalence, and Jean d'Antioche's freer *sensus de sensu* adaptation.

Louis G. Kelly's "Medieval Psalm Translation and Literality" outlines the history of Psalm translation into the vernacular during the Middle Ages. The four groups of source-versions (the *Vetus latina*, the Roman, the Gallican, and the *Psalterium iuxta Hebraeos*) yielded a variety of descendants. Further variety resulted from the differing purposes envisaged by each translator. Lexical choices were dictated by the pastoral responsibilities that the translator assumed toward his readers.

Rita Copeland proposes a model for Lollard translation in "Toward a Social Genealogy of Translation Theory: Classical Property Law and Lollard Property Reform." Positing that later resignifications of ancient theories of translation may be political transformations of the function of translation, she sees Horace's "difficile est proprie communia dicere" as acquiring new connotations in the Lollard context, so that a text is seen as collective property.

In "Written French and Latin at the Court of France at the End of the Middle Ages," Serge Lusignan analyzes the relation between French and Latin in the milieu of the royal court of France in the fourteenth and early fifteenth centuries. In a situation of diglossia where each language had its own areas of specialization (French being less suited to the high style of rhetoric, and Latin lacking words to convey oral information from legal testimony), the less fit language had a mimetic relationship with the other.

Lusignan concludes that in this particular context of bilingualism, Latin was the secondary language.

Bilingualism is again a central issue of Brian Merrilees' "Translation and Definition in the Medieval Bilingual Dictionary." Taking several extant dictionaries, the *Abavus* and the *Aalma*, the *Glossarium gallico-latinum*, the Latin-French Lexicon in Montpellier H110 and Stockholm N78, and the *Dictionarius* of Firmin Le Ver, Merrilees assesses the degree of bilingual competence implied by each and, thus, the nature and use of the Latin and French languages within the dictionary structure. These bilingual dictionaries provide evidence of the increasing growth and importance of the French language—the full use of that language in a unilingual dictionary was not many decades away.

The theme of Christopher Baswell's "*Troy Book*: How Lydgate Translates Chaucer into Latin" is *translatio imperii* in Europe in the later fourteenth and fifteenth centuries. Baswell sees Lydgate's *Troy Book*, ostensibly a translation of Guido delle Colonne's *Historia destructionis Troiae*, as a vehicle for the transmission of an imperial message. Its translator, registering England's imperial ambitions to replicate Arthur's conquests and to reverse the *translatio imperium* that brought Brutus to England, inserted a native rhetorical authority, Chaucer, within the Latin framework of the *Troy Book*. In translating Guido's Troy for Henry V, Lydgate attempted to revive Troy's empire for Britain.

Ian Johnson also explores the empowerment of the vernacular and the interaction of source-culture and target-culture in "Vernacular Valorizing: Functions and Fashionings of Literary Theory in Middle English Translation of Authority." Using as examples Nicholas Love's *Mirrour of the Blessed Lyf of Jesu Christ*, a "confident bid for vernacular canonicity" with its anglicized terminology derived from Latin prologues, and the Lollard Bible with its "take-away home exegesis kit" as clinching moments of vernacularity's self-awareness, Johnson compares the Latin-vernacular interaction to the dialectic between the rhetorical and hermeneutic aspects of translation.

In a final shift, the volume moves from the translation of works *in* the Middle Ages to modern translation of works *from* the Middle Ages. Two translators, William W. Kibler and David Staines, whose renderings of the complete works of Chrétien de Troyes appeared almost simultaneously, discuss translation from a modern perspective. Their chapters, "Translating Chrétien de Troyes: How Faithful?" and "On Translating Chrétien de Troyes," reveal that the theory and practice of translation continue to stimulate the same debates and display the same preoccupations that were evident in the theory and practice of translation in the Middle Ages.

Translation between Latin and Romance in the Early Middle Ages

Roger Wright

The Problem

The word *translate* in an English dictionary is usually glossed as "change from one language to another." This definition, however, raises the more basic question of how we can tell whether two related forms of speech are or are not different languages. The conclusion of this present paper is going to be that literal translation between Latin and any variety of Romance did not occur until the twelfth-century Renaissance. The earliest surviving texts of translations are of that date. This dating may at first seem surprisingly late, but I will argue that the reason for this apparent lateness is simply that before that century Latin and Romance were not the two independent languages required for translation to be needed, in the normal sense of the word.

The point at issue is this: how are we to explain, and when are we to date, the rise of the conceptual distinction between Medieval Latin and Early Romance? The first observation to make is that the advent of such a distinction is not inevitable. A single language can contain enormous variation within itself without this variation necessarily implying that the language has split into more than one separate and independent language. Modern English is one such single language; it may well be the case that in three hundred years' time it will no longer be normal to speak of American English, British English, Pakistani English, Australian English, etc., as different phenomena included within the single wide ambit of "English," but instead to refer to American, British, Pakistani and Australian, etc., as independent languages. That stage has not been reached

7

yet. If, indeed, by the year 2300 these separate entities develop their own phonetic individuality, systematized spelling, grammars, and vocabulary, then we might be justified in seeing those entities and others as having become actual separate languages. Only then would it begin to be sensible to consider the literal existence of translations between them. This would be a reasonable analogy for the emergence of the separate Romance languages as different conceptual entities out of the wide and heterogeneous single speech community originally known as Latin. However, the present English-speaking world offers no parallel to the subject under present consideration: translations between Latin and Romance.

From the perspective of a historical linguist, the strange and complicating factor in the Latin-Romance situation of the Middle Ages is not the development of the Romance languages but the existence of Medieval Latin. For there is a difference in modern academic perspectives here; to a medieval historian the emergence of the Romance languages seems strange, mysterious, and unnecessary, but the existence of Medieval Latin is simple and obvious; there it is, in hundreds of texts. To a historical linguist, the arrival of new linguistic features, such as those which we can now identify as being Romance, is only to be expected; all spoken languages evolve over time. Not only that, it seems to be natural for them to evolve in different ways in different places. The conceptual establishment of separately identified Romance languages, and the official elaboration of new written systems to represent them, are comprehensible phenomena; we understand the way in which new written systems can be invented, established, and eventually standardized, by authoritative writers, intellectuals, administrators, and educators, as happened in the later medieval Romance-speaking kingdoms. The question that seems in comparison baffling is this: why and how did the archaic language, which we now know as Medieval Latin, come to be both written and spoken alongside the Romance languages, as a conceptually separate entity? Why did people just not stop using the old written forms entirely? After all, the reason for inventing the new ones had been precisely that the old ones were so cumbersome. Furthermore, how could this old-fashioned Latin manage to maintain a separate phonetic existence, to such an extent that words which were historically the same came to have two pronunciations in the same geographical place, one

"Latin" and the other "Romance"? These are the phenomena that need explanation, although the consequent convenience of still having an international language with established pedagogical traditions is as obvious to the linguist as it is to the historian, and is indeed part of the answer.

Early Romance: Phonetics

It has proved tempting to investigators in the field of language history to be seduced by the idea that language evolution is comparable to the growth of a tree. A tree trunk splits naturally into different branches, the branches diverge and split again, etc. As a very rough approximation this image has some value, but unfortunately many Romance philologists have been tempted to apply this metaphor to far too early a date. Several have dated the earliest splits between separate Romance languages to two or three centuries before Christ. The split between Latin and Romance also often is thought (in this scholarly tradition) to be equally early. But slight divergences of pronunciation and vocabulary do not make for different languages, and this theory of early divergence is coming to seem increasingly unattractive, at a time when study after study is stressing the essential linguistic unity, both geographical and stylistic, of the early Middle Ages in the Romance-speaking area. Indeed, it now seems reasonable to argue that the later Roman Empire was a period of not only linguistic evolution but also linguistic convergence, rather than divergence. József Herman has argued, on the basis of minutely examined epigraphic evidence, and Alberto Varvaro has also deduced, on the basis of sociolinguistic argumentation, that even though there may well have been considerable intrinsic linguistic variation within any one geographical area in the first six or seven centuries A.D., there was no great divergence overall, nor any clear linguistic frontier between separable geographical areas (with the possible exception of Sardinia, which has natural borders);[1] that is to say, most of

---

[1] See József Herman, *Du latin aux langues romanes: Études de linguistique historique* (Tübingen: Niemeyer, 1990); and Alberto Varvaro, "Latin and Romance: Fragmentation or Restructuring?" in *Latin and the Romance Languages in the Early Middle Ages*, ed. Roger

the important developments of colloquial Early Romance speech at that time could be found over most of the former Empire, rather than being confined to the areas where they were destined, much later, to be promoted to a role in one of the eventual Romance standards. Thus the preaching expertise of Martín de Braga, who came originally from sixth-century Pannonia to preach in the western part of the Iberian Peninsula, implies a continuing linguistic unity in the whole Romance area (since they understood him and he also understood them); in a similar way, St. Eligius, in seventh-century France, had wide contacts—although not, probably, from Pannonia—with similar comprehensibility.[2]

Another metaphor often suggested for the evolution of Early Romance is that of the lake, in which waves of change originating in one place can ripple out and affect the whole.[3] Varvaro has also used a building image, and written of the gradual collapse of the universal standard "dome" that kept the geographically separate supporting arches together in one construction as part of the same Romance ensemble (an image I myself have attempted to draw).[4] Whatever image of the linguistic state of the Early Medieval Romance-speaking world we have in mind, though, it is being increasingly accepted by the specialists in the field that at least until the late eighth century it formed one speech community, with the social and stylistic internal variation that is normal in all such wide speech communities.

Wright (London and New York: Routledge, 1991; paperback repr., Philadelphia: Penn State Press, 1996), pp. 44–51.

[2]Michel Banniard, "Normes culturelles et réalisme langagier en Galice au VIᵉ siècle: les Choix de Martín de Braga," in *Congreso Internacional: XIV Centenario del Concilio III de Toledo* (Toledo: Diputacíon Provincial, 1991), pp. 661–76, and "Latin et communication orale en Gaule franque: le témoignage de la 'Vita Eligii'," in *Le Septième Siècle: Changement et Continuités*, ed. Jacques Fontaine and J. N. Hillgarth (London: Warburg Institute, 1992), pp. 58–86.

[3]Yakov Malkiel, "Alternatives to the Classic Dichotomy Family Tree/Wave Theory? The Romance Evidence," in *Language Change*, ed. Irmengard Rauch and Gerald F. Carr (Bloomington: Indiana University Press, 1983), pp. 192–256.

[4]See Varvaro, "Latin and Romance"; and Roger Wright, "Los cambios lingüísticos medievales," in *Actes du XXᵉ Congrès international de linguistique et philologie romanes: Université de Zurich, 6–11 avril 1992*, ed. Gerold Hilty, 5 vols. (Tübingen: Francke, 1993), 2: 609–20.

The point that concerns us directly is that some Romance philologists have postulated not only that there were separate Romance languages in existence by the end of the Roman Empire, but in addition that there was already then in existence a spoken archaic Latin language conceptually separate from those Romance languages, in the same way as Latin and the Romance languages are conceptually separate now. Since there has been no convincing evidence adduced in favor of this idea, it might be expected that it would have been discarded by now. I have been trying to weaken the hold of this idea that Latin coexisted with Early Romance in these earliest medieval centuries, in approximately thirty studies prepared over the last fifteen years.[5] What the reconstruction philologists had indeed succeeded in doing was show, beyond any doubt at all, that the phonetic characteristics of Romance speech in the early Middle Ages were rather different from those of spoken Latin as we know it now, that is, as we have known it for the last thousand years or more. For example—to be technical for a moment—phonemic vowel quantity had disappeared; velar consonants had been fronted before a front vowel; final [-m] had disappeared; many intervocalic plosives had voiced, and subsequently many double consonants had been simplified, in western areas. The early date for these phonetic developments is undeniable, and this realization is Robert Hall's great achievement.[6] However, the next step taken in the argument, that is, to state that Latin and Romance were phonetically quite different in the very early Middle Ages, as they are now, depends on the prior and unargued assumption that a separate Latin language, with distinct phonetics, already existed by then alongside this evolving Early Romance. This assumption is unjustifiable and *a priori* improbable. In 1982 I pointed out that the genuine phonetic discoveries made with the Romance philological reconstruction techniques can still be preserved even if we postpone the postulation of a separate coexisting spoken Latin non-Romance phonetic system until the end of the eighth century, which is the date at which it

---

[5]Many of my studies are collected in *Early Ibero-Romance* (Newark, Del.: Juan de la Cuesta, 1995).

[6]See Robert A. Hall, Jr., *Proto-Romance Phonology* (New York: Elsevier, 1976).

seems to have been reinvented for the purpose which has sustained it to the present day, as an international standard.[7]

Early Romance: Grammar

The nature of linguistic evolution is not identical at all levels, however, and in the realms of grammar, as opposed to phonetics, the situation is rather more interesting in detail and complex in chronology. Reconstruction of Early Romance grammar has made considerable advances, to the extent that we can be fairly sure that many of the grammatical developments that characterize Romance already existed in the seventh century and probably earlier, for example, the periphrastic future and perfect tenses formed with the auxiliary *habeo* (and others); the use of *ille* and *ipse* as definite articles; the spread of prepositions with weakened meanings to compensate for the increasingly unfashionable oblique case endings (genitive, dative, and ablative); the preference for *quod* clauses over *ut* clauses; etc. In the case of phonetic evolution, the reconstruction scholars have assumed that the arrival of new pronunciations was usually accompanied by the loss of the corresponding old phonetic phenomena, and on the whole that assumption may well be largely justified; but regarding grammar, there is no reason to presume that existing features disappeared quickly from normal usage merely because new features had arisen. The periphrastic perfect forms, for example, have still not ousted the already existing preterite forms in spoken Romance, except in northern France and parts of Catalonia, and they are still more rare than the original preterite tense forms in northwestern Spain. Many of the already existing grammatical features almost certainly continued to be used in vernacular speech for a long time alongside the new ones, and even after they came to be spoken more rarely, if that is what indeed happened to them, they were still going to be intelligible for several centuries by virtue of being found in existing texts and being continually read aloud.

---

[7]Roger Wright, *Late Latin and Early Romance in Spain and Carolingian France* (Liverpool: Cairns, 1982).

Reading Aloud

Reading aloud was an important activity in these centuries. It united the written word with an unlettered audience. Even the liturgy was mostly intelligible as a result, if read aloud sympathetically. Jacques Fontaine calls it "une culture liturgique donnée et reçue dans l'oralité."[8] Malcolm Parkes has shown that much of the energy of linguists in the early Middle Ages went into developing what he calls a "Grammar of Legibility," as they moved over time from using *scripta continua* without punctuation symbols or even gaps between the words, towards the production of texts with diacritics of various kinds designed to aid comprehensible reading aloud;[9] in the Early Medieval period it seems that liturgical manuscripts were particularly likely to have the stressed syllables diacritically marked to aid both reading aloud and comprehension by the congregation. Isidore of Seville himself referred to reading aloud from a *codex distinctus,* that is, one endowed with such punctuation symbols. Careful grammar and careful reading are, of course, aids to comprehension rather than a hindrance.

Historians are increasingly coming to the conclusion that reading aloud in the Early Medieval Romance-speaking areas still made texts of any kind intelligible to interested but illiterate listeners. (This is a diametrically different conclusion from the much-repeated and previously influential perspective presented by Ferdinand Lot in 1931.[10]) Indeed, society was still able to function on a basis of written documentation for precisely that reason. We know, for example, that the reading of saints' lives (and deaths, *Passiones*) was often a highly emotional event for the listeners; Peter Brown

---

[8]Jacques Fontaine, "Bilan du Colloque," in *Le Septième Siècle*, ed. Fontaine and Hillgarth, p. 278.

[9]Malcolm Parkes, *Scribes, Scripts and Readers: Studies in the Communication, Presentation, and Dissemination of Medieval Texts* (London: Hambledon, 1991); and idem, *Pause and Effect* (Aldershot: Scolar, 1992).

[10]Ferdinand Lot, "A quelle époque a-t-on cessé de parler latin?" *Bulletin du Cange* 6 (1931): 97–159.

even called it a "psychodrame."[11] This assumption of the intelligibility of the read text also applied to ninth-century France; as McKitterick points out, countless Carolingian documents prepared in Latin were intended to be read aloud there to all sorts of people, rather than being the exclusive intellectual preserve of an educated élite.[12] Kelly has studied the tax-exemption documents carried by Carolingian merchants to be shown to toll-collectors en route; Nelson has shown that the whole of Nithard's *History*, not merely the Strasbourg Oaths, was intended to be read aloud to his largely unlettered military colleagues.[13] The same assumption applied in Early Medieval Spain, up to and including the twelfth century in many respects, where interested parties regularly signed or marked documents to indicate that they had heard the text read aloud and could confirm its correctness.

This topic forms the substance of the exceptionally important work of the French linguistic historian Michel Banniard. In his book *Viva Voce*, Banniard has shown from a minute reading of textual detail, and beyond any doubt at all, that St. Augustine, Gregory the Great, and St. Isidore of Seville wrote on the assumption that their own work would be intelligible when read aloud to the Early Romance speakers of North Africa, Italy, and Spain, respectively; and that the eighth-century Merovingian hagiographers still felt the same, although they were by then increasingly conscious of a need to write in a comparatively simple style in order to achieve this.[14]

There is no sign that any translators were needed in these Early Romance communities in order to convey written texts to the illiterate. What indeed were needed, and often were mentioned explicitly, were good

---

[11]Peter Brown, *The Cult of the Saints: Its Rise and Function in Latin Christianity* (Chicago: University of Chicago Press, 1982), p. 82.

[12]Rosamond McKitterick, *The Carolingians and the Written Word* (Cambridge: Cambridge University Press, 1989).

[13]See Susan Kelly, "Trading Privileges from Eighth-Century England," *Early Medieval Europe* 1 (1992): 3–28; and Janet Nelson, "Public *Histories* and Private History in the Work of Nithard," *Speculum* 60 (1985): 251–93.

[14]Michel Banniard, *Viva Voce: Communication écrite et communication orale du IVᵉ siècle au IXᵉ siècle en occident latin* (Paris: Institut des Études Augustiniennes, 1992); see also his "Latin et communication orale," in *Le Septième Siècle*, ed. Fontaine and Hillgarth.

readers-aloud, *lectores*. Isidore of Seville regarded being a *lector* as one of the basic stages in training for the Church, which would imply that in seventh-century Spain this was a skill acquired by many people. Readers-aloud were given instructions to be competent, clear, interested, and persuasive, as is desirable for any language; but they were never told to translate. On the contrary, they had to stick to the words of the written text. So did preachers.

There are several linguistically interesting consequences we can draw from the insistence on *lectores* but the absence of reference to translators. First, on the whole, listeners understood most of the morphology and grammar, even if not many of them would have been likely often to use actively ablative endings on nouns or synthetic passive verb forms, etc. Second, the pronunciation of the individual words was intelligible enough for an unlettered audience to recognize those words; this in turn implies that the *lectores* spoke the words carefully, yes, but with their normal vernacular pronunciation of the time and place, overcoming naturally any detailed discrepancies between speech and writing (such as silent letters) in the same way as English-readers do now; once the readers recognized what word the written form represented, they read that word with its normal pronunciation in the ordinary way. Third, though—and this is a consequence that modern scholars (including Banniard) have been less ready to grasp— we have to conclude that our modern projection into those centuries of a distinction between two linguistic systems, Latin and Romance, is anachronistic. It is not the case that Latin and Romance existed then as separate systems that could be distinguished then, or can be distinguished now; nor is it the case that they were separate systems but with many coinciding features and mutual interferences, as Bruguera and others suggest.[15] It is not the case, either, that Latin and Romance both existed but then mixed together into a single "ensemble," as Banniard tends to suggest.[16] Rather, I suggest, such a distinction between two systems had not been invented yet, and all the linguistic features in use were part of the same language. Stylistic and sociolinguistic variation existed, naturally, but not neatly

---

[15]Jordi Bruguera, *Història del lèxic català* (Barcelona: Enciclopedia Catalana, 1985), p. 19.

[16]In particular in his *Genèse culturelle de l'Europe: V^e–VIIIe siècle* (Paris: Du Seuil, 1989).

between one stratum that we would now think of as Latin and another that we would now think of as Romance. The complex speech of the eighth-century Romance area was monolingual; it had its own status and its own internal validity, which should not be merely measured in terms of the perspectives of other ages.[17] Eighth-century Romance indeed did contain linguistic features—in pronunciation, grammar, and vocabulary—that were destined to die out later; it indeed did contain other features that had only arrived since the end of the Roman Empire, and would continue into later Romance languages; but nobody then thought of their own language in those terms. Their language was a contemporary language in itself, alive, versatile, vital, flexible, just as modern English is. It makes no more sense to say that the language of these Early Medieval communities was a mixture of Latin and Romance than it would be to say that twentieth-century English is a mixture of sixteenth-century English and twenty-fourth-century English. They had their own single contemporary language, and operated as well with that as we do with ours, as Díaz y Díaz has argued for seventh-century Spain and Alarcos Llorach for tenth-century Spain.[18]

There is one further important consequence of this perspective that is worth pointing out: that the uneducated population of the Early Romance world were not necessarily thereby cut off from written culture, since texts could be communicated to them orally. In a more general way, modern scholars working in a number of medieval European areas, from Iceland (where Njál's Saga has echoes of Gregory the Great's *Dialogues*) down to Spain, are coming to see that there was no clear strict divide between clerical and non-clerical culture.[19] An Early Medieval image is still

---

[17]See my "Complex Monolingualism in Early Romance," in *Linguistic Perspectives on the Romance Languages: Selected Papers from the 21st Linguistic Symposium on Romance Languages* (Amsterdam and Philadelphia: John Benjamins, 1993), pp. 377–88 (now in *Early Ibero-Romance*, chap. 1; see n. 5).

[18]See Manuel C. Díaz y Díaz, "El latín de España en el siglo VII: lengua y escritura según los textos documentales," in *Le Septième Siècle*, ed. Fontaine and Hillgarth, pp. 25–40; and Emilio Alarcos Llorach, *El español, lengua milenaria (y otros escritos castellanos)* (Valladolid: Ámbito, 1982).

[19]See Lars Lönnroth, *Njál's Saga: A Critical Introduction* (Berkeley: University of California Press, 1976), pp. 121–23; and Roger Collins, "Literacy and the Laity in Early Mediaeval

sometimes presented to us, even now, of a tiny number of educated monks separated from the mass of other inhabitants who had no part in their world; but this image can only be wrong. Sermons, letters, documents, wills, orders, saints' lives, histories, tax certificates, epitaphs, etc., were communicable and communicated. Conversely, it appears that *lectores* and notaries were also available for general hire if anyone needed anything to be written down. Literacy itself was more widespread in seventh-century Spain than is usually allowed, as can be seen from the texts on slates that survived only because they were not as biodegradable as papyrus or wax;[20] but an individual's lack of literacy does not now, and certainly did not then, imply stupidity. Let us at last give back some dignity, and allow some participation in their own society, to the hundreds of thousands of Early Romance speakers, for whom written texts were accessible in oral form, without any need for translation.

Writing

The hypothesis of Latin-Romance translation in reading aloud is thus, in my view, untenable. The hypothesis of the existence of translation in the reverse direction, however, that is, when writing, is altogether more interesting. Some scholars have confidently stated that this period contained one spoken language (Romance) and a different written language (Latin). Some believe this to be inevitably so in any society; Parkes states baldly that "to convert the spoken word into the written word is a process of translation";[21] it has been said that transcribing oral literature onto paper is inevitably a kind of translation.[22] George Steiner, in *After Babel*, sees all

---

Spain," in *The Uses of Literacy in Early Mediaeval Europe*, ed. Rosamond McKitterick (Cambridge: Cambridge University Press, 1990), pp. 109–33.

[20]Isabel Velázquez Soriano, *Las Pizarras Visigodas: edición crítica y estudio* (Murcia: Universidad de Murcia, 1989).

[21]Parkes, *Scribes, Scripts and Readers*, p. 25. See also Helmut Bertschin, "Mittellatein und Romanisch: I," *Zeitschrift für Romanische Philologie* 103 (1987): 1–7.

[22]See, for example, Harriet Goldberg, "Another Look at Folk Narrative Classification: The Judeo-Spanish *Romancero*," in *Hispanic Medieval Studies in Honor of Samuel G. Armistead*,

communication even within the same language as a kind of translation, and while I see what he means, that is not the normal sense of the word *translation,* as being used in this paper.[23] I prefer Díaz y Díaz's reference to the "stylization that the written language always presupposes."[24]

Writing in the Early Romance area became increasingly complicated as the centuries went by. Words had traditional spellings deemed to be not only traditional but also "correct," and as a consequence any other spelling was deemed "incorrect," especially if it was closer to the spoken form. Spellings were not attempts at phonetic transcriptions of actual speech any more than they are now; written forms represented attempts to achieve the traditionally correct spelling;[25] it is worth remembering that the word *(cor)rectus* originally meant not just "correct" but, further, "corrected." Orthography must have been taught, somehow. I have examined elsewhere what surviving evidence can tell us about the orthographical training of scribes in tenth-century Galicia, in northwestern Spain, and concluded that the spelling of some words was taught to apprentices as whole units, but that for writing words not on that list, vernacular syllables and individual sounds were taught as requiring specified written counterparts.[26] This is not a surprising conclusion, since the same mixture of techniques is found in English-speaking primary schools today. Such writing and reading abilities are part of many people's native speaker competence within their vernacular, rather than representing different languages entirely. What complicates our assessment of the tenth-century Romance data, however, is that the correct method of writing involved the addition to nouns and adjectives of

---

ed. E. Michael Gerli and Harvey L. Sharrer (Madison, Wisc.: Hispanic Seminary of Medieval Studies, 1992), pp. 153–62, where she quotes Elizabeth C. Fine, *The Folklore Text: From Performance to Print* (Bloomington: Indiana University Press, 1984).

[23]George Steiner, *After Babel: Aspects of Language and Translation*, 2nd ed. (Oxford and New York: Oxford University Press, 1992).

[24]Díaz y Díaz, "El latín de España," p. 27, n. 6.

[25]See Carmen Pensado Ruiz, "How Was Leonese Vulgar Latin Read?" in *Latin and the Romance Languages*, ed. Wright, pp. 190–204.

[26]Roger Wright, "La enseñanza de la ortografía en la Galicia de hace mil años," *Verba* 18 (1991): 5–25 (English version in *Early Ibero-Romance*, chap. 14).

several case-endings, and to verbs of several inflectional endings, that were rarely, if at all, used actively in speech; and also involved the avoidance, where reasonable, of several other morphological and syntactic phenomena that indeed were used actively in speech. That is, the stark Latin-Romance dichotomy did not exist then, but there did exist a theoretical distinction between, on one hand, those linguistic phenomena that were strictly allowed to appear on papyrus, wax tablet, slate, or parchment, as decreed in the *Ars Minor* of Donatus and the linguists in his tradition, and, on the other hand, those phenomena of the language that were not supposed to be thus recorded. This inherited distinction was part of the basis on which a later distinction, between separate written languages, would be built.

It is not reasonable, then, to claim that for an Early Romance speaker in ninth- and tenth-century Spain to compose a text in writing was an act of translation, just as it would not be reasonable to claim that writing acceptable English today involves translation from a different language we can call spoken English. Writing involved polishing, formalizing, adding certain well-known details, such as grafting passive morphology on to verbs. Once again, Banniard's work indicates the key; when discussing the voluble Christian writers of ninth-century Moslem Spain, some of whom wrote in an exaggeratedly formal manner, Banniard points out that they thought of themselves as "polishing" their language in their texts.[27] To refer to a comparatively unformalized text, Álvaro de Córdoba uses the phrase *impolito textu*;[28] to refer to a more formalized text, he uses the phrase *sententiis per Artem Donati politis*;[29] Álvaro thus used the verb *polire*, "to polish," to refer to his own process of written composition, as indeed Martín de Braga had done three centuries earlier.

We can glimpse the polishing process actually in operation in the late ninth-century *Chronicle of Alfonso III*, written at the instruction of, and conceivably even by, King Alfonso III of Asturias. Several manuscripts of this

---

[27]Banniard, *Viva Voce*, chap. 8.

[28]See Álvaro de Córdoba, *Epistola* 9.1, ed. Juan Gil, *Corpus Scriptorum Muzarabicorum* (Madrid: CSIC, 1973), p. 211; and Banniard, *Viva Voce*, p. 445.

[29]Álvaro de Córdoba, *Epistola* 2.1, in Gil, *Corpus Scriptorum*, p. 151; and Banniard, *Viva Voce*, p. 447.

Chronicle survive, and we can see how successive versions gain more and more passive verbs, for example; or we can see that at least in the modern editions that preserve the manuscript readings.[30] Now that we can be sure that the least formalized surviving version of this *Chronicle* is actually the one composed earliest, the process we have to envisage is a polishing of their native vernacular Early Medieval Romance into a smarter written form.[31] This has other parallels: modern Shakespeare scholars often now interpret textual variation as a symptom of authorial revision rather than of scribal or printerly corruption. Any casual jottings that survive by chance, such as the tenth-century list of cheeses from León, or the scraps in Merovingian votive offerings, have not been smartened in such an obsessive way; such texts represent an earlier and less rigorous stage of scribal self-satisfaction.[32]

This insight has important consequences for our study of those works that deliberately adopt a comparatively simple style; in the case of the Merovingian hagiographers studied by Banniard and Van Uytfanghe, or of the syntactic characteristics of the sermons of Martín de Braga as studied by Carmen Codoñer, or the lexical characteristics of the same sermons as studied by Banniard, the point is not that the authors deliberately have simplified an originally more complex production but that the authors have not bothered to take the usual formalizing and polishing steps that in other cases they would have deemed desirable.[33] That is, a

---

[30]See Jan Prelog, *Die Chronik Alfons' III: Untersuchung und Kritische Edition der vier Redaktionen* (Frankfurt a.m.: P. D. Lang, 1980); and *Crónicas asturianas: crónica de Alfonso III (Rotense y "A Sebastián"): crónica albeldense (y "profética")*, ed. Juan Gil Fernández et al. (Oviedo: Servicio de Publicaciones, Universidad de Oviedo, 1985).

[31]See Roger Wright, "Textos asturianos de los siglos IX y X: ¿latín bárbaro o romance escrito?" *Lletres Asturianes: boletin oficial de l'Academia de la Llingua Asturiana* 41 (1991): 20–34 (English version in *Early Ibero-Romance*, chap. 11).

[32]For the cheeses see Ramón Menéndez Pidal, *Orígenes del español, estado lingüístico de la Península ibérica hasta el siglo XI* (Madrid: Espasa-Calpe, 1926), pp. 24–25; for Merovingian offerings see David Ganz and Walter Goffart, "Charters Earlier than 800 from French Collections," *Speculum* 65 (1990): 906–32.

[33]See Banniard, *Viva Voce*, chap. 7; Marc Van Uytfanghe, "Le latin des hagiographes mérovingiens et la protohistoire du français," *Études Médiévales* (Ghent: Romanica Gandensia, 1976), pp. 5–89; Carmen Codoñer, "Rasgos configuradores de un estilo 'popular',"

text of this kind is closer to the writers' own native speech as well as to that of their audience.

Even in the eleventh century, the famous Riojan Glosses of San Millán and Silos are still in the same way best interpreted as being, sometimes at least, deliberately not formalized into traditional morphology and orthography. The conclusions of much of the recent research into these Glosses supports the theory that their purpose is to aid the comprehensible reading aloud of the text. Birte Stengaard showed how this purpose was sometimes facilitated by reading the words in a more accessible order, under the stimulus of written diacritics invented to aid that process (as had become common practice elsewhere, e.g., in the British Isles);[34] and perhaps, as Emiliano proposes, with occasional word-substitution (what Emiliano calls "conversión grafolexémica").[35] Despite these eleventh-century sophistications, however, even the more adventurous glosses are evidence not of interlingual translation but of the absence of the usual formalization; except for the two phrases in Basque, the equivalents chosen by the glossers are still alternatives from within the same language. The majority of the words in the manuscript text are left unglossed. The one completely new sentence among the Glosses, however, in *Em.* 89, shows an extended syntactic equivalent and is certainly significant. It can be seen as representing another small but vital step along the road to eventual conceptual separation in those monasteries, as Alvar's recent account implies.[36] It is, incidentally, essential for literary scholars who wish to comment on linguistic matters of this sort to keep up to date with the research of the historical Hispanic

---

in *Estudios de lingüística y lengua literaria*, vol. 1 of *Serta Philologica F. Lázaro Carreter: Natalem diem sexagesimum celebranti dicata* (Madrid: Cátedra, 1983), pp. 109–18; and Banniard, "Normes culturelles."

[34]Birte Stengaard, "The Combination of Glosses in the *Códice Emilianense 60* (*Glosas Emilianenses*)," in *Latin and the Romance Languages*, ed. Wright, pp. 177–89.

[35]Antònio Emiliano, "'Latín y romance' y las glosas de S. Millán y de Silos," in *Actas del Primer Congreso Anglo-Hispano*, vol. 1, *Lingüística*, ed. Ralph Penny (Madrid: Castalia, 1993), pp. 235–44.

[36]Manuel Alvar, "De las Glosas Emilianenses a Gonzalo de Berceo," *Revista de Filología Española* 69 (1989): 5–38.

linguists (in this case also including, in addition to Stengaard and Emiliano, Díaz y Díaz, Alarcos Llorach, Wright, Bézler, and Cano Aguilar[37]). John Walsh, in his recently published posthumous article co-written with Alan Deyermond, for example, accepts both the tenth-century date now known to be wrong and Menéndez Pidal's view, expressed in 1926, that these glosses were transcribed from pre-existing Latin-Romance glossaries, a suggestion that is, for several reasons, impossible to support now.[38]

Although the process of Early Medieval composition through formalization as visualized here may seem complex, for those scribes used to it, it must at a later time have seemed hard to avoid putting on this veneer when at last it became respectable to write complete texts without applying such formalization; the thirteenth-century Leonese documentation analysed by Emiliano shows that notarial expertise in avoiding the Latinate disguise on all levels (spelling, morphology, syntax, and vocabulary) did not come all at once.[39] For in northwestern Spain, the traditional written composition process survived well into the twelfth century, even in important legal documents such as the *Fueros*; for an example, see my rephrasing of Lapesa's conclusions concerning the *Fuero de Valfermoso de las Monjas* of 1189, as representing a case of only partial formalization rather than of incompetent Latinization.[40] There is a famous tale of Peter of

[37] See especially Díaz y Díaz, "El latín de España"; Llorach, *El español*, Part I; Wright, *Late Latin and Early Romance* and "La función de las Glosas de San Millán y de Silos" in *Critique et édition des textes*, vol. 9 of *Actes du XVIIͤ Congrès International de Linguistique et de Philologie Romanes* (Aix-en-Provence and Marseille: Université de Provence, 1986), pp. 211–19 (English version in *Early Ibero-Romance*, chap. 15); François Bézler, "Pour une revision de la date des Gloses de Silos," *Recherches Ibériques* 2/2 (1984): 1–10, and "Pénitence chrétienne et or musulman dans l'Espagne du Cid," *Recherches Ibériques* 2/3 (1985): 68–90; and Rafael Cano Aguilar, *Análisis filológico de textos* (Madrid: Taurus, 1991), chap. 2.

[38] John K. Walsh and Alan D. Deyermond, "*Locus* and Literature in the Spanish Middle Ages," *Journal of Hispanic Research* 1 (1992): 35–52 (at 39–40); Menéndez Pidal, *Orígenes del Español*.

[39] Emiliano, "Latin or Romance? Graphemic Variation and Scripto-Linguistic Change in Medieval Spain," in *Latin and the Romance Languages*, ed. Wright, pp. 233–47.

[40] Roger Wright, "El latín y el ladino (siglos XI–XII)," *Actas del XIX Congreso Internacional de Lingüística y Filología Románicas*, vol. 5 (Coruña: Barrié de la Maza, 1993), pp. 61–70

Cluny hiring a Maestro Pedro de Toledo to translate a text from Arabic into Romance speech in Toledo in 1142, and also hiring Peter of Poitiers to polish that Romance speech into writing, using the verb *polire* as usual;[41] this phraseology shows that the distinction being made in the present paper between translating (e.g., turning Arabic into Romance) and polishing (e.g., from vernacular Romance into formal style) was a genuine distinction that was felt in those terms at the time. It was the normal practice.[42] Even later in that century, Gerard of Cremona had the same task of listening to a *mozárabe* translating orally an Arabic original and then polishing that vernacular into the internationally accepted written standard.[43] The gestation process of the Latin-Romance conceptual dichotomy took so long in the Iberian Peninsula that evidence from the Peninsula is crucial to our modern understanding of that process, from Martín de Braga, Isidore, Álvaro de Córdoba, Alfonso III to the Glosses and beyond, right through to the Toledo scholars and the texts of the early thirteenth century.

Medieval Latin

Yet we still have not come up with an answer to the initial conundrum, of the existence in the later Middle Ages of Medieval Latin as a separate language alongside the normal vernacular Romance. In order to explain what brought that situation about, with its eventual cumbersome need for Latin-Romance translations, we can follow a time-honored tradition: we can blame it on the English. As we have seen, in the Romance-speaking world, learning *Grammatica* meant learning to write the language one already

---

(English version in *Early Ibero-Romance*, chap. 17); Rafael Lapesa, "El Fuero de Valfermoso de las Monjas," in *Homenaje a Álvaro Galmés de Fuentes*, vol. 1 (Oviedo: Universidad de Oviedo, 1985), pp. 43–98.

[41]James Kritzeck, *Peter the Venerable and Islam* (Princeton: Princeton University Press, 1964), p. 212.

[42]Clara Foz, "Pratique de la traduction en Espagne au Moyen Âge: les travaux tolédans," in *The Medieval Translator: II*, ed. Roger Ellis (London: Center for Medieval Studies, Queen Mary and Westfield College, University of London, 1991), pp. 29–44.

[43]Richard Fletcher, *Moorish Spain* (London: Weidenfeld & Nicolson, 1992), esp. p. 151.

spoke. The British Isles, however, already at the time of Bede, were no longer a native Romance-speaking community, and *Grammatica* had to be taught and learned there as a foreign language. The difference between Anglo-Saxon and Latin, and between Celtic and Latin, was obvious. For a while they were even written with separate symbols (runes versus an alphabet). Translation was necessary whenever a Latin text, such as a sermon, had to be communicated outside the Church. Translation was also necessary in the other direction, whenever a native Anglo-Saxon speaker wrote in Latin. In the British Isles, *Grammatica* was taught and learnt *ab initio* on the basis of the reading aloud of written forms, and the pronunciations taught, insofar as we can reconstruct them, involved a peculiar and unnatural habit, viz., the oral production of a specified sound for each already written letter. Hence Latin Grammar was called in Anglo-Saxon *Staefcraft*, where *staef* meant "written letter." This technique, giving a sound to each letter, is how we all read Latin aloud now, but that was certainly not the case in the Early Romance-speaking world. The decisive point at which we can see the conceptual difference between Latin and Romance starting to take root is when this Anglo-Saxon tradition became politically powerful in the Romance cultural world; that is, when Alcuin of York and his colleagues tried to impose this artificial *Grammatica* as the norm in the Carolingian realms, around the year A.D. 800. Banniard suggested (in *Viva Voce*) that Alcuin tried to make absolutely everybody speak that way, but soon abandoned the attempt on discovering that in that case penitents could not address, and in turn could not understand, their confessors; I have suggested, more cautiously, and along similar lines to those being elaborated at the same time by Anita Guerreau-Jalabert, that it was only in the church services that this newly introduced pronunciation was required, and that the famous seventeenth edict of the Council of Tours of 813 (to the effect that preachers should *transferre* their homilies into *rustica romana lingua* or Germanic) represents the consequences of the discovery that sermons were widely unintelligible in the new reading pronunciation.[44] That edict was

---

[44]Wright, *Late Latin and Early Romance*, chap. 3; Anita Guerreau-Jalabert, "La 'Renaissance Carolingienne': modèles culturels, usages linguistiques et structures sociales," *Bibliothèque de l'École des Chartes* 139 (1981): 5–36.

republished verbatim by Alcuin's star pupil Hrabanus Maurus on his accession to the bishopric of Mainz in 847, and Hrabanus may indeed be a key figure in the process we are considering; Banniard has recently suggested that Hrabanus's increasingly positive attitude towards the value of a written form for Germanic was in the event an important catalyst in the gradual growth of the idea that there was a need for another new written mode, the one which we would now call written Romance.[45] Attitudes varied widely in ninth-century France; writers were not homogeneous in their outlook on this issue, as Van Uytfanghe has graphically demonstrated.[46]

Janson suggests that both the invention of a conceptual distinction between Latin and Romance in general and the invention of distinctions between individual Romance languages were allied aspects of the same wider shift in the medieval conceptualization of languages and their names, and that the establishment of separate written forms and norms precedes rather than follows the conceptual division.[47] In this he differs from Banniard,[48] who feels that the decision to invent autonomous written forms of Romance was inspired by the previous arrival of the new idea that Romance and Latin were separate languages. I prefer[49] Janson's perspective here, and point out that Latin-Romance translation can only have arisen later still. The role of the Germanic speakers as catalysts in the whole process is becoming clearer to modern investigators; if it had not been for the need to have Germanic speakers reading aloud in an intelligible vernacular manner, there would have been no point in preparing the

---

[45]Michel Banniard, "Rhabanus Maurus and the Vernacular Languages," in *Latin and the Romance Languages*, ed. Wright, pp. 164–71.

[46]Marc Van Uytfanghe, "Les expressions du type *quod vulgo vocant* dans des textes latines antérieurs au Concile de Tours et aux Serments de Strasbourg," *Zeitschrift für Romanische Philologie* 105 (1989): 28–48, and "The Consciousness of a Linguistic Dichotomy (Latin-Romance) in Carolingian Gaul: The Contradictions of the Sources and Their Interpretation," in *Latin and the Romance Languages*, ed. Wright, pp. 114–29.

[47]Tore Janson, "Language Change and Metalinguistic Change: Latin to Romance and Other Cases," in *Latin and the Romance Languages*, ed. Wright, pp. 19–28.

[48]Banniard, "Rhabanus Maurus."

[49]Wright, *Late Latin and Early Romance*, chaps. 3, 4, and 5.

Strasbourg Oaths in the written form they now have, in which the Anglo-Saxon Latin letter-sound correspondences were applied to establishing appropriate written symbols for the ninth-century Romance words' pronunciations; similarly, it seems reasonable to suspect that it was the Germanic speakers at St. Amand who needed the *Eulalie* sequence to be written the way it was.[50]

In order to illustrate the central role played by the Germanic-speakers in the shift that took place in France between A.D. 800 and 1000, I shall make use of an analogy that I have used before.[51] Imagine that in the year 2000 a politically powerful group of Arabs are invited into the United States to reform the education system, as Alcuin was invited by Charlemagne. The native Arabic-speakers concerned have learned English as a foreign language, with a pronunciation based on a sound for each written letter (which would lead them to pronounce, for example, the phrase "The Wright Brothers" as [the wright brothers]), instead of the present normal [ðəɹajtbɹʌðəz], and with a handwriting technique that, for this reason, required each letter always to be written separately and clearly and with little variation (like the *litterae absolutae* that the eighth-century Anglo-Saxon scribes preferred, but those in eighth-century Gaul did not), and using only the most formal English grammar as found in the most hidebound textbooks of the last century; and further imagine that these Arabic-speakers have the political power to impose this very strange style of English for use in all serious American intellectual life. This new introduction, which we can call *Grammar,* is quite alien to the present population of the United States, who will carry on speaking as they do now but will only be allowed to write in the formal way, which admits some but not all of the phenomena of their normal spoken usage. Some time later, for some purposes, in some places, enterprising and literate Americans think up a new mode for representing on paper works, such as Oaths, Sermon notes, Songs, etc., that need to be read or sung aloud with ordinary non-

---

[50]See Wright, *Late Latin and Early Romance,* chap. 3.

[51]In "On Editing 'Latin' Texts Written by Romance-speakers," in *Linguistic Studies in Medieval Spanish,* ed. Ray Harris-Northall and Thomas D. Cravens (Madison: Hispanic Seminary of Medieval Studies, 1991), pp. 191–208 (*Early Ibero-Romance,* chap. 9).

Grammar pronunciation, using written forms that follow quite accurately the sound-letter correspondences introduced by the Arabs. That is, the first texts in the new written mode will come from well-educated writers, just as the earliest texts in the new Romance scripta all come notoriously from centers of expert Latinity. This newly invented written mode, however, might well vary from place to place in the present English-speaking world, to suit local speech habits, and thus might come in time to be called separately "British," "American," "Indian," "Jamaican," "Australian," etc., just as French, Occitan, Castilian, Italian, Catalan, and Portuguese came to be allotted separate names. Whereupon the coexisting presence of these different written modes with that of official and formal *Grammar* might well lead in due course to the idea that they are all actually different languages. At which point, but not before, it becomes possible to envisage translations between Grammar and American, Grammar and British, and so forth; and Latin and Romance.

Translation between Latin and Romance

Even under this scenario, the advent of a need for translations takes time. I suggest that we should only envisage the possibility of translation between Latin and Romance at a time for which we actually have evidence of the existence of two written versions of exactly the same text, one Latin, one Romance. If so, then it is an innovation of the so-called Twelfth-Century Renaissance. Translations did not occur before, because Latin had not existed separately as a different system from ordinary spoken Romance. A complex but monolingual Romance was all that had existed before. Thus the absence of translation enterprises between Romance and Latin in earlier years is not a sign of lack of intellect, nor of indolence; on the contrary, the previous ability to combine all the available variety in one monolingual competence required linguistic versatility and sophistication, such as we already know the inhabitants of eleventh- and twelfth-century Europe to have been endowed with. The concept and practice of translation itself was, of course, ancient in these societies; into Latin from Greek, Arabic, and Hebrew on a written level, and from Germanic, Celtic, Basque, and elsewhere on a practical level in bilingual communities.

If the refrain of the apparently bilingual *Alba* from Fleury were to be shown, as it has not yet been, to be a direct translation of a more formal Latinate original, then it might be possible to advance the date and pinpoint a crucial stage in the process at early eleventh-century Fleury-sur-Loire. This center seems to have been exceptionally interesting from our point of view, to judge from the earliest Romance manuscripts, in the decades that followed Abbo's abbacy; yet even so, translation seems not to be explicitly mentioned in the lengthy *Vita* of his successor Gauzlin.[52] The earlier Romance and Latin *Eulalie* sequences, for example, found in the same manuscript, are not translations one of the other but independent compositions on the same theme. The *Jonah sermon* notes are not precise Romance translations of a Latin original but at most an extended paraphrase, despite Jeanette Beer's reference to them as involving "translative processes."[53] I do, however, share Beer's belief that these were preachers' notes aimed at subsequent delivery, rather than Parkes's suggestion that these were notes taken by a listener.[54] And the fact that these notes weave in and out of the two written modes with no clear transitional boundaries supports my view that there were still not two clearly separated metalinguistic entities in the mind of the writer. The Clermont-Ferrand compositions (the *Vie de St. Léger* and the *Passio*) are similarly not translations, so far as we can tell; what we see as a language distinction was still seen by writers at the time as a genre distinction, which implies a lack of a need for translation. In France, translation from Latin into French, apparently initiated in the 1120s with biblical texts, was under way in the twelfth century, and, as Michel pointed out, there may have been even earlier translations, now lost.[55] In official circles, in France and Castille, normal

---

[52]See Robert-Henri Bautier and Gillette Labory, *Vie de Gauzlin, Abbé de Fleury* (Paris: Éditions du CNRS, 1969).

[53]Jeanette M. A. Beer, *Early Prose in France: Contexts of Bilingualism and Authority* (Kalamazoo: Medieval Institute Publications, 1992), chap. 2.

[54]Parkes, *Scribes, Scripts and Readers*, p. 27.

[55]See *Libri Psalmorum versio antiqua Gallica e cod. ms. in Bibl. Bodleiana asservato*, ed. François Michel (Oxford: Oxford University Press, 1989); Jeanette Beer, *Medieval Translators and Their Craft* (Kalamazoo: Medieval Institute Publications, 1989). For Provence see

redaction of official documents in the vernacular rather than Latin only begins at approximately the turn of the thirteenth century (which is why the invaluable studies of Anthonij Dees start no earlier than that).[56] The same seems to hold true for Italy, Navarra, and Portugal. This is probably part of the early thirteenth-century trend towards professional specialization that we can also see at work in the founding of the earliest universities.

There is also evidence from the post-Carolingian centuries concerning the nature of the reading aloud of official texts. Not all aspects of reading pronunciation in the newly prescribed system were actually covered by Alcuin's simple sound-letter correspondences, but reading aloud, often in unison, played an essential role in the ninth-century training of young monks, so ideally every detail had to be clarified in advance.[57] In particular, uncertainty about the purpose of digraphs such as *ch,* and of the letter *h* in general; the phonetic equivalents of the Greek symbols; the decision concerning which syllable in a word should be given the word-stress, and the attendant need for specific diacritics; the pauses in reading that could be indicated by features of punctuation; even after Alcuin's instructions, these uncertainties needed, and were given, further elaboration, as we can see, for example, from the topics chosen for discussion by Abbo of Fleury in his *Quaestiones Grammaticales* of ca. 982, Hildemar of Corbie (of Civate), and others.[58] Such special expertise helped widen further the gap between vernacular Romance and *Grammatica.*

Michel Banniard, "Naissance et conscience de la langue d'oc, VIIIe–IXe siècles," in *La Catalogne et la France méridionale autour de l'an mil,* comp. Xavier Barral i Altet (Barcelona: University of Barcelona, 1992), pp. 351–61.

[56]See Anthonij Dees, *Atlas des formes et des constructions des chartes françaises du 13e siècle* (Tübingen: Niemeyer, 1980).

[57]Mayke De Jong, "Growing Up in a Carolingian Monastery: Magister Hildemar and His Oblates," *Journal of Medieval History* 9 (1983): 99–128.

[58]See Abbo Floriacensis, *Quaestiones Grammaticales,* ed. Anita Guerreau-Jalabert (Paris: Belles Lettres, 1982); David Ganz, "The Preconditions for Caroline Minuscule," *Viator* 18 (1987): 23–43; John Contreni, "The Carolingian School: Letters from the Classroom," in *Giovanni Scoto nel suo tempo: l'organizzazione del sapere in età Carolingia* (Spoleto: Centro di Studi sull'alto Medioevo, 1989), pp. 81–111; and Parkes, *Scribes, Scripts and Readers.*

The final stages in the development of a need for translation will be exemplified here from central Spain. The first extant official document in autonomous written Spanish vernacular whose original date in that form we can be entirely sure of comes from the Royal Chancery of Palencia in 1206 (the Treaty of Cabreros), and the next from the Cortes of Toledo of January 1207 (which is also where Hernández plausibly suggests that the version we now have of the *Poem of the Cid* was first performed).[59] These texts are not in themselves translations, but the existence of such important documentation in almost completely non-formalized form seems to have acted as the impulse to take existing legal documents, prepared earlier in the formal guise we now call Latin, and recast them in what we would now call Old Castilian. That is indeed translation. It is not at all clear when the first of these translations of *Fueros* began; although they are often ascribed to the start of the reign of Fernando III of Castilla (1217–52), it may be more likely that Romance translations of existing Latin documents (as opposed to new documents drawn up *ab initio* in Romance) were not commissioned or prepared until the 1240s, as part of the preparations for Alfonso X's *Fuero Real*, eventually finalized in 1255. Although most translations in thirteenth-century Castile were made into Castilian from Arabic or from Hebrew, this model for Latin-Romance translation had been set at the highest official level for later expansion, in, for example, the Alfonsine histories. Since Latin works had been translated for centuries into Arabic in Moslem Spain, the idea of Latin-Romance translation in the Iberian Peninsula may have been partly catalyzed from the Arabic south, as it had been from the Germanic north in the Carolingian realms. Or the presence of German-speakers in the twelfth-century Toledo translation enterprises might again be significant.

The osmotic connection between Latin and Romance in Spain may not have been entirely severed until the time of Nebrija, however, in the late fifteenth century. Nebrija claimed to be the first writer in Spain not to

---

[59]Francisco Hernández, "Las Cortes de Toledo de 1207," in *Las Cortes de Castilla y León en la Edad Media*, vol. 1, ed. J. Valdeón (Valladolid: Cortes de Castilla y León, 1988), pp. 221–63.

approach writing Latin as being essentially writing Romance with a few tricks added on,[60] as though all thirteenth- to fifteenth-century writers in Latin in Spain had still been continuing the normal earlier practice of formalizing and polishing a vernacular base. There is a probably fourteenth-century Latin grammar in the *Biblioteca Nacional* in Madrid (MS 10.073), said by the catalogue to be *Una gramática del Siglo XIV* and on the manuscript itself to be *Arte de Priscian y Castellano,* where some of the sample sentences on folios 16 to 18 are actually translated into Castilian. This looks like bilingualism until we notice that the same grammar is there thought to explain both Latin and Castilian. But Nebrija had his own axe to grind. In fact, even though Alfonso X at times seems not to make a clear distinction between Latin and Romance, as Niederehe showed,[61] some thirteenth-century writers in the Peninsula did. Berceo did, although even Berceo's copious works are not yet translations of their sources, still being independent compositions on the same theme. Yet *Fueros* were being translated, of necessity closely and literally, in Berceo's lifetime, and by 1300 the metalinguistics of the early Middle Ages were almost over. Thus the fourteenth century is the one that sees a translation into Castilian of the Benedictine Rule, Franciscan hymn translations, and prose translations of saints' lives.[62] But it must be realized that the reason why such translations were not needed before is merely that in previous centuries their original form had largely been accessible anyway.

Conclusions

Remember that the linguistic situation in the Romance world changed greatly between the tenth and the thirteenth centuries. Do not generalize about the relationship between Latin and Romance without being careful

---

[60]Francisco Rico, *Nebrija frente a los bárbaros: el canon de gramáticos nefastos en las polémicas del humanismo* (Salamanca: Universidad de Salamanca, 1978).

[61]Hans-Josef Niederehe, *Alfonso X el Sabio y la lingüística de su tiempo* (Madrid: Sociedad General Española de Librería, 1987).

[62]See Walsh and Deyermond, *"Locus* and Literature," pp. 36–37, 43.

about the time and place of the data being referred to. Bear in mind that it is absurd to talk of the "emerging" Romance of that period, since "Romance" had existed for centuries in everybody's mind and on everybody's lips, not least in a flourishing tradition of oral literature,[63] and the only "emerging" phenomenon during this period was the autonomous status of what we now call Medieval Latin. Consequently it would be best for modern investigators to avoid using either the word or the concept of "translation," between Latin and Romance, until well into the twelfth-century Renaissance.

---

[63]Roger Wright, "Several Ballads, One Epic and Two Chronicles (1100–1250)," *La Corónica* 18 (1990): 21–38, and 19 (1991): xiii–xiv.

The (M)other Tongue:
Translation Theory and Old English

Robert Stanton

Alfred the Great, king of Wessex in the late ninth century, wrote concerning his ambitious translation program:

> Forðy me ðyncð betre, gif iow swa ðyncð, þæt we eac suma bec, ða þe nidbeðyrfsta sien eallum monnum to witanne, þæt we þa on ðæt geðeode wenden þe we ealle gecnawan mægen.[1]
> [Therefore it seems better to me—if it seems so to you—that we too should turn into the language that we can all understand certain books which are the most necessary for all people to know.]

Alfred obviously believed that by translating a few very important religious works from Latin into Old English and by sprucing up the English educational system, he could improve the sad state of learning at the time. His translation program marks a watershed in the early development of English. Before Alfred's time, there is no firm evidence for any substantial amount of written English; after Alfred's reforms, translations began to appear at a rapid pace; indeed, Old English literature as a whole includes few texts that are not translations or adaptations of Latin works.[2] Thus, English as a

---

[1] *King Alfred's West Saxon Version of Gregory's Pastoral Care*, 2 vols. in 1, ed. Henry Sweet, EETS, o.s., 45, 50 (London: Oxford University Press, 1871), p. 6. All translations are my own.

[2] Currently two research projects, *Sources of Anglo-Saxon Literary Culture* and *Fontes Anglo-Saxonici,* are attempting to identify the Latin sources used by Anglo-Saxon writers. See the *Old English Newsletter* for progress reports of both projects. See also *Sources of Anglo-Saxon Literary Culture: A Trial Version,* ed. Frederick M. Biggs, Thomas D. Hill, and Paul E. Szarmach, with the assistance of Karen Hammond, Medieval and Renaissance Texts and

literary language was born out of a program of translation, and defined itself largely in terms of differences between itself and the Latin language. Given all this, it is both a surprise and a disappointment that medieval English does not occupy a more prominent place in the history of translation.

Histories of translation tend to give quite short shrift to the early English period.[3] Likewise, books on the history of the English language do not sufficiently emphasize the fact that Old English developed largely as a medium of translation from Latin, and Middle English partly as a language of translation from French.[4] Similarly, grammars, syntax and vocabulary studies, and other language handbooks dealing with Old English often gloss over or totally ignore the development of the language as a tool of translators.[5]

Research in the Old English field has also been disappointing in this respect. Louis Kelly has said in the introduction to his book on translation

Studies 74 (Binghamton: Center for Medieval and Early Renaissance Studies, State University of New York at Binghamton, 1990).

[3]On the history of translation see Louis G. Kelly, *The True Interpreter: A History of Translation Theory and Practice in the West* (Oxford: Blackwell, 1979); Eric Jacobsen, *Translation: A Traditional Craft; An Introductional Craft* (Copenhagen: Gyldendal, 1958); Werner Schwarz, *Principles and Problems of Biblical Translation: Some Reformation Controversies and Their Background* (London: Cambridge University Press, 1955); Flora Ross Amos, *Early Theories of Translation* (New York: Columbia University Press, 1920); H. Hargreaves, "From Bede to Wyclif: Medieval English Bible Translations," *Bulletin of the John Rylands Library* 48 (1965): 118–40; and Frederick M. Rener, *Interpretatio: Language and Translation from Cicero to Tytler* (Amsterdam and Atlanta, Ga.: Rodopi, 1989).

[4]On the history of English see Celia M. Millward, *A Biography of the English Language*, 2nd ed. (Fort Worth: Harcourt Brace, 1996); Albert C. Baugh and Thomas Cable, *A History of the English Language*, 3rd ed. (Englewood Cliffs, N.J.: Prentice-Hall, 1978); and Thomas Pyles and John Algeo, *The Origins and Development of the English Language*, 4th ed. (New York: Harcourt Brace Jovanovich, 1993).

[5]See at random Bruce Mitchell and Fred C. Robinson, *A Guide to Old English*, 5th ed. (Oxford and Cambridge, Mass.: Blackwell, 1992); Orrin W. Robinson, *Old English and Its Closest Relatives: A Survey of the Earliest Germanic Languages* (Stanford: Stanford University Press, 1992); Victor L. Strite, *Old English Semantic-Field Studies* (New York: Peter Lang, 1989); and Bruce Mitchell, *Old English Syntax* (Oxford: Clarendon and New York: Oxford University Press, 1985).

history that a complete theory of translation has three components: specification of function and goal; description and analysis of operations; and
critical comment on relationships between goal and operations.[6] According
to Kelly, most theories of translation treat one of these aspects to the exclu-
sion of others. Clearly, a theoretically based approach to a particular group
of translations, or to a historical period of translation, should also combine
these three elements. In the Old English field, which has been so inimical
to explicit theory until quite recently, there has been very little of Kelly's
first component (that is, specification of function and goal), with the
notable exception of King Alfred's translation program;[7] most Old English
translation studies can be grouped under the second category (that is, analysis of operations, largely the province of linguists and historical linguists);
and there has been almost none of the third sort (namely, a coherent
commentary on the relationship between goals and operations).[8]

It is time to correct this situation. With the history of the English
language being studied and taught more and more, and both translation
history and translation theory enjoying ever more intelligent and coherent
study, we need to formulate a series of theoretical approaches to the
problem of early English translation. One possible reason for the meager-
ness of theoretical work in this field is the relative scarcity of explicit
translation theory in Anglo-Saxon England itself. It is a truism that
medieval translators do not talk much about what they do, they simply do
it; and the early English period is no exception. But we must not be afraid

---

[6]Kelly, *The True Interpreter*, pp. 1–2.

[7]Kurt Otten, *König Alfreds Boethius* (Tübingen: Niemeyer, 1964); and F. Anne Payne,
King Alfred & Boethius: An Analysis of the Old English Version of the Consolation of Philosophy
(Madison: University of Wisconsin Press, 1968).

[8]A notable exception is Phyllis Wright's excellent 1984 University of Toronto thesis,
"Literary Translation in Anglo-Saxon England." Ælfric's translation theory has also come
under scrutiny: see Ann Eljenholm Nichols, "*Awendan*: A Note on Ælfric's Vocabulary,"
Journal of English and Germanic Philology 63 (1964): 7–13; Harvey Minkoff, "Some Stylistic
Consequences of Ælfric's Theory of Translation," *Studies in Philology* 73 (1976): 29–41; and
Richard Marsden, "Ælfric as Translator: The Old English Prose *Genesis*," *Anglia* 109 (1991):
319–58.

of importing theory that is anachronistic, or nothing will get done. A lack of explicit translation theory in the medieval period is not the same as an absence of theoretical principles. It is the responsibility of the modern critic of translation to formulate theory that does justice to the texts being studied: to extrapolate, as it were, from practice to theory.

One way to do this is to look closely at the translation theory of the classical and patristic periods, which had both direct and indirect influence on medieval English translation. Examining these older views, one quickly discovers a central core of translation issues that have remained relevant since the classical period at least. At the same time, a lot has happened in translation theory over the last thousand years or so, and a sustained use of some post-medieval translation theory is essential if the field is ever to attain any theoretical rigor. Modern literary theory, thoroughly studied and critically and conscientiously applied, has much to offer medieval literary studies, and much remains to be done. But somehow, amidst the flurry of new theoretical approaches and their deployment in the medieval English period, translation theory seems to have been largely forgotten—it must have been behind the door when "new approaches to medieval English literature" were making their move. In the concluding portion of this essay, I would like to hint at a few more recent approaches that could be helpful.

But first to the classical period. The most famous legacy of ancient Rome to subsequent translation theory is the distinction between word-for-word (or "literal") translation and sense-for-sense (or "loose" translation), which first comes up in Roman times, was cited in the Middle Ages, and is still with us today. The most famous users of the phrase *non verbum pro verbo* were Cicero and Horace. The formula was picked up by Jerome, who espoused sense-for-sense translation except in the case of Holy Scripture where, he said, the very order of the words was a sacred mystery. But Rita Copeland has recently shown, first in an article on the "word for word" formula and more recently in her book *Rhetoric, Hermeneutics, and Translation in the Middle Ages,* that this formula did not pass from the ancient period to the patristic without radical modification. Specifically, she demonstrates that Cicero used sense-for-sense translation as a plank in his aggressive platform of cultural appropriation: Cicero conceived of a contest between the eloquence of his Greek originals and the rhetorical power of *latinitas.* Although St. Jerome inherits the idea of sense-for-sense translation from Cicero, he uses it in a fundamentally different way. Jerome advocates this method in order to conserve an immanent meaning untroubled by linguistic differences, and not in order to valorize the target language or displace the authority of the source. Copeland's achievement is to have demonstrated that patristic translation theory borrowed the language of classical theory while fundamentally rejecting all of the assumptions behind that language.[9]

Students of Old English literature should be equally careful when thinking about the translation theory of King Alfred. Alfred probably picked up the *sensum pro sensu* formula from Gregory the Great, who said he had real trouble understanding word-for-word translations and advocated sometimes sense-for-sense translation, sometimes word-for-word.[10] The

---

[9]Rita Copeland, "The Fortunes of 'Non Verbum pro Verbo': Or, Why Jerome Is Not a Ciceronian," in *The Medieval Translator: The Theory and Practice of Translation in the Middle Ages,* ed. Roger Ellis (Woodbridge, Suff., and Wolfeboro, N.H.: Brewer, 1989), pp. 15–35; and *Rhetoric, Hermeneutics, and Translation in the Middle Ages: Academic Traditions and Vernacular Texts* (Cambridge and New York: Cambridge University Press, 1991), pp. 42–55. See also Schwarz, *Principles and Problems* (27–37); and A. Condamin, "Les Caractères de la Traduction de la Bible par Saint Jérôme," *Recherches de Science Religieuse* 2 (1911): 425–40, and 3 (1912): 105–38.

[10]*Epistula* 10.21, *S. Gregorii Magni Registrum Epistularum,* ed. Dag Norberg, CCSL 140A (Turnhout: Brepols, 1982), p. 855: "Indicamus praeterea, quia gravem hic interpretum difficultatem patimur. Dum enim non sunt, qui sensum de sensu exprimunt, sed transferre verborum semper proprietatem volunt, omnem dictorum sensum confundunt. Unde agitur, ut ea quae translata fuerint nisi cum gravi labore intellegere nullo modo valeamus" [Moreover, I declare that I suffer serious difficulty with translators here. For as long as there is no one who expresses sense for sense, but only those who always want to translate the idiom of the words, they confuse the whole meaning of the writers. Thus it happens that I cannot understand translated works except by hard work]. See also *Dialogi,* 1. prol. 10 (Gregory I, *Dialogues,* ed. Adalbert de Vogüé and Paul Antin [Paris: Éditions du Cerf, 1979], pp. 16–18): "Hoc uero scire te cupio quia in quibusdam sensum solummodo, in quibusdam uero et uerba cum sensu teneo, quia se de personis omnibus ipsa specialiter et uerba tenere uoluissem, haec rusticano usu prolata stilus scribentis non apte susciperet" [I would also like you to know that in some (stories), I keep only the sense, in some both the

preface to his translation of Gregory's *Cura pastoralis* says:

> hwilum word be worde, hwilum ondgit of andgite, swæ swæ ic hie geleornode æt
> Plegmunde minum ærcebiscepe & æt Asserie minum biscepe & æt Grimbolde
> minum mæssepreoste & æt Iohanne minum mæssepreoste. Siððan ic hie þa
> geleornod hæfde, swæ swæ ic hie forstod, & swæ ic hie andgitfullicost areccean
> meahte, ic hie on Englisc awende.[11]
>
> [(I translated) sometimes word for word, sometimes sense for sense, as I learned
> it from Plegmund my archbishop, and from Asser my bishop, and from Grimbald
> my mass-priest and from John my mass-priest. After I had mastered it, I translated
> it into English as best I understood it and as I could most meaningfully render it.]

We should take a lesson from Copeland and be very cautious in interpreting this passage. First, it is clear that Alfred is engaging in a fascinating
collaborative enterprise, whereby he consults closely with his advisors on the
meaning of the text before rendering it into English. Such a mediated
engagement with the text would seem, on the face of it, to rule out any
explicit motive of "Ciceronian" contestation or displacement on Alfred's
part. Second, we cannot attribute to Alfred a purely "Hieronymian"
outlook, whereby he would aim to conserve, or replicate, an immanent
meaning. Alfred's translation practice, and that of his colleagues, is too
loose to allow such an interpretation. Alfred's translation of Boethius's
Consolation of Philosophy is an excellent example of free translation, with a
great many additions, deletions, and substantial changes.[12]

---

words and the sense, because if I wished to keep the very words of each individual character,
the writer's pen would not properly sustain their rustic expressions].

[11]Alfred, preface to *Cura Pastoralis*, in Sweet, p. 6.

[12]Alfred's free translations have led at least one critic to say that King Alfred's prose was
not translation at all but "transformation." This kind of euphemism implies that translation
must be close and literal, and masks the range and complexity of medieval translation
techniques. See Janet Bately, *The Literary Prose of King Alfred's Reign: Translation or
Transformation?* An inaugural lecture in the Chair of English Language and Medieval
Literature delivered at University of London King's College on 4th March 1980
(Binghamton: CEMERS, SUNY–Binghamton, 1984). See also Nichols, "*Awendan*," and
Marsden, "Ælfric as Translator" (n. 8 above).

So we should be wary of situating Alfred in either the classical or the patristic camp, although he is closer to the latter. In the end, Alfred's translation program should be judged against his own justification for it. He perceived a grave deficiency in Latin literacy at the time, and his English translations were meant to make available important works that people should have been able to read in Latin but could not. His ultimate aim was the resuscitation of the ideal of wisdom among his royal officials and clergy. Translation into English was but a step along that road. There is much more to be said about King Alfred; the main point is that we must not assume that he is the direct inheritor of either classical or patristic translation theory; we need to look at his translations in the context of his own very novel project.

The real paradox of translation is the tension that exists within it between two different aspects.[13] The first is the subservient function of replication, where the translation is viewed simply as a reproduction of the original text. The second is the creative tendency, where the translation does not reproduce but actually displaces the source text, replacing it with an original text of its own. This was a continuing worry for Old English translators. Alfred worried about it, and it was certainly of great concern to Ælfric, the second most famous translator in Anglo-Saxon England. Ælfric flourished in the late tenth century: he translated portions of the Old Testament and numerous saints' lives; he wrote a great many homilies in English, which could certainly be called translations; he wrote the first Latin grammar in English; and he composed numerous works in Latin. Ælfric had grave concerns about translating religious works into English; he feared disrupting the lineal continuity of the Latin tradition by introducing linguistic multiplicity.[14] Here is the danger in the paradox of translation:

---

[13]This has also been brilliantly argued by Rita Copeland in the works cited in n. 9 above. See also Kelly, *The True Interpreter*, pp. 34–67.

[14]See especially Ælfric's preface to his *Lives of Saints*, 4 vols., ed. Walter W. Skeat, EETS, o.s., 76, 82, 94, 114 (London: Oxford University Press, 1881; repr. 1966 in 2 vols.), 1: 2, lines 9–12: "Nec tamen plura promitto me scripturum hac lingua, quia nec conuenit huic sermocinationi plura inseri; ne forte despectui habeantur margarite christi" [But I do not promise to write anything more in this language, because it is not fitting that anything more

the translator may wish to preserve identity, and may even attempt to do so, but a smart translator knows that this is not possible. A clever translator (and Ælfric was certainly that) will know that the creative, disjunctive aspect of translation cannot be denied. Ælfric expressed such fears in concrete, contemporary terms: his real fear, he says, is that heretical doctrine will arise out of English writings.[15] This can only happen if something new has been created in the vernacular.

Most of these considerations will apply throughout medieval Europe, but in some respects Anglo-Saxon England was unique. First, a lot of things were written down in Old English several centuries before any substantial vernacular writing elsewhere in Europe. There is evidence that the Venerable Bede, at the time of his death in 735, was engaged in translating the Gospel of St. John into Old English.[16] This has led at least one scholar to conclude enthusiastically that "Anglo-Saxon was the first western language that was neither sacred nor Latin to be given (by Bede) its cultural consecration and intellectual status."[17] This may be overstating the case, since we know neither the scale nor the exact purpose of Bede's translation efforts; nonetheless, the use of the vernacular in a religious context by such

---

be brought out in this speech, lest perhaps the pearls of Christ should be held in disrespect]. See also his preface to *Genesis* (*The Old English Version of the Heptateuch, Ælfric's Treatise on the Old and New Testament and His Preface to Genesis*, ed. Samuel J. Crawford, EETS, o.s., 160 [London: Oxford University Press, 1922]), p. 79: "We ne durron na mare awritan on Englisc þonne ðæt Leden hæfð" [We do not dare write any more in English than the Latin has].

[15] See Ælfric's preface to the first series of Catholic Homilies (*The Homilies of the Anglo-Saxon Church. The First Part, Containing the Sermones catholici, or Homilies of Ælfric*, 2 vols., ed. Benjamin Thorpe [London: Ælfric Society 1844–46; Hildesheim: Olms, 1983], 1: 2): "Ic geseah and gehyrde mycel gedwyld on manegum Engliscum bocum, þe ungelærede menn þurh heora bilewitnysse to micclum wisdome tealdon" [I saw and heard much error in many English books, which unlearned people, through their innocence, took to be great wisdom].

[16] Cuthbert, *Letter to Cuthwine*, in *Symeonis monachi opera omnia*, 2 vols., ed. Thomas Arnold (London: Longman, 1882–85), 1: 3–135.

[17] Michel Banniard, "Rhabanus Maurus and the Vernacular Languages," in *Latin and the Romance Languages in the Early Middle Ages*, ed. Roger Wright (London and New York: Routledge, 1991), p. 165.

an illustrious scholar is an indication of the status of the language at the time and its perceived suitability for rendering canonical texts. Or perhaps it would be better to say that for various religious and social reasons, there was a *need* for English translations at an early date. The language had *de facto* to acquire the status of an appropriate medium of religious discourse.

Related to this linguistic precocity is the obvious fact that Old English is a Germanic language. Thus, it differed from Latin in the significant respect that no one in England after the fifth century had Latin as a first language. The driving force behind early English translation was not only social and religious but also linguistic. The situation was utterly different from the Romance-speaking countries, where Latin could be read aloud and understood to varying degrees during the centuries of transition from Latin to Romance.[18] In England, if circumstances demanded that a Latin text be made available for a public that could not understand Latin read aloud, then it had to be translated.

Is it possible to evaluate linguistically the differences between Latin and Old English as literary languages, or as vehicles of religious expression? Indeed, *should* we evaluate them this way? It used to be said that Old English was a blunt instrument, lacking the range and subtlety of Latin. Subsequent generations have largely modified this view, pointing to the seemingly endless capacity of the language to form compounds and derivatives. If we did want to make a judgement about linguistic difference here, one way we could do it would be to follow the twentieth-century French school of *stylistique* originating with Charles Bally.[19] Bally saw differences between languages as differences in modes of seeing peculiar to each nation (and, of course, in this he followed nineteenth-century linguists affected by the Romantic movement). Bally said that words in Germanic languages tend to be image-based, reflecting a physical type of vision, while those in Romance languages define, reflecting a more intellectual vision. An

---

[18]On the Romance situation see Roger Wright, *Late Latin and Early Romance in Spain and Carolingian France* (Liverpool: F. Cairns, 1982); his *Latin and the Romance Languages*; and his essay in this volume.

[19]Charles Bally, "Stylistique et linguistique générale," *Archiv für das Studium der neueren Sprachen* 128 (1912): 87–126. See also Kelly, *The True Interpreter*, p. 13.

example would be the translation of the Latin word *classis*, which bears the primary meaning "a class or category." By extension in a logical, non-spatial fashion, it also means "army" or "fleet." An Old English writer would probably translate *classis* as *sciphere,* "ship-army," which uses the concrete noun *scip* as the first term, creating a visual image rather than a logical association. One would certainly want to be very cautious in using this as evidence of the difference between the English and their contemporaries in Latin/Romance areas; I rather think the most interesting use of this kind of "national psychology" would be the study of subsequent Old English scholarship as it has evolved in England, Germany, and the United States, each country having its own sociopolitical agenda and its own putative links with the Anglo-Saxon soul.[20]

In the remainder of this essay, I would like to mention a few other modern critical approaches which may help "firm up" the study of Old English translation. One of the most influential early modern translation theorists was John Dryden. Dryden distinguished three types of translation. The first he called "metaphrase, or turning an author word by word, and line by line, from one language into another." The second was "paraphrase, or translation with latitude, where the author is kept in view by the translator so as never to be lost, but his words are not so strictly followed as his sense." Finally, there was "imitation, where the translator (if now he has not lost that name) assumes the liberty not only to vary from the words and sense but also to forsake them both as he sees occasion; and taking only some general hints from the original, to run division on the ground-work, as he pleases."[21]

Dryden warns against the use of his first type (metaphrase, or literal translation), especially when translating Latin:

---

[20]See Allen J. Frantzen, *Desire for Origins: New Language, Old English, and Teaching the Tradition* (New Brunswick, N.J., and London: Rutgers University Press, 1990), pp. 27–61 and 201–26.

[21]From the preface to Dryden's translation of *Ovid's Epistles* (1680), repr. in *Theories of Translation: An Anthology of Essays from Dryden to Derrida,* ed. Rainer Schulte and John Biguenet (Chicago: University of Chicago Press, 1992), p. 17.

[Virgil] had the advantage of a language wherein much may be comprehended in a little space. We, and all the modern tongues, have more articles and pronouns, besides signs of tenses and cases, and other barbarities on which our speech is built by the faults of our forefathers. The Romans founded theirs upon the Greek: and the Greeks, we know, were labouring many hundred years upon their language, before they brought it to perfection. They rejected all those signs, and cut off as many articles as they could spare; comprehending in one word what we are constrained to express in two; which is one reason why we cannot write so concisely as they have done.[22]

Dryden's complaint is a common one among English translators of Latin; indeed, such comments formed the basis for much of the debate over the inferiority of English in the early modern period and into the eighteenth century.[23] If this comment was true in 1697 when Dryden wrote it, it was no less true in the ninth and tenth centuries, when English translation was in its infancy. Old English is much closer to being a synthetic language than is modern English; but in comparison to Latin, it is heavily weighed down with articles, prepositions, and adverbs, and its syntax is frequently sprawling and awkward. And where vocabulary is concerned, Old English translators were considerably worse off than Dryden, who had the use of all the English words borrowed from Latin in the medieval and early modern periods—a massive shift towards a Latinate vocabulary, and a vast increase in the number of words available.

Dryden also disliked overly free translations, or imitations as he called them: "Imitation of an author is the most advantageous way for a translator to show himself, but the greatest wrong which can be done to the memory and reputation of the dead."[24] This comment expresses succinctly the fear of being unfaithful to an authoritative writer, of doing a disservice or even a blasphemy to a canonical text. Dryden's fears about translating Virgil and Ovid were doubtless different in many respects from

---

[22]From the dedication of the *Aeneis* (1697), repr. in *Theories of Translation*, ed. Schulte and Biguenet, p. 25.

[23]See Charles Barber, *Early Modern English* (London: Deutsch, 1976), pp. 65–142.

[24]From the preface to *Ovid's Epistles* (1680), repr. in *Theories of Translation*, ed. Schulte and Biguenet, p. 20.

Ælfric's about translating the Bible. But both show a similar fear about language, a suspicion that something newly created actually displaces the original, and that the text in the new language becomes too much of an event in itself.

Related to these fears about displacing the source text is the question of equivalence. If the translator is consciously aiming to replicate rather than replace the original, then he or she will be aiming at some sort of equivalence. This problem is a complex one; for the moment I want to focus on the notions of formal and dynamic equivalence as outlined by Eugene Nida.[25] Formal equivalence means a correspondence of linguistic units: word, phrase, clause, and sentence. Old English translators were naturally conscious of the differences between their language and Latin, but this did not stop them from imitating Latinate structures; a good example comes from the Old English translation of Bede's *Historia ecclesiastica* (the translation formed part of King Alfred's program).[26] For the Latin "respondens ipse uoce humillima . . . inquit" [he, answering in a humble voice, said . . .], the translator has "ða ondsworede he eaðmodre stefne" [then he answered in a humble voice].[27] The translator has attempted to find an Old English equivalent to the ablative of manner; as frequently happens, the dative case is pressed into service, without the help of a preposition like *mid* (which would give "with a humble voice"). The result is unidiomatic Old English. This kind of formal literalism may owe something to the Anglo-Saxon gloss tradition, which flourished throughout the period. Word-by-word glossing represents the logical extreme of formal equivalence; if (and it is a big if) the subsequent course of Old English translation owed something to a kind of "glossing sensibility," this would

---

[25] Eugene A. Nida, *Toward a Science of Translating, with Special Reference to Principles and Procedures Involved in Bible Translating* (Leiden: Brill, 1964), pp. 159–77.

[26] The Latin original is from *Bede's Ecclesiastical History of the English People*, ed. Bertram Colgrave and R. A. B. Mynors, repr. with corrections (Oxford: Clarendon, 1969). The Old English is from *The Old English Version of Bede's Ecclesiastical History of the English People*, 4 vols., ed. Thomas Miller, EETS, o.s., 95, 96, 110, 111 (1890–98; London: Oxford University Press, 1959).

[27] Bede 4.26; Colgrave and Mynors, p. 334; Miller, p. 260.

help account for the strain of awkward literalism that persists until the very end of the period.

Dynamic equivalence is an even thornier problem. Nida defines it as a translation that has the same effect on its audience as the original text had on its audience. It would be hard to look at small units of text and say that translators were attempting to reproduce an effect. Nonetheless, if we look at larger chunks of highly formalized works such as saints' lives and homilies, we can see an attempt to reproduce a rhetorical effect. In a saint's life, for example, the introductory material, accounts of the saint's birth and early life, death, and performance of miracles may be matched section by section in source and translation. A didactic work such as this aims at a very specific effect, and "dynamic equivalence" is at least a starting point in understanding vernacular translation of such audience-oriented texts.

Finally, the study of medieval vernacular translation cannot proceed without some consideration of orality. The early Middle Ages was a time when writing was steadily gaining ground and establishing itself as a rival to speech in many spheres—religious, commercial, legal, ceremonial, liturgical. In all walks of life, the power of the oral and the power of the written were coexisting, contesting, and influencing one another.[28] Some of what was written down in the medieval period was being written for the first time—that is, it represented a first transcription of a previously oral

---

[28]See Brian Stock, *The Implications of Literacy: Written Language and Models of Interpretation in the Eleventh and Twelfth Centuries* (Princeton: Princeton University Press, 1983); Evelyn Birge Vitz, "Vie, légende, littérature: Traditions orales et écrites dans les histoires des saints," *Poétique* 18 (1987): 387–402; Jack Goody, *The Domestication of the Savage Mind* (Cambridge and New York: Cambridge University Press, 1977); Goody, *The Logic of Writing and the Organization of Society* (Cambridge and New York: Cambridge University Press, 1986); and Walter Ong, *Orality and Literacy: The Technologizing of the Word* (London and New York: Methuen, 1982). For England see Susan Kelly, "Anglo-Saxon Lay Society and the Written Word," in *The Uses of Literacy in Early Mediaeval Europe*, ed. Rosamond McKitterick (Cambridge and New York: Cambridge University Press, 1990), pp. 36–62; Katherine O'Brien O'Keeffe, *Visible Song: Transitional Literacy in Old English Verse* (Cambridge and New York: Cambridge University Press, 1990); and M. T. Clanchy, *From Memory to Written Record in England, 1066–1307*, 2nd ed. (Oxford and Cambridge, Mass.: Blackwell, 1993).

entity. It is possible that most of the Old English poetry we have was composed and performed orally. Unfortunately, we cannot say for certain how far removed our manuscripts of Old English poetry are from actual oral performance. Other texts—including religious works such as prayers and sermons—existed in a written milieu but were intended to be read aloud in public. Still other texts would have been read aloud, but in private. In fact, all reading at this time was out loud; silent reading was a somewhat later development.

Again, England differs significantly from the Romance areas in this respect. The act of translation was highly significant in that it entailed the transference, not just of particular works but of an entire Christian Latin tradition, into a language that was previously a mainly oral milieu and was just finding its feet as a written language. Expanding the audience of a work to include anyone who could understand English introduced an oral authority that drew on everyday practice and secular experience and necessarily involved larger numbers of lay people. Old English represented at once the first attempt to buy into the authority of the Latin tradition in the medieval West and the first challenge to that authority. A more extensive and open-minded use of orality theory will help clarify and develop this line of research.

To list all the fundamental precepts, concepts, differences, distinctions, and categorizations devised by translation theorists that I think can benefit the study of Old English would be beyond the scope of this study. The few approaches that I have mentioned are certainly not the only ways to go about this task; they may not even be the best ones. But if we are to fill in a lacuna in the history of translation, and if Anglo-Saxon scholarship is to progress to a mature study of Old English translation, then these two fields must begin speaking to one another.

The *Fidus interpres*: Aid or Impediment to Medieval Translation and *Translatio*?

Douglas Kelly

Horace uses the expression *fidus interpres* in the sense of "faithful translator" when, in the *Ad Pisones,* his Art of Poetry, he tells the reader how to rewrite a Greek original in Latin:

> publica materies privati iuris erit, si
> non circa vilem patulumque moraberis orbem,
> *nec* verbo verbum curabis reddere fidus
> interpres,[1]
> [in ground open to all you will win private rights <that is: common matter will become original> if you do not linger along the easy and open pathway, if you do *not* seek to render word for word as a slavish translator].

Interpretatio in Classical and Medieval Latin could mean "translation from one language to another."[2] However, *interpretatio, interpres,* and their

---

[1]*Q. Horati Flacci opera,* 2nd ed., ed. Edward C. Wickham and H. W. Garrod (Oxford: Clarendon, 1901), *Ars poetica,* vv. 131–34; emphasis mine. After presenting the paper upon which this chapter is based, I discovered that Rita Copeland also discusses the reception of Horace's notion of the *fidus interpres* in her *Rhetoric, Hermeneutics, and Translation in the Middle Ages: Academic Traditions and Vernacular Texts* (Cambridge and New York: Cambridge University Press, 1991), esp. pp. 168–78. See also John V. Fleming, "The *Fidus Interpres,* or from Horace to Pandarus," in *Interpretation: Medieval and Modern,* ed. Piero Boitani and Anna Torti, The J. A. W. Bennett Memorial Lectures, Perugia 1992 (Cambridge: D. S. Brewer, 1993), pp. 189–200; Alexandru N. Cizek, *Imitatio et tractatio: die literarisch-rhetorischen Grundlagen der Nachahmung in Antike und Mittelalter* (Tübingen: Niemeyer, 1994).

[2]*Thesaurus linguae latinae* (Leipzig: Teubner, 1941), 7.1: 2256–57.

cognates connote more than just "translation, rendering." Besides the sense
that interests us here *interpretatio* can, according to the *Oxford Latin
Dictionary*, also convey the following meanings: "exposition," explanation
by synonyms, an "interpretation," and the "signification, meaning (of a
word or expression)."[3] These meanings carry over into the Middle Ages, as
we shall see. What I propose to investigate in this chapter are the ways in
which this wider range of meanings of *interpretatio* allows for a broader
notion of "translation" in medieval writing, or, more precisely, rewriting.

In lines 133–34 of the *Ad Pisones,* where Horace uses the expression
fidus interpres, he is referring to the word-for-word translator or close para-
phraser: "verbo verbum curabis reddere fidus / interpres." Clearly, Horace
is not speaking about the Ciceronian kind of translation.[4] Cicero favored
translation that renders correctly the sense of the original, but not necessarily
word-for-word. Horace's injunction goes even further. What he is arguing
has major implications for the use medieval authors made of sources and,
more specifically, for the medieval standards of translating from Latin to the
vernacular. Such translations transfer past works to the medieval present by
rewriting. Such rewriting is "translation" as literary invention, using
pre-existent source material. It is a variety of *translatio studii.*[5]

Horace's words appear in the section of the *Ad Pisones* in which he
counsels the writer to take up subjects that have already been treated rather
than something new: "rectius Iliacum carmen deducis in actus, / quam si
proferres ignota indictaque primus" (lines 129–30) [you are doing better in
relating a song of Troy than if for the first time you were recounting things
unknown or unsung]. But the new version should *not* be a faithful translation or paraphrase of the earlier one. For in lines 133–34 Horace *negates*
the *fidus interpres* statement quoted above: "*nec* verbo verbum curabis
reddere fidus / interpres." Lest the work be a failure because of constraints
that impede progress, constraints deriving from too great fidelity to

---

[3] *Oxford Latin Dictionary* (Oxford: Clarendon, 1982), p. 947.

[4] See W. Schwarz, "The Meaning of *Fidus interpres* in Medieval Translation," *The Journal
of Theological Studies* 45/2 (1944): 73–78.

[5] See my "*Translatio studii*: Translation, Adaptation, and Allegory in Medieval French
Literature," *Philological Quarterly* 57 (1978): 287–310.

antecedent sources, or, Horace continues, lest it fail because the new author attempts to grasp too broad a design—retelling the Trojan War *ab ovo* [from the very beginnings]—the *interpres* or "translator" interpreting and rewriting his or her material should leave out what is unnecessary or inept, and even insert falsehoods in order to produce a new version that is coherent, consistent, and credible from beginning to end. Macrobius gives an example of such "false" insertions in the *Saturnalia*. Vergil, he states, added to his material the mendacious story of Dido borrowed from the *Argonautica*, and his readers have believed in and been moved by her story ever since.[6] In doing so the author still represents persons and their actions in ways that are credible. Horace illustrates this further by a *cursus aetatum* [ages of life or of man] scheme: *puer, adolescens, vir, senex* (lines 156–78) [boy, young man, man, old man]. The technique for such invention is the identification and elaboration of circumstantial topoi: "semper in adiunctis aevoque morabimur aptis" (line 178) [we shall ever linger over features that are connected and fitted to the age] for the topos "age" [*aetas*], or for whatever the topos chosen calls for: gender, nationality, language, social order, profession, fortune and chance, and so on.[7]

Horace is speaking about theater in these lines. The Middle Ages seem to have known little about Roman theater. Accordingly, Horace's injunction was extended, by the twelfth and thirteenth centuries, to refer to any public reading. The broadening began in glosses on Horace's word *scaena* itself, as in line 125: "si quid inexpertum *scaenae* committis" [if it is untried theme that you entrust to the *stage*; emphasis mine]. The Pseudo-Acro scholia already take this line to refer to any poem, glossing it as: "si nouum poema scribis" [if you write a new poem].[8] The extension in meaning was no

---

[6]*Ambrosii Theodosii Macrobii Saturnalia*, ed. Jacob Willis (Leipzig: Teubner, 1963), 5.17.4–6.

[7]These circumstantial topoi are taken from Matthew of Vendôme's *Ars versificatoria*; see 1.77 in vol. 3, *Mathei Vindocinensis opera*, ed. Franco Munari (Rome: Edizioni di Storia e Letteratura, 1988). Professor Munari has retained the book and paragraph divisions in Faral's heretofore standard edition of the *Ars versificatoria*.

[8]*Pseudacronis scholia in Horatium vetustiora*, ed. Otto Keller, 2 vols. (Leipzig: Teubner, 1902–04), 2: 330.5–6.

doubt facilitated by the ensuing example of the *Iliacum carmen*, which suggests epic narrative rather than drama. Medieval readers would have been more familiar with epic examples than with those from theater.

A recently published edition of twelfth-century glosses on the *Ad Pisones* makes the broader application of Horace's line explicit by glossing his *scaena* as follows:

> scenon obumbraculum; inde scena quidam locus in theatro iuxta recitatorem, ubi erant cortine[9] extente infra quas latitabant persone, que prodibant ad suos gestus representandos, et inde scena theatrum uel recitatio uel scriptura recitanda appellatur.[10]
>
> [*scenon* is a shaded area; hence *scena* is a place in the theater next to the reader or reciter covered with curtains (?) in which actors hid, emerging to mime their gestures; hence *scena* means "theater" or "reading" or "recital" or a "written work intended for public reading or recitation."]

The drift in meaning of *scaena* from ancient stage to medieval public reading is readily apparent in this passage. The twelfth- and thirteenth-century arts of poetry and prose retain this broader sense of Horace's injunction regarding the *fidus interpres*, extending it to all written compositions.[11] Thus, glosses, scholia, and commentaries kept Horace's injunctions alive and meaningful beyond the end of Antiquity through to the arts of poetry and prose written in the twelfth and thirteenth centuries.

I should like to highlight a few of the interesting interpretations of *Ad Pisones* lines 133–34 that have been published. The most important issue in interpreting these lines is how to render sources, especially good sources, with originality—Horace's "proprie communia dicere" (*Ad Pisones* line 128) [to treat in your own way what is common]. A ninth-century scholia

---

[9]Taken in the medieval sense of "curtains" or "hangings" on a stage; see Jan F. Niermeyer, *Mediae latinitatis lexicon minus: lexique latin medieval-français/anglais* (Leiden: Brill, 1984), s.v. *cortina* (277).

[10]Karsten Friis-Jensen, "The *Ars Poetica* in Twelfth-Century France: The Horace of Matthew of Vendôme, Geoffrey of Vinsauf, and John of Garland," *Université de Copenhague: Cahiers de l'Institut du Moyen-Âge Grec et Latin* 60 (1990): 353.

[11]The major examples are discussed below.

attributed to Heiric of Auxerre states that the new poet must work new meaning and new language into the original. For example, he continues, if the new writer preserves Vergil's meaning even though using different words, the resulting work will not be original; it must have new meaning as well.[12] A medieval example of such unoriginal rewriting might be the twelfth-century poem entitled *Historia Troyana* by its editor.[13] The *Historia Troyana* is, as it were, anonymous. This is because the anonymous author thinks that this new version of Dares' *De excidio Troiae* does not really change anything found in the source. As the prologue points out to justify the anonymous *interpres*'s decision not to reveal his name but to sign the work with Dares': "Quia vero in ordinata Troyani belli historia Daretem Frigium auctorem habui, additis tamen quibusdam per preparacionem et per etopoiiam, quod personarum loquencium informacionem dicunt, hoc opusculum illius nomine inscribendum esse statui" [because in truth in the account of the Trojan War I took Dares the Phrygian as my source, despite the presence of some additions meant to prepare for events or clarify thoughts and sentiments through the contrived words of some characters].[14]

Let us return to Heiric of Auxerre's ninth-century scholia. If the poet adopts the same matter but expresses new meanings through or in it with different language, then the new work will be original: "si eandem materiam haberet et alias sententias et alia verba ex toto poneret, tunc de communi faceret propriam materiam" (465.11–13) [if one took the same matter and

---

[12] *Scholia in Horatium*, vol. 4, *Scholia in Horatium in codicibus parisinis latinis 17897 et 8223 obvia, quae ab Heirico Autissiodorensi profecta esse videntur,* ed. Hendrik J. Botschuyver (Amsterdam: Bottenberg, 1942), 465.9–13. See also Copeland, *Rhetoric, Hermeneutics, and Translation,* p. 176.

[13] *Anonymi historia Troyana Daretis Frigii,* ed. Jürgen Stohlmann (Wuppertal, Ratingen, Düsseldorf: Henn, 1968).

[14] *Historia Troyana,* 266.12–17. On this passage see my "Le patron et l'auteur dans l'invention romanesque," in *Théories et pratiques de l'écriture au moyen âge,* Actes du Colloque, Palais du Luxembourg-Sénat, 5 et 6 mars 1987, ed. Emmanuèle Baumgartner and Christiane Marchello-Nizia (Nanterre and Saint-Cloud: Centre de Recherches du Département de Français de Paris X-Nanterre and Centre Espace-Temps-Histoire de l'E.N.S. Fontenay/Saint-Cloud, 1988), pp. 34–36.

construed the whole with other meanings and language, then one would have one's own version of a common theme]. But to do so is difficult!

In his twelfth-century *Ars versificatoria* Matthew of Vendôme takes Horace's lines 133–34 as text to introduce the fourth part of his treatise on how to rewrite a given matter. He castigates those ill-prepared versifiers whose compositions rewrite poetic fables word for word, as if they had set out to comment in verse on their sources: "qui in scolastico exercitio fabulas circinantes poeticas verbum verbo sigillatim exprimunt tanquam super auctores metrice proposuerint commentare" (4.1) [in school exercises they grind out stories, ransacking poems word for word for images, just as if they were setting out to write a verse commentary upon their authors]. Matthew then quotes Horace's lines 133–34 to authorize the instruction he is imparting to his own pupils to rewrite in conformity with customary actions and sentiments in order to achieve truth or verisimilitude without falling into the word-for-word excesses of the *fidus interpres*.

Matthew is here codifying and lending authority to instruction and training in composition like that which John of Salisbury, in the *Metalogicon,* says characterized Bernard of Chartres's pedagogy. In preparation for their *praeexercitamina,* or exercises in prose and verse composition, Bernard had his pupils study carefully and in great detail—even memorize—the authors in verse and prose whom they were going to imitate by rewriting them. These assignments prepared Bernard's pupils to follow in the footsteps of the ancients, as John puts it, by "imitating" them. Such imitation required special attention to how the original conjoins words ("iuncturas dictionum") and uses elegant phrasing ("elegantes sermonum clausulas").[15] However, this kind of imitation does not allow for what we might call plagiary, or word-for-word copying! The patchwork quilt is not a work of art in Bernard of Chartres's classroom. He is after something else, something which seems to coincide with Horace's admonitions against the *fidus interpres* and Matthew's against paraphrase.

When Bernard found a pupil guilty of such patchwork plagiary the fault was corrected if the inept insertion merited it. Bernard then urged the

---

[15] *Ioannis Saresberiensis episcopi carnotensis Metalogicon libri IIII*, ed. Clement C. J. Webb (Oxford: Clarendon, 1929), 56/fol. 855b.

offending pupil not to copy but to imitate the image of the authors found in the sources.

> Sic uero redargutum, si hoc tamen meruerat inepta positio ad exprimendam auctorum imaginem, modesta indulgentia conscendere iubebat. (56/fol. 855b) [Thus reprimanded when inept composition justified it, with modest indulgence in the fault he ordered them to strive to express (in their compositions) the image of the authors (they imitated).]

It is noteworthy in the context of the twelfth-century gloss on *scaena* in the *Ad Pisones* as "scriptura recitanda" that Bernard included not only writing but public recitation as part of his pupils' assignments. They had to memorize and then recite what they had heard the day before in evening declamations, or *collationes*. After a year of such study, John claims that pupils acquired the "rationem loquendi et scribendi" (55/fol. 855a) [the principles of speaking and writing].

Another passage in the fourth book of Matthew's *Ars versificatoria* can help us get a better grasp of the character of such *interpretationes*. Matthew teaches that in describing a person one should strive to represent that person as one has "imagined" him or her. That is, the object of description should conform to the mental image the author has drawn up of that person in the context of the work being rewritten. For example, to describe an attractive young woman one should dwell on those features that make her attractive. This is invention using the circumstantial topoi referred to above. Matthew generalizes as follows: "in descriptione talis exprimatur persona qualis ymaginarie[16] descriptionis vel opinionis preconcipitur argumento" (4.18) [in description a person will be set forth in conformity with the import of the preconceived imaginary description or point of view]. Matthew's example of the attractive young woman is taken from Ovid's *Ars amatoria*: "Elige, cui dicas: 'Tu mihi sola places'" (4.18) [choose to whom you will say: "you alone please me"].[17] The artist as Pygmalion will reconstruct the pleasing qualities by imitating Ovid's 'imaginary idea'

---

[16]Cf. John of Salisbury's "ad exprimendam auctorum imaginem." (See n. 15.)

[17]See Munari, ed., *Ars versificatoria*, p. 203 n. 18.

and making it visible to the mind's eye in the new work. Such imitation of a source author's image is consistent with Bernard of Chartres's pedagogy as described by John of Salisbury. It is also a pedagogy which can be practiced; and it can produce something new from old matter. A description of the attractive young woman will contain new words that detail her attractiveness as the new author imagines it—that is, as he draws a mental picture from appropriate topoi and then turns that picture into words.[18] The new image may carry a new meaning, as when the person or the entire Ovidian seduction is praised, blamed, or adapted to a different kind of love from that which Ovid represents.

Matthew's *Ars versificatoria* is not the only medieval treatise to expound on Horace's *fidus interpres* and its context. Geoffrey of Vinsauf also takes the expression up in the short version of his *Documentum*. Here he offers specific suggestions on how to avoid word-for-word translation or paraphrase.[19] First, be brief when the source is dilated, and vice-versa. This applies especially to digressions and descriptions found in the source; these should be dispatched and passed over expeditiously in the new source, or, if brief in the original, be expanded, much as Matthew suggests for Ovid's "Tu mihi sola places." Second, the new authors should not follow in the steps of their predecessors. Geoffrey seems to mean the same thing that Heiric of Auxerre does, who reads Horace's admonition as giving new meaning and new language to the source by rewriting it. Geoffrey also wants the new work to reorder the source-matter according to the principles of natural and artificial order, and—in an extension of the first item—elaborate on what the source leaves out or excise material that in the new version would be unnecessary or inappropriate. This would presumably satisfy

---

[18] This is the "archetypal" or "mental" image that is basic to all phases of invention in both Matthew and Geoffrey of Vinsauf; see my *The Arts of Poetry and Prose* (Turnhout: Brepols, 1991), pp. 64–68. Invention begins anew in each phase of rewriting.

[19] *Documentum de modo et arte dictandi et versificandi* II.3.132–37, in Edmond Faral, *Les arts poétiques du XIIᵉ et du XIIIᵉ siècle: recherches et documents sur la technique littéraire du moyen âge* (Paris: Champion, 1958), pp. 309–10. See now Karsten Friis-Jensen, "Horace and the Early Writers of Arts of Poetry," in *Sprachtheorien in Spätantike und Mittelalter*, ed. Sten Ebbesen (Tübingen: Narr, 1995), pp. 360–401.

Horace's "veris falsa remiscet" (*Ad Pisones* line 151) [let the author blend fact with fiction (as Vergil did with Dido, according to Macrobius)]. Third, one must not introduce digressions from which one is unable to return to the principal matter. Fourth and last, one should avoid a bombastic, supercilious *entrée en matière*. Geoffrey continues to develop these ideas along the lines Horace does after the *fidus interpres* reference. In fact, his words here are a virtual commentary on those lines, as Faral's edition shows.

These diverse treatments of the Horatian rejection of the *fidus interpres* of old matter give some insight into the ways medieval schools practiced translation, taught composition, and formed habits of rewriting in their pupils and future authors. The intensity and detail of that study, illustrated by the context and scope of the medieval arts of poetry and prose as well as by Bernard of Chartres's systematic program of daily exercise, were aided and abetted by, alternately, corporal punishment, praise, and encouragement. If one acquired some proficiency in the Latin language after a year of such immersion, then surely after five or ten years habits of composition —or rather habits of rewriting—would have become ingrained. As the gifted or lucky pupils moved beyond the schools and attempted their own masterpieces, the injunction to favor extant sources, combined with a second injunction not to be a *fidus interpres* of those sources, led to a special sense of "translation" that I shall consider briefly in conclusion.

The medieval translation topic in its various guises—from *translatio imperii et studii* to the transfer of *chevalerie* and *clergie*—posits the use of *translatio*. *Translatio* is a term ranging in meaning from translation through adaptation to metaphorical transfer and allegory.[20] Yet all these terms presume some restatement, from Horace's rejected word-for-word translation through rewriting to rehearse the same matter with new words and meaning to, finally, metaphorical transfer itself as allegory. They all illustrate *interpretatio*. Depending on our specialties, diverse examples of these varieties will occur to all of us.

Does this special kind of translation—an "unfaithful" yet artful interpretation or reinterpretation—actually occur? Two kinds of evidence

---

[20]See my "*Translatio studii*," pp. 287–310.

support the contention that it did, in fact, exist and point in directions where we might confirm it. The two kinds of evidence are: 1) the concept of *interpretatio* in the medieval arts of poetry and prose; and 2) actual practice in works for which we know the sources and can be reasonably certain that our editions of them correspond to the versions the "rewriters" knew and used.

I shall begin with *interpretatio* in the arts of poetry and prose. In its simplest sense, *interpretatio* as a figure of diction refers to the way by which a sentence is restated—rewritten—using different words: "Est . . . interpretatio color quando eamdem sententiam per diversas clausulas interpretamur" (*Documentum* II.2.29/p. 277) [*Interpretatio* is a figure of speech by which we restate the same idea in different sentences]. By extension it becomes one of the devices for amplification in Geoffrey of Vinsauf's treatises. But, in fact, as I have tried to show elsewhere, all the devices for amplification are species of restatement.[21] If one takes the list in the *Poetria nova,* this is obvious in the case of periphrase, comparison, apostrophe, prosopopeia, description, and opposition. All these canonical devices of amplification restate in new words or new modes an initial statement and—by implication—an initial subject-matter or source. The different modes can in fact counterpoint one another. The one apparent exception is digression. Yet here too most varieties (I exclude the so-called *digressio inutilis*) either restate another part of the subject-matter or bring to the original subject-matter new material that produces a new version and, thus, restatement of it. All of this points to the general proposition that, in rewriting, one should dwell on what is brief, shorten what is lengthy, and complete what is incomplete. The last kind—the so-called *digressio utilis,* or digression proper—may even make the digression a kind of *mise en abyme* subsuming the entire work. There are striking examples of this in both parts of the *Roman de la rose.*[22]

---

[21] See my *Medieval Imagination: Rhetoric and the Poetry of Courtly Love* (Madison: University of Wisconsin Press, 1978), pp. 43–44.

[22] See my study of the *Rose, Internal Difference and Meanings in the "Roman de la rose"* (Madison: University of Wisconsin Press, 1995), pp. 125–27.

To be sure, length and brevity are relative categories. This brings us to the second kind of evidence mentioned above for "unfaithful" translation: actual rewriting of sources extant today. This kind of material helps us to appreciate the relative value of length and brevity as well as the complex strategies that went into lengthening and abbreviating sources for writers in search of new meaning. For example, when Benoît de Sainte-Maure and Joseph of Exeter rewrote Dares and Dictys, they obviously lengthened these sources while filling them out with other secondary sources, perhaps with glosses too, and with their own inventions. Briseida's presence in Dares becomes meaningful in Benoît. The battles are lengthier than in the source work as well, especially the first battle, which takes up a little more than 600 lines (lines 6979–7596) in Benoît. Yet in Konrad von Würzburg's Middle High German adaptation of Benoît, the *Trojanerkrieg*, the first battle extends over thousands of lines. This makes Benoît's version "brief," Konrad's "lengthy." Konrad also develops Achilles' story with earlier material that is missing in Benoît. Is not his invention an unfaithful translation of Benoît analogous to Benoît's own invention of Briseida's story?[23]

In conclusion, I should like to support the preceding discussion of unfaithful translation by pointing briefly to a few additional instances of "unfaithful" interpretation in rewriting. I will not explain them here but simply will show the obvious: something has changed in rewriting, the change is important, and it falls under the category of unfaithful translation of the antecedent work such that the new work becomes an original version of their common subject matter. One example, like Horace's, is from one language to another. It makes a great difference in how we read the Erec and Enide story whether Erec pardons Enide or asks his wife's forgiveness. The former occurs in Chrétien de Troyes's *Erec,* the latter in Hartmann von Aue's. A major "translation" also occurs when, near the midpoint of the *Roman de la rose,* Amant drops the God of love's commandment to be open and true and opts for deceit and infidelity—a decision restated (*interpretatio!*) and amplified when the God of love admits Faux Semblant

---

[23]On the Briseida invention, see my "The Invention of Briseida's Story in Benoît de Sainte-Maure's *Troie," Romance Philology* 48 (1995): 221–41.

into his army. Similarly, the various explanations offered for Lancelot's inability to achieve the Grail Quest in the *Lancelot en prose*—the sin of his father, love for Guenevere, the corrupting effect of that love on his own virtues—are so many new translations of the same issue. They emerge as explanations and are set aside as Lancelot comes to know his own moral state. Whether one sees these as the rewrite of successive continuators of the *Lancelot,* or of new versions proposed by the same author, they illustrate the principle of rewriting as unfaithful translation. "Unfaithful" translation, yet artful interpretation, is also at work in Froissart's reinventions of Ovidian fables. Not only does Froissart show Narcissus indifferent to Echo, the traditional version, but also he shows Narcissus spurned by Echo and dying of lovesickness because of unrequited love. Yet Froissart goes even further, conjoining elements of various Ovidian myths to write new fables about Neptisphelé and Pynoteus in the *Prison amoureuse,* Papyrus and Ydoree in the *Espinette amoureuse,* and Ydrophus and Neptiphoras in the *Joli buisson de jonece.* The mysterious Enclimpostair in the *Paradis d'amour* is an "unfaithful" interpretation of Machaut's Morphee in the *Fonteinne amoureuse.* Enclimpostair is Morphee's son.

These examples suggest that infidelity to source, and thus unfaithful translation, is what we must expect and, in all its intertextual implications, what we must look for and study. Translation and *interpretatio* are fundamental strategies in medieval composition. The discovery of mere borrowing or paraphrase is, by these standards, erroneous, or it is a fortuitous coincidence, or—by medieval standards and practice—it is writing as bad as that of Bernard of Chartres's inept pupils. Does not the critic who extols such works deserve the same flogging Bernard of Chartres meted out to his inept pupils?

Translating Job as Female

Ann W. Astell

The act of translation had, as Rita Copeland has demonstrated, two distinct but overlapping meanings in late Antiquity and the Middle Ages. In the grammarian tradition, translation virtually was synonymous with interpretation and thus a "form of commentary," inclusive of gloss, allegoresis, and paraphrase. Among rhetoricians, in contrast, translation was a means of invention and "a special form of imitation." These two aspects of *translatio*—interpretation and imitation—are, of course, connected intimately in the process of literary production because the "copy" of the "model" text emerges from an interpretive community and inevitably displays not so much "the conspicuous likeness of the original, but rather what is understood and revalued in the original."[1] The historical reception of a text, in short, determines the form of its literary afterlife.

This chapter, therefore, begins by considering how biblical exegesis—in particular, St. Gregory the Great's influential *Moralia in Job* (ca. A.D. 595)—translated, that is, interpreted, Job as feminine.[2] It then addresses a

---

[1] See Rita Copeland, *Rhetoric, Hermeneutics, and Translation in the Middle Ages: Academic Traditions and Vernacular Texts* (Cambridge and New York: Cambridge University Press, 1991), pp. 10 and 27.

[2] In addition to the broad meanings of interpretation and imitation, the word *translatio* had, of course, a variety of narrower denotations in the Middle Ages. With respect to things (*res*), translation implied physical movement from place to place; the changing of outward form and bodily appearance (metamorphosis); the transmutation of actual substance; and the elevation from a lower to a higher state of being (transfiguration, apotheosis, or sainthood). With respect to words (*verba*), translation designated paraphrase in the same language (rewording), expression in another natural language, and the use of words in a metaphorical or transferred sense.

59

single notable imitation of Job as female in the person of Chaucer's Patient Griselda. As we shall see, Gregory's allegorical interpretation of the Book of Job simultaneously genders and displaces its literal meaning as feminine in a way that admits and invites a Chaucerian reversal of that reading and, thus, the return of a female Job in the form of Walter's sorely tried wife.

As I have argued elsewhere, Gregory's peculiar interpretation of Job and its commonplace medieval classification as a biblical instance of heroic poetry comparable to the pagan epics of Homer and Virgil depend not on any outward, formal similarity between and among these works but, rather, on the commentary tradition that contextualized the Greek and Roman epics and discovered in them hidden meanings consonant with Stoic and Neoplatonic moral philosophy.[3] To use Copeland's phrase, the "larger framework of interpretive consanguinity" obviates the "need for conspicuous resemblance,"[4] not only synchronically (between pagan and Christian works) but also diachronically (between any literary model and its copy). The important thing joining the texts as a single set and thus determining their literary kind is that they teach the same truth, convey the same moral lesson.

Within this interpretive frame, gender symbolism plays an important role, given the dominant cultural understanding of heroic poetry as a masculine genre. Plato criticizes Homer and wishes even his poetry to be banned from the Republic for the specific reason that Homer's heroes display "a woman's reaction, not a man's" to bereavement, delivering long speeches of lamentation, singing, weeping, or beating their breasts, and thus "nourish and water" the passions of their auditors, evoking them and giving them rulership "when they ought to be under control."[5] Aristotle, unlike Plato, finds a social value in *pathos* and calls attention to notable examples of heroic virtue in Homer's poetry, but he defines fortitude in a narrow, martial way that demands a public occasion and thus effectively excludes

---

[3]See my *Job, Boethius, and Epic Truth* (Ithaca: Cornell University Press, 1994).

[4]Copeland, *Rhetoric, Hermeneutics, and Translation*, p. 28.

[5]Plato, *Republic* 10, *Classical Literary Criticism*, trans. Donald A. Russell, ed. Donald A. Russell and Michael Winterbottom (Oxford and New York: Oxford University Press, 1989), pp. 48–49.

women from heroism.[6] Cicero derives the word *virtus* from *vir*, on the grounds that a man's most characteristic quality is strength: "viri autem propria maxime est fortitudo."[7] Isidore of Seville, following in this same line, links *virtus* with *vir*, observing that strength (*vis*) is greater in a man than in a woman.[8] Although the Stoic, Neoplatonic, and Christian allegoresis of Homer and Virgil in late Antiquity gradually effected a semantic shift in the meaning of "virtue"—from physical prowess in a public arena to spiritual endurance in a private one—the imagery used to represent that inward truth remained the same: martial and male.

Given this set of gendered criteria for heroism, the classification of the Book of Job as a *heroicum carmen* is necessarily problematic. The Book records the serial sufferings of a just man confronted with the sudden loss of his property, his seven sons and three daughters, and his health. With the exception of a single verse which compares our earthly life to warfare (Job 7:1), the Book makes no mention of martial action and sets no public occasion for a freely chosen act of courage.[9] The so-called frame story (Chapters 1, 2, and the last part of 42) features a self-controlled Job who silently bows to the will of God, but the central Dialogue (Job 3:3–42:6) depicts a passionate Job who curses the day of his birth, protests his innocence, complains bitterly, and prays for death. In Platonic terms, the Job of the frame story has "a man's reaction" to his misfortune, whereas the Job of the Dialogue speaks and weeps like a woman.

In order to interpret the Book of Job as a whole as a *heroicum carmen*, therefore, medieval readers necessarily had to subordinate the feminine text

---

[6]See Aristotle, *The Nicomachean Ethics,* trans. H. Rackham, Loeb Classical Library 73 (1926; repr. London and New York: Putnam, 1962), III.vi–ix, pp. 152–73. Aristotle excludes drowning and disease as "occasions" for courage. He goes on to enumerate five kinds of fortitude, all illustrated with examples of fighting men, after giving this general definition of the hero: "The courageous man, therefore, in the proper sense of the term, will be he who fearlessly confronts a noble death, or some sudden peril that threatens death; and the perils of war answer this description most fully" (p. 157).

[7]Cicero, *Tusculan Disputations,* trans. John E. King, Loeb Classical Library 141 (1927; repr. Cambridge, Mass.: Harvard University Press, 1971), II.xviii.43, pp. 194–95.

[8]Isidore of Seville, *Etymologiae* XI.ii.17, PL 82: 417.

[9]Here and elsewhere, I use the Douay translation of the Vulgate.

of the Dialogue to the masculine text of the frame story and interpret the former from the perspective of the latter. Christian exegetes, who had learned to discover in mythological figures such as Odysseus and Hercules the veiled image of the Stoic sage enduring misfortune with *apatheia,* were eager to find in the biblical letter the heroic truth to which the pagan poets obliquely referred. Gregory, for one, does this in three ways.

First, he takes his cue from Job 7:1 and Prudentius's *Psychomachia* (A.D. 405) and constructs in the opening pages of his commentary on Job an elaborate allegory, wherein Job appears as a combatant in a cosmic theater, fighting alternatively as a wrestler or a gladiator to champion God's cause against Satan's attack. Job's sinews are virtues; his helmet, faith; his shield, patience; his sword and spear, love. The pagan "otherness" of Iliadic poetry thus confirms the literal truth of Job's (masculine) heroism under trial. Gregory's commentary in this way "serves" the sacred Scripture it purports to elucidate, even as it effectively translates and displaces the biblical narrative to make it more comparable to its Homeric and Virgilian counterparts.[10]

Second, Gregory uses the figure of Job's wife to protect Job himself from the charge of womanish behavior. In the enigmatic biblical account, Job's unnamed wife appears and speaks only once, advising her afflicted husband to "curse God and die" (Job 2:9). Job rebukes her for speaking "like one of the foolish women" and asks her, "If we take happiness from God's hand, must we not take sorrow too?" (Job 2:10). Gregory comments at length on the brief exchange, finding in it a re-enactment of Eve's temptation of Adam: "verba sua Eva repetit."[11] According to Gregory, Job's wife, at the instigation of Satan, not only speaks words "of a bad persuasion" (III.viii.14, p. 123: "male suadentis verba") but also seduces Job with blandishments (III.viii.13, p. 122: "per . . . verba blandiens") and,

---

[10]Cf. Copeland's remark that a "chief maneuver of academic hermeneutics is to displace the very text that it purposes to serve. Medieval arts commentary does not simply 'serve' its 'master' texts: it also rewrites and supplants them" (3).

[11]Gregory I, *Moralia in Job,* ed. Marcus Adriaen, CCSL 143, 143A, 143B (Turnhout: Brepols, 1979–85), III.viii.14, p. 123. Subsequent citations by book, chapter, subchapter, and page number are parenthetical.

appealing to his sensuality, pierces his heart with the force of love: "uis amoris cor perforat."

Like Shakespeare's Hamlet, who translates the "name" of "frailty" as "woman,"[12] Gregory glosses "woman" to mean "weakness." Distinguishing between the categories of sex and gender, Gregory explains that the word *woman* in Scripture either literally designates a member of the female sex or figuratively names weakness: "In sacro eloquio mulier aut pro sexu ponitur aut pro infirmitate" (XI.xlix.65, p. 623). Thus, as the *Moralia* translates the passage, Job's wife encourages her husband to yield to his passions, to give a carnal, emotional response to his losses. Siren, like the meretricious Muses who attend the bedside of Boethius, she tempts Job to moral weakness, weeping despair, and suicide.

Within the larger scheme of Gregorian gender symbolism, therefore, Job's rebuke of his wife and his syllogistic defense of divine justice constitute the victory of his higher, masculine nature over his passionate, feminine self. As Gregory explains it, a man is commonly called ("vocatur") strong and discreet, whereas a woman is considered ("accipitur") weak and indiscreet, and therefore the words *vir* and *mulier* can be translated as mental strength and weakness, respectively: "Vir etenim fortis quilibet et discretus vocatur, mulier uero mens infirma uel indiscreta accipitur" (XI.xlix.65, p. 623).[13] Elsewhere Gregory interprets the creation of Eve during the sleep of Adam in a way that explicitly associates woman's nature with a man's emotional and instinctive sphere, his carnal unconscious, his "animal part." Echoing a long misogynist tradition, Gregory insists that self-knowledge requires a man to recognize that there is within himself something virile and something infirm; something rational, which ought to rule like a man, and something passionate, to be ruled like a woman: "ut aliud in illo sit quod regere ualeat tamquam vir, aliud tamquam femina quod regatur" (XXX.xvi.54, p. 1528).[14]

---

[12]William Shakespeare, *Hamlet, Prince of Denmark,* in *The Complete Works,* ed. Alfred Harbage, revised Pelican text (New York: Viking, 1977; repr. 1979), I,ii.146.

[13]Gregory uses this equation to explicate the proverb, "Melior est iniquitas viri, quam benefaciens mulier" (literally, "The wickedness of a man is better than a woman doing good").

[14]For a similar gendered distinction between the higher and lower parts of the soul see Cicero, *Tusculan Disputations* II.xxi, pp. 200–05.

Gregory's elaborate exposition of the exchange between a wise Job and his unruly wife prepares the way for his allegorical interpretation of the central dialogue, where Job, shortly after rejecting his wife's advice to "curse God and die," utters a series of blasphemous complaints, curses the day of his birth, and prays for death. Privileging the masculine text of the frame story as literally true, Gregory treats the Joban outcries as a deliberate allegory, wherein Job, the inspired author of his own story, presents orthodox dogma hidden under the veil of a double-meaning, deceptive, carnal, and feminine text. If we understand Job's words correctly, Gregory insists, his malediction actually expresses the right judgement of a man not bitter with despair, not stirred by wrath, but rather tranquil with true teaching: "non est ira commoti sed doctrina tranquilli" (IV.i.3, p. 165). Although he speaks outwardly ("foras") in sorrow, he administers allegorically ("intus") the power of a healing medicine to the wounded: "uulneratis intus ostendit uirtutem medicaminis" (IV.i.3, p. 166).

By developing an allegory of spiritual warfare, commenting extensively on Job's rebuke of his temptress wife, and treating the passionate Joban protests as intentional allegory, Gregory's *Moralia* translates—in the sense of an interpretive displacement—the Book of Job to align it closely with the Stoic moralizations of Homer and Virgil and distance it from a possible feminine, non-heroic reading. At the same time, however, Gregory recognizes a fundamental incompatibility between the Stoic sage and the Christian saint and the heroic ideals they embody. Emphasizing that difference forces him again and again to overturn his masculine gendering of Job and translate his hero ("bellator noster") anew in feminine terms, which have in the process been paradoxically revalued. Carole Straw observes that for Gregory wisdom is the Pauline foolishness of the cross, a wisdom that, unlike the *constantia mentis* of the Stoics, "demands not *apatheia*, but *passio*,"[15] the painfully felt and freely accepted experience of suffering, loss, and infirmity. According to Gregory, Job's very name translates into Latin ("latino eloquio") as *dolens*, so that the Redeemer's suffering might be signified by both Job's name and his wounds: "per eius

---

[15]Carole Straw, *Gregory the Great: Perfection in Imperfection* (Berkeley: University of California Press, 1988), p. 199.

et nomen et uulnera" (VI.i.1, p. 284). As a figure or type of Christ crucified, the very meaning of Job—his *significatio* translated into time—depends on the historical truth of his affliction and the literal truth of his lamentations.

The *Moralia*'s treatment of Job at discontinuous levels of interpretation—literal and allegorical (Christological and moral/tropological)—thus sustains the manifold contradictions in Gregory's depiction of Job as both an invincible, well-armed warrior and a sword-pierced sufferer, images that engender Job as both masculine and feminine in a fluid array of possibilities. When this interpretive *translatio* itself translates into a literary translation of Job, however, the multiple exegetical levels and metanarratives are forced to occupy a single narrative line. The vertical discontinuities among discrete hermeneutical levels tend in the process to become "gaps" in the horizontal account of things, ordered chronologically in a Joban retelling. This, as we shall see, is especially apparent in Chaucer's version of the story of Patient Griselda.

When the commentary's Christological gendering of Job as feminine is reliteralized in The Clerk's Tale, the heroine Griselda appears as Job's female *translatio*. Like Job, she is a virtuous figure, subjected to a mysterious series of cruel trials. First her infant daughter, then her newborn son, are wrenched from her arms at the orders of her husband the Marquis, presumably to be murdered. Then, after years of marriage, Walter publicly divorces Griselda, sending her, clad only in a smock, away from the palace. Finally he asks her to return to court to oversee the arrangements for his remarriage to a much younger woman. Only after Griselda has borne all these afflictions patiently does Walter relent, reveal that his new bride is in fact their daughter, restore to a fainting Griselda their two children, and renew his marriage bond with her.

Chaucer's language explicitly likens Griselda to both Christ and Job throughout the tale. When Walter proposes marriage, Griselda, like Mary at the hour of the Annunciation, kneels to hear "what was the lordes wille."[16]

---

[16]Geoffrey Chaucer, *The Canterbury Tales,* in *The Riverside Chaucer,* 3rd ed., ed. Larry D. Benson (Boston: Houghton Mifflin, 1987), 4.294. Subsequent citations by fragment and line number are parenthetical.

"Translated" (4.385) from the "oxes stalle" (4.291) into the court, out of her peasant garb into royal attire, Griselda reigns at Walter's side with such pacific wisdom that she, like Christ, "from hevene sent was, as men wende, / Peple to save and every wrong t'amende" (4.440–41). "[A]s a lamb . . . meke and stille" (4.538), she suffers the loss of her children, offering them to the Heavenly Father like the dolorous Mother on Calvary. Divorced and dismissed by Walter, Griselda paraphrases Job 1:21: "'Naked out of my fadres hous,' quod she, / 'I cam, and naked moot I turne agayn'" (4.871–72). Indeed, according to the Clerk, Griselda's "pacient benyngnytee" (4.929) surpasses the much acclaimed "humblesse" of Job himself (4.932–38).

Introducing the Joban intertext into his translation of his Petrarchan source, Chaucer converts a classical Stoic exemplum of *constantia mentis* into a Christian legend of salvific suffering and all-conquering love.[17] Doing so requires Chaucer to give emotive expression to Griselda's suffering while retaining the necessary plot element of the premarital vow that binds Griselda never to oppose Walter's wishes "'[n]either by word ne frownyng contenance'" (4.356). Chaucer accomplishes this in two ways.

First, as Lawrence Besserman has noted, Chaucer displaces onto male characters the display of emotion that is typically gendered as feminine.[18] Unlike Griselda, who walks silent and dry-eyed away from the palace, her father, Janicula, takes upon his lips the lamentation of Job and "[c]urseth the day and tyme that Nature / Shoop hym to been a lyves creature"

---

[17]In 1371 Petrarch wrote a Latin version of the Griselda story that Boccaccio had used to conclude his *Decameron* (1353). Petrarch's Griselda (*Epistolae seniles* 17.3) reflects his commitment to what Charlotte C. Morse has termed "a heavily Stoic, practical moral philosophy" ("The Exemplary Griselda," *Studies in the Age of Chaucer* 7 [1985]: 57). As Morse observes, "Petrarch accommodates the story to classical rhetoric," keeping "overt Christian references" to a minimum (58). Petrarch does not name Job. Indeed, after examining over sixty manuscripts of Petrarch's Latin story of Griselda, J. Burke Severs found an explicit mention of Job in only one fifteenth-century manuscript. See "The Job Passage in the *Clerkes Tale*," *Modern Language Notes* 49 (1934): 461–62.

[18]Lawrence L. Besserman, *The Legend of Job in the Middle Ages* (Cambridge, Mass.: Harvard University Press, 1979), p. 112.

(4.902–03). Similarly, Chaucer's Clerk, unlike Petrarch's narrator, repeatedly interjects pathetic commentary, sympathizing with Griselda, speaking for her, and blaming Walter. Indeed, he castigates the latter for sadism in a way that aligns Walter more with the cruel Satan of Gregory's Job than with the benevolent (albeit inscrutable) God of Petrarch.

Second, Chaucer allows Griselda herself to speak more than Petrarch's heroine does—both in touching prayer, as when she kisses her infant daughter farewell—and in double-meaning responses to Walter. When, for instance, he intimates that her second child must also be killed, she replies, "Deth may nought make no comparisoun / Unto youre love" (4.666–67). Later, when he divorces her, she announces her intention never to remarry: "God shilde swich a lordes wyf to take / Another man to housbonde or to make!" (4.839–40). Taken at face value, her words honor Walter and fulfill the vow he has enforced upon her; read ironically, they translate into a sharp-tongued indictment of him. Chaucer thus parodies Gregory's allegoresis of Joban outcry and inverts it, representing Griselda's words as carefully controlled outwardly but veiling inwardly the depth of her pain under torture. At the same time, Chaucer anticipates in his echoic portrayal of Griselda's speech the insight of feminist theorists who speak of women's discourse as a form of double-speaking that mimics the dominant, patriarchal discourse in order to subvert it.[19]

The troubling tale of Chaucer's Clerk similarly undermines the Gregorian scriptural model it echoes and imitates. When a Christlike Job who has been gendered as feminine in biblical commentary is reliteralized as a female protagonist in Chaucer's imitation of the Job story, the inherent contradictions and the implicit and explicit misogyny of Gregorian exegesis stand exposed. As we have seen, Gregory ostensibly distinguishes between the categories of sex and gender, yet he tends to equate and conflate them in practice; to ascribe fortitude to men, weakness (moral, mental, and physical) to women. Chaucer's Clerk therefore answers the Wife of Bath's

---

[19]See Barbara Godard, "Theorizing Feminist Discourse-Translation," in *Translation, History, and Culture*, ed. Susan Bassnett and André Lefevere (London and New York: Pinter, 1990), pp. 87–96.

charge that "no womman of no clerk is preysed" (3.706) by explicitly countering the clerical tendency to discover virtue only in men such as Job, while they "preise wommen but a lite" (4.935). The Clerk's storied praise of a fictive Griselda, however, elevates her so high above other women that Chaucer cautions the married men in his audience against testing their wives' patience "in trust to fynde / Grisildis" (4.1181–82). No such discovery, however marvelous, can justify the Walter-like cruelty upon which it depends. If, as Chaucer declares in his envoy, "Grisilde is deed, and eek hire pacience" (4.1177), both Walter and her Clerk-narrator seemingly have gone too far in their treatment of her.

In making Griselda an answer to the Wife of Bath, Chaucer calls attention to the incontrovertible binary in feminine gender symbolism.[20] At one extreme, *woman* translates into carnality, weakness, foolishness, emotion, and loquacity; at the other, into the soul, sanctity, intuitive wisdom, mercy, justice, and silence. Thus in Gregory's commentary the biblical hero Job both is and is not feminine. Distanced from his despairing wife, Job enters into his own despair. Metamorphosized into a female form in Chaucer's Griselda, he/she loses none of the polarized ambiguity of his/her gendering. Indeed, it is precisely the translative interchange of emotive outcry and silence, suffering and self-control, *pathos* and endurance in the (direct and indirect) characterization of Chaucer's Joblike Griselda that makes her, unlike Petrarch's Stoic heroine, the agent of genuine conversion.

In Griselda Chaucer presents the joining together of two extremes: physical and social vulnerability, on the one hand, and divine grace, on the other—feminine extremes that tempt Walter at first to exercise absolute domination over his wife and thus debase himself; then draw him upward to reconcile himself to Griselda and her tested goodness. Although Walter attempts to justify his actions, the narrative indicates that he, moved by

---

[20]For a treatment of the Joban connection between the Wife of Bath and Griselda see my "Job's Wife, Walter's Wife, and the Wife of Bath," in *Old Testament Women in Western Literature,* ed. Raymond-Jean Frontain and Jan Wojcik (Conway, Ark.: University of Central Arkansas Press, 1991), pp. 92–107.

Griselda's virtue, repents of his "crueel purpos" (4.734) and actually changes in the end, whereas Petrarch's Godlike husband never really converts but only discloses to Griselda the true benevolence behind his seeming malice. At the lower and upper margins of Walter's world, Griselda enters it through a translation that ultimately effects Walter's own.

As Sherry B. Ortner and others have shown, this meeting of extremes, this confluence of "completely polarized and apparently contradictory meanings" reflects a "single system of cultural thought"[21] inclusive of other related binaries, such as the dualism of body and soul. If, as Gregory the Great tells us, *woman* means "weakness," that simple equation conceals a union of contraries subsumed under a single term. *Woman* means opposite things, because "weakness" points to what is both the lowest and the highest; to the carnal sensuality of an Eve, on the one hand, and the self-sacrifice of Christ, on the other. As this paper has suggested, the meeting of opposites in gender symbolism assumes a special force in the paradoxical language of Scripture, scriptural exegesis, and biblical imitation. United by a copulative verb or the *id est* of an exegete, folly is wisdom; weakness, strength; death, life; the last, first; the servant, the master; and a female Job, greater than Job.[22]

---

[21] Sherry B. Ortner, "Is Female to Male as Nature Is to Culture?" in *Woman, Culture, and Society,* ed. Michelle Zimbalist Rosaldo and Louise Lamphere (Stanford: Stanford University Press, 1974), pp. 67–87; quotation from 85.

[22] The paratactic evocation of opposites in this last sentence, like the ten enigmatic pairings in the Pythagorean Table of Opposites, highlights the incommensurability of opposition as such. Not all opposites are opposites in the same way; that is, they do not all stand at the same "distance" from each other, nor do they occupy the same ontological plane. Immortality is not to Mortality what Life is to Death, Hot to Cold, Day to Night, Good to Evil, Right to Left, Youth to Age, and Male to Female. Some opposites are absolutely distinct; others meet; others overlap. In the Aristotelian tradition, paired terms are generally contraries in the sense that one is a positive term, the other a privative. See G. E. R. Lloyd, *Polarity and Analogy: Two Types of Argumentation in Early Greek Thought* (Cambridge: Cambridge University Press, 1966), pp. 16–17, 48–65.

Gender Symbolism
and Text Image Relationships:
Hildegard of Bingen's *Scivias*

Madeline H. Caviness

The conventional view of illustrations seems to be that they represent a kind of pictorial translation of a text, of secondary if supplemental interest, generally marred by the inadequacies and ambiguities of visual representation and, possibly also, by "misunderstandings." This version is something like a gospel, beginning "In the beginning was the word, and the word was translated into pictures." This is the *a priori* position from which Christel Meier began her analysis of the illuminations in the lost Rupertsberg manuscript of the *Scivias,* summed up in the phrase "Transformation von Wort ins Bild."[1]

The severing of text from image reflects our modern disciplinary separations. The Latinists who have edited texts often chose to ignore the pictorial images that accompanied the words in some recensions of the work. Art historians traditionally concentrated on pictorial sources for pictures, typically reproducing them as if literally cut out of the medieval book, and when they did consider "textual sources" they took textual primacy for granted. More recently, under the fashionable tag "text and image," scholars have identified many instances of the indivisibility of one from another.[2]

---

[1]Christel Meier, "Zum Verhältnis von Text und Illustration im überlieferten Werk Hildegards von Bingen," in *Hildegard von Bingen, 1179–1979: Festschrift zum 800. Todestag der Heiligen*, ed. Anton P. Brück (Mainz: Selbstverlag der Gesellschaft für mittelrheinische Kirchengeschichte, 1979), p. 168.

[2]For instance, see the collection of papers edited by Christel Meier and Uwe Ruberg, *Text und Bild: Aspekte des Zusammenwirkens zweier Künste in Mittelalter und früher Neuzeit* (Wiesbaden: L. Reichert, 1980). The journal *Word and Image* was founded in 1985, and

Some significant examples involved the simultaneous creation of verbal and pictorial records of recent events, for instance by the English chroniclers Gerald of Wales and Matthew Paris in the late twelfth and early thirteenth centuries. Both monastic writers evidently made notes and sketches at the same time, recording their observations of details in costume or equipment. Each presumably worked up these field notes into a finished book, in one case probably still autograph, in the other, perhaps written and illustrated by an assistant.[3] The exotic elephant that arrived in London in 1255 as a royal gift was closely observed by Matthew Paris, and his autograph drawing is an important case of imagistic primacy—not only was part of the archaic bestiary text written in the spaces already defined by the magnificent beast's contour but also the draughtsman's eye overrode the biases it might have taught him about elephants having no knee joints (fig. 1).[4] His drawing in fact questioned the authority of the text in a way that is at once more convincing than a verbal refutation, and less risky; but to confirm its authority, he states flatly that the elephant itself served as his model. Hildegard's visionary works validated seeing of a different kind, but in the lost *Scivias* too, a radically new imagery was created that I maintain complements and supplements the text.

---

one of the three volumes of papers from the 1986 art history congress in Washington concerned "The Written Word as Art and in Art"; see *World Art: Themes of Unity in Diversity: Acts of the XXVIth International Congress of the History of Art*, vol. 2, ed. Irving Lavin (University Park: Pennsylvania State University Press, 1989).

[3]A manuscript of Gerald of Wales's *Topographia Hibernica,* containing many marginal sketches of the peoples he encountered in Ireland in 1187–88, was probably very close to the original version: British Library, MS Royal 13 B VIII; see T. S. R. Boase, *English Art, 1100–1216* (Oxford: Clarendon, 1953), p. 197 and pl. 31e. See also Antonia Gransden, *Historical Writing in England: c. 550 to c. 1307* (Ithaca: Cornell University Press, 1973), pp. 242–44, pl. VIII.

[4]Gransden, *Historical Writing*, p. 365, refers to the verisimilitude of the drawings in the *Chronica Majora*. More recently, the drawing in the miscellany, British Library Cotton MS Nero D I, fol. 169v, has been claimed as the first sketch; see Suzanne Lewis, *The Art of Matthew Paris in the Chronica Majora* (Berkeley: University of California Press in collaboration with Corpus Christi College, Cambridge, 1987), p. 215, and Madeline H. Caviness, "'The Simple Perception of Matter' and the Representation of Narrative, ca. 1180–1280," *Gesta* 30 (1991): 52.

In this short, exploratory chapter I argue that text and image were inseparably linked together as bearers of meaning in the lost illuminated manuscript of the *Scivias* (formerly Wiesbaden, Hessisches Landesbibliothek, MS 1). It is generally accepted that this book was made under Hildegard's direction, most probably at Rupertsberg Abbey about 1165, but I will argue that Hildegard began to make sketches at the same time that she began to take notes, perhaps reworking them as the text took shape in the 1140s, and that these were the basis for the illuminations. Thus we can recognize in them Hildegard's personal record of her visions. The odd proportions of the frames, curious abstract forms, truncated human figures (some gigantesque, some diminutive), and the fragmentation of architectural forms and compositions that have no consistent right side up, are the products of an eccentric and very specific visual cognitive process on the part of the designer, regardless of how many craftspersons aided in the final execution of the illuminations. Furthermore, in several cases the images in the lost *Scivias* manuscript add information that is not in the text (or that is a corrective to it), but these changes depend on other works of Hildegard. Some of these instances make even more claims for female deity than does the text.

I will also speculate on why this set of illuminations appears not to have been copied, and why a far more conventional series is to be seen in the later recension from the Cistercian Abbey of Salem (Heidelberg, Universitätsbibliothek Cod. Salem X, 16). This later set of pictures depends on various identifiable traditions, including standard Apocalypse illustrations, and serves to point up the originality of the Rupertsberg images (figs. 2, 3, 4).[5]

[5] See *Die Zeit der Staufer: Geschichte, Kunst, Kultur: Katalog der Austellung,* ed. Reiner Haussherr, vol. 1 (Stuttgart: Württemburgisches Landesmuseum, 1977), pp. 553–55, no. 732 (catalogue entry by Renate Kroos, with bibliography). The most complete description and discussion of sources is still that of Adolf von Oechelhaeuser, *Die Miniaturen der Universitäts-bibliothek zu Heidelberg,* vol. 1 of *Heidelberger Habilitationsschrift* (Heidelberg: Gustav Koester, 1887), pp. 75–107, pls. 11–17. Some sources are discussed by C. Hand Kessler, "A Problematic Illumination of the Heidelberg Liber Scivias," *Marsyas* 8 (1957–59): 7–21. Meier, *Festschrift,* figs. 15–16, uses the same example (fol. 111) for comparison with the Rupertsberg manuscript (my figs. 2, 3). This manuscript, which Kroos dated to the first quarter of the thirteenth century, cannot be the one Abbot Gottfried of Salem (1165–68)

Comparison is made here with the Bamberg Apocalypse of about A.D. 1000, which is a more likely source of inspiration than the Spanish manuscripts with Beatus's Commentary, although these too provide parallels.[6]

First, a clear review is needed of the extent of our knowledge of the lost manuscript, which disappeared from storage in Dresden during World War II. Barring its rediscovery, of which there is some hope with the reunification of Germany and the opening up of collections in the Soviet Republics, there are, on the one hand, excellent black-and-white photographs of all thirty-five illuminations, taken about 1925 (the negatives are in the Rheinisches Bildarchiv in Cologne) and reproduced in the first edition of Maura Böckler's German translation.[7] These are the only authentic images we have, but of course they lack color (figs. 2, 5, 7, 10, 12–15, 17, 18, 20). The modeling and contours read well enough in the photographs to establish that the figure drawing follows twelfth-century conventions in the somewhat crude abstractions of wet-fold drapery; similar drawing is seen for instance in the Stammheim Missal made for the Benedictine Abbey of

acknowledged "seeing and reading" when he received it from Hildegard; see *Hildegardis Scivias*, ed. Adelgundis Führkötter and Angela Carlevaris, *Corpus Christianorum Continuatio Mediaevalis* 43 and 43A (Turnhout: Brepols, 1978), p. xl.

[6]Hildegard herself preached in Bamberg between 1158 and 1161 and could have seen the Ottonian manuscript, but I prefer to think the Salem images were created independently of her; see *Das Leben der Heiligen Hildegard von Bingen*, ed. Adelgundis Führkötter (Düsseldorf: Patmos, 1968), p. 132. Several pages from the Bamberg Apocalypse are illustrated in Frederick van der Meer, *Apocalypse: Visions from the Book of Revelation in Western Art* (New York: Alpine Fine Arts Collections, 1978), pp. 102–08. A more general comparison is to the late tenth-century Escorial Beatus manuscript, Escorial, Biblioteca del Monasterio, &.II.5, fol. 120; see John Williams, *Early Spanish Manuscript Illumination* (New York: Braziller, 1977), pl. 26.

[7]Maura Böckler, *Hildegard of Bingen, Wisse die Wege, Scivias* (Salzburg: Otto Müller, 1928). Unfortunately, the later edition (1954) uses the modern copies. Some of each appear to be used by Charles Singer, "The Visions of Hildegard of Bingen," in his *From Magic to Science: Essays on the Scientific Twilight* (London: Ernest Benn, 1928), pls. I, XI–XIV, figs. 95, 97, 99, 106–08, though the poor color reproductions might be from hand-colored photographs. An earlier set of black-and-white photographs was reproduced by Louis Baillet, "Les Miniatures du 'Scivias' de Sainte Hildegarde conservé à la bibliothèque de Wiesbaden," *Académie des inscriptions et belles lettres, monuments et mémoires* [Paris] 19 (1911): 49–149.

St. Michael's Hildesheim about 1160, which also has the plain shaded frames that are frequently used in the *Scivias* manuscript (figs. 5, 6, 20).[8] No other illuminated manuscript from Hildegard's Rupertsberg has been authenticated, so comparisons cannot be made with other illuminated books from her scriptorium.[9]

A hand-made copy in full color supplements the photographs of the lost *Scivias;* Josepha Knips, working in the revived Benedictine monastery of Eibingen in 1927–33, made a very close copy of all the illuminations, and three nuns copied the script of the original text.[10] Thus we can also reconstruct accurately the text pages, and understand the compositional relationships of text lines and picture frames. The illuminated pages of this copy were reproduced in facsimile by Adelgundis Führkötter in 1977.[11] Knips's colors appear authentic in relation to manuscripts of the period, especially in the light greens, blues, orange-reds, and purples of the drapery, and the deep blue or gold of the grounds. A similar palette is seen, for instance, in a Psalter made in Hamersleben about 1175 and in the Admont Bible of ca. 1140 from Salzburg.[12] The amount of silver in the *Scivias* illuminations is very unusual, however—and unwise, in that the metal tarnishes (figs. 2, 7, 10, 14). Some of the *Scivias* pages follow the layout of the Admont Bible type, with framed illuminations filling the equivalent of a column of script, or half the page, but some of the layouts are more

---

[8]See Haussherr, ed., *Die Zeit der Staufer*, 1: 588–89, no. 758, and vol. 2, pl. 552. Barbara Newman, *Sister of Wisdom: St. Hildegard's Theology of the Feminine* (Berkeley: University of California Press, 1987), p. 58, fig. 1, has discussed thematic similarities to Hildegard's work.

[9]Elisabeth Klemm, "Das sogenannte Gebetbuch der Hildegard von Bingen," *Jahrbuch der Kunsthistorischen Sammlungen in Wien* 74, n.s., 38 (1978): 29–78, has concluded that this book was not Hildegard's.

[10]Eibingen, Abtei St. Hildegard, Cod. 1.

[11]Adelgundis Führkötter, *The Miniatures from the Book Scivias—Know the Ways—of St Hildegard of Bingen from the Illuminated Rupertsberg Codex* (Turnhout: Brepols, 1977).

[12]Wolfenbüttel, Herzog August-Bibliothek, cod. Guelf. 1075 Helmst, described and illustrated in Haussherr, ed., *Die Zeit der Staufer*, 1: 590–91 no. 760, and vol. 2, pl. 553. For the Admont Bible, Vienna, Österreichische Nationalbibliothek, N.S. Cod. 2701–02, see Walter Cahn, *Romanesque Bible Illumination* (Ithaca: Cornell University Press, 1982), pp. 159–60, 258–59 no. 26, pl. 121.

eccentric, as we shall see; the text was organized to accommodate a great variety of picture frames, and the lack of a modular pictorial field is one of the salient characteristics of the book design.

Thus the modern copy is a useful adjunct to the black-and-white photographs of the original manuscript, but its accuracy must be controlled by comparisons with contemporary material. The gold and silver look very bright in the modern copy, and the paint appears to have been rubbed off both metals in the original so that losses have been made good in the process of copying; it is very evident, for instance, that details of the face and genital mask of the Virgin Ecclesia threatened by Antichrist have been filled in by the copyist, whether or not she was able to decipher much of this detail in the damaged original (figs. 10, 11). At times, when missing linear detail had to be supplied, the facial expression looks distinctly modern, reminiscent of the work of Gustave Klimt (figs. 8, 9).[13] It is much to be regretted that neither of the recent paperback translations of the text has reproduced the photographs of the original, instead of drawings that are yet further removed from it.[14]

The issue of Hildegard's role in the creation of the illuminations in the lost Rupertsberg recension of the *Scivias* has not been explored in detail despite the recent explosion of scholarship, which began with the *Corpus Christianorum* edition of the original Latin text (1978), and includes monographs by Barbara Newman (1987) and Sabina Flanagan (1989), and finally the complete English translation of Mother Columba Hart and Jane Bishop (1990).[15] Chapters by Peter Dronke (1984), Elizabeth Petroff (1986),

---

[13]Fritz Novotny and Johannes Dobai, *Gustav Klimt: With a Catalogue Raisonné of His Paintings*, 2nd English ed. (Boston: Little, Brown for the New York Graphic Society, 1975), p. 307, no. 93. It is also true that Klimt seems to have found inspiration for several facets of his work in medieval illumination.

[14]Saint Hildegard, *Scivias*, trans. Bruce Hozeski (Santa Fe: Bear, 1986) (with drawings by Angela Werneke); and Hildegard of Bingen, *Scivias*, trans. Columba Hart and Jane Bishop (with plates by Placid Dempsey) (New York: Paulist, 1990). The Latin edition reprints the facsimile plates of the modern copy; see *Hildegardis Scivias*, ed. Führkötter and Carlevaris.

[15]*Hildegardis Scivias*, ed. Führkötter and Carlevaris; Newman, *Sister of Wisdom*; Sabina Flanagan, *Hildegard of Bingen, 1098–1179: A Visionary Life* (London and New York: Routledge, 1989); and *Scivias*, trans. Hart and Bishop.

Emilie Zum Brunn and Georgette Epiney-Burgard (1988), and Frances Beer (1992) have integrated Hildegard's writings into "women's visionary literature" and "mystical experience."[16] Prudence Allen (1985) and Mary Ellen Waithe (1989) and others have included her works in the history of philosophy.[17] I have elsewhere suggested that Hildegard's claim to see her visions with her eyes open had a major impact on the validation of sight as a source of truth in the late twelfth century.[18] It remains to firmly ascribe to her the "invention" of the unusual pictures in the Rupertsberg *Scivias* manuscript, whose images complement and expand upon the text in ways that suggest they constituted part of Hildegard's own cognitive process.

Before presenting my argument, it is worth noticing that a good deal of vagueness and confusion exists in published statements about the relationship of the Rupertsberg images to Hildegard; a variety of unarticulated possibilities are hidden under the repeated formula that she directed the production of this manuscript.[19] According to Führkötter, the illuminations

---

[16]Peter Dronke, *Women Writers of the Middle Ages: A Critical Study of Texts from Perpetua (†203) to Marguerite Porete (†1310)* (Cambridge and New York: Cambridge University Press, 1984), pp. 144–201; Elizabeth Petroff, ed., *Medieval Women's Visionary Literature* (Oxford: Oxford University Press, 1986), pp. 151–58; Emilie Zum Brunn and Georgette Epiney-Burgard, trans. Sheila Hughes, *Women Mystics in Medieval Europe* (New York: Paragon, 1989), pp. 19–36 (originally *Femmes Troubadours de Dieu* [Turnhout: Brepols, 1988]); and Frances Beer, *Women and Mystical Experience in the Middle Ages* (Woodbridge: Boydell, 1992).

[17]Prudence Allen, *The Concept of Woman: The Aristotelian Revolution, 750 BC–AD 1250* (Montreal: Eden, 1985), pp. 292–315; and Elisabeth Gössmann, "Hildegard of Bingen," in *A History of Women Philosophers*, vol. 2, *Medieval, Renaissance, and Enlightenment Women Philosophers, A.D. 500–1600*, ed. Mary Ellen Waithe (Dordrecht: Kluwer, 1989), pp. 27–65. For more in this vein, see the review articles by Joan Gibson, "Women in/and Medieval Philosophy: A Survey and Bibliography," *Medieval Feminist Newsletter* 14 (Fall 1992): 1–12; and Helen J. John, "Hildegard of Bingen: A New Twelfth-century Woman Philosopher?" *Hypatia* 7/1 (Winter 1992): 115–23.

[18]Madeline H. Caviness, "The Rationalization of Sight *and* the Authority of Visions? A Feminist (Re)vision," *Museu Nacional d'Art de Catalunya Bulletin* (forthcoming).

[19]I have not established when this idea was first expressed; an early study of text-image relationships—Josef Schomer, *Die Illustrationen zu den Visionen der hl. Hiildegard von Bingen als künstlerische Neuschöpfung* (Bonn: Stodieck-Druck, 1937)—has not been available to me.

must have been done by monks, whereas Peterson and Wilson asserted they were done by nuns in Hildegard's abbey;[20] more recently Newman has tentatively attributed them to a nun in Hildegard's house.[21] Even though Beer allowed that Hildegard might have painted the miniatures herself, she treats them as illustrations.[22] The case for textual or visual primacy has been obfuscated by Pächt's argument that the text mediates between the original visual image (the vision itself) and the illustration.[23] His ambiguous statements seem to have confused Sur, who voiced opinions similar to my own, yet did not rigorously address the question of the genesis of the images.[24] On the other hand, the artist who illustrated the most recent

---

[20]Führkötter, *Miniatures from the Book Scivias*, pp. 9–10, considered Hildegard the "spiritual inspiration behind the miniatures," while attributing their execution to monks from a neighboring monastery; compare Karen Peterson and J. J. Wilson, *Women Artists: Recognition and Reappraisal from the Early Middle Ages to the Twentieth Century* (New York: Harper & Row, 1976), p. 15.

[21]Newman, *Sister of Wisdom*, pp. 17–18, suggested that the manuscript was produced under Hildegard's supervision, and she posited "a close working relationship between the visionary and the unknown artist—possibly one of Hildegard's nuns."

[22]"The visual nature of Hildegard's revelation cannot be stressed strongly enough. Every one of her visions was literally that: visual; an elaborate, static, iconic tableau, which she first described, then allegorized. Finally she painted, or had paintings done, of these images, to complete the record and to serve in themselves as objects of further contemplation" (Beer, *Women and Mystical Experience*, p. 30).

[23]Otto Pächt, *Book Illumination in the Middle Ages: An Introduction* (London and New York: Harvey Miller and Oxford University Press, 1986). He makes apparently contradictory statements: "The picture in this instance is not, as it were, a crutch; as visionary inspiration it is the original form of all the complexities of thought, and the painted picture is an attempt to make accessible to the external eye what the inner eye has perceived. . . . Hildegard's text is both a vision and a meaningful commentary. The illustrator has attempted to reinterpret the most important visions in her work, but in so doing it was inevitable that his [*sic*] pictures would contain translations of non-visual and purely symbolic elements" (pp. 159–60).

[24]Carolyn Wörman Sur, *The Feminine Images of God in the Visions of Saint Hildegard of Bingen's 'Scivias'* (Lewiston, Queenston, and Lampeter: Mellen, 1993): "One may say, that, given Hildegard's involvement in the supervision of the illuminations, the *text* of *Scivias* could be considered a commentary upon the miniatures, in that the visions were the source

edition of the *Scivias* rejected the idea of Hildegard's supervision, arguing instead that differences in style in the original compositions suggest "not merely different artists but entirely different historical periods"; having set aside the author's control, her "copies" are extremely free.[25]

The complementarity of word and image is well demonstrated in the sixth and last vision of Book I, concerning the choirs of angels, since the illumination cancels out lacunae and even visually inappropriate elements in the text (fig. 12). The description, which begins with the outer two "armies," "arrayed in the shape of a crown," and goes on to describe five more inside (one with feet, that are happily not represented in the interest of the composition), the fifth appearing like the dawn. The design is clarified by its circular configuration, surely essential to its understanding in relation to the heavenly sphere, and by the ingenious representation of the dawn as several auras radiating into a deep blue star-lit sky; and by the use of a blank center ("And I saw no other shape") corresponding to a standard category of non-figural essence according to the fourth mode of seeing of Richard of St. Victor.[26] Yet the rectangular frame is not co-opted to the regular geometries preferred in that tradition of visionary images. I conclude tentatively that the visual representation is an important complement to the description here, and that it is slightly eccentric, hinting that it may be original to the author.

Some of the more eccentric images privilege the feminine (fig. 13). As noted by Newman, there is no lack of male imaging of God in the text and

---

of the text" (p. 17; emphasis textual); cf: "Hildegard's visions, and the illuminations which concretized them, are her guidelines for the description of the text. Though the text may have preceeded the illuminations, the visions preceded the text or her verbalization of the text" (41). She seems to stretch the point to agree with other authorities that the existing illuminations are later than the composition of the text (pp. 18–19).

[25]Placid Dempsey, in *Scivias*, trans. Hart and Bishop, p. vi.

[26]Madeline H. Caviness, "Images of the Divine Order and the Third Mode of Seeing," *Gesta* 22 (1983): 103–10. I do not agree with Dronke, *Women Writers*, p. 146, that Hildegard's visions belong neatly to the Victorine's category of seeing with the inner eye, nor do they generally conform to the geometries that I have demonstrated are used in designs of the third and fourth mode; even here the rectangular frame cuts awkwardly into the circle instead of playing on the perfect geometric relationship of circle to square.

illustrations, but there are several instances of the feminine as Life Giver. Hildegard commonly used *homo* (person rather than man) to denote figures of the divinity, humankind, and even of herself. In most cases, Bishop amended the English translation to reflect this lack of gender, but the description of the second vision of Book II should read: "Then I saw a bright light, and in this light the figure of a person (not man) the color of sapphire, which was all blazing with a gentle glowing fire.[27] And that bright light bathed the whole of the glowing fire, and the glowing fire bathed the bright light; and the bright light and the glowing fire poured over the whole human figure, so that the three were one light in one power of potential." The frontal figure, entirely blue, is beardless, with long black hair, the hands held in an orans gesture; the silver halo that follows its contour is one light, but the other two are rendered in concentric circles, a band of silver surrounding a gold sphere that contains the figure; a gratuitous deep blue ground sets off the outer silver zone, and this is framed in a rectangular border with palmettes—again, the circle is not in the neat square or lozenge that the visionary geometries preferred. The prototype for the beardless long-haired figure may have been an image of Christ as sometimes represented in Carolingian and Ottonian paintings, but the type was not common in the later twelfth century.[28] The rendering here, though figuring the Trinity, seems deliberately androgynous, which means it can be thought

---

[27]Singer, "The Visions of Hildegard of Bingen," p. 233, translates: ". . . appearance of a human form of a sapphire color . . ."; so also does Newman, *Sister of Wisdom*, p. 57. The whole passage in *Hildegardis Scivias*, ed. Führkötter and Carlevaris, p. 124: "Deinde vidi serenissimam lucem et in ipsa sapphirini coloris speciem hominis, quae tota suauissimo rutilante igne flagrabat. Et illa serena lux perfudit totum illum rutilantem ignem, et ille rutilans ignis totam illam serenam lucem, ac eadem serena lux et idem rutilans ignis totam speciem eiusdem hominis, ita lumen unum in una ui possibilitatis exsistentes."

[28]The Bamberg Apocalypse, and the Pericope Book of 1002–14 that Emperor Henry II gave to Bamberg Cathedral (Munich, Staatsbibliothek Clm 4452), might have been seen by Hildegard herself in 1158–61, after the composition of the *Scivias* text and presumably when the full compositions of the pictures were still being worked up; see John Beckwith, *Early Medieval Art: Carolingian, Ottonian, Romanesque* (1969; New York and London: Oxford University Press and Thames and Hudson, 1974), pp. 111–14, pl. 94 (fol. 2); see also pl. 46. For Hildegard's preaching in Bamberg see Führkötter, ed., *Das Leben*, p. 132.

of as female—the hand position hides the breasts, and the ankle-length garment is given elsewhere to figures designated as female, such as Synagogue
in Book I, vision 5.[29] Intervisuality creates a link with another orans figure
that signifies Hildegard herself in the first vision of Book I (fig. 14).

Further examples indicate that the pictorial representation is selective,
and privileges the feminine in ways that are not mandated by the words:
Vision 5 in Book II begins with the image of a huge crowned woman
(fig. 7), and the description:

> After this I saw that a splendor white as snow and translucent as crystal had shone
> around the image of that woman from the top of her head to her throat [it is so
> in the picture]. And from her throat to her navel another splendor, red in color,
> had encircled her, glowing like the dawn from her throat to her breasts and shining
> from her breasts to her navel mixed with purple and blue [this is uniformly gold,
> though flame-shapes are delineated in red within this zone; the red and blue, with
> green instead of purple are appropriated for the crowd of women]. And where it
> glowed like the dawn, its brightness shone forth as high as the secret places of
> Heaven [the gold flames reach to the top of the frame]; and in this brightness
> appeared a most beautiful image of a maiden, with bare head and black hair,
> wearing a red tunic, which flowed down about her feet [her outstretched arms,
> with hands in an open orans position, and her *blond* hair mimic the posture and
> coloring of Ecclesia].
>
> And I heard a voice. . . .
>
> And around that maiden I saw standing a great crowd of people, brighter
> than the sun, all wonderfully adorned with gold and gems. Some of these had their
> heads veiled in white, adorned with a gold circlet [these are crowned *women*, with
> long loose hair, in the foreground]; and above them, as if sculpted on the veils, was
> the likeness of the glorious and ineffable Trinity as it was represented to me earlier
> [i.e., orans—the hands stretch out in gold silhouette to either side, but this fuses
> the female Ecclesia-queen with the idea of the Trinity, perhaps also abstractly
> expressed in the three central flames of brilliant light], and on their foreheads the
> Lamb of God, and on their necks a human figure, and on the right ear cherubim,
> and on the left ear the other kinds of angels [apparently omitted, unless they
> rubbed off the silver ground]; and from the likeness of the glorious and supernal
> Trinity golden rays extended to these other images [the three central gold flames
> again]. And among these people were some who had miters on their heads and

---

[29]One of the worst travesties in the illustrations to the Hart and Bishop translation is the
addition of a beard to this figure! (p. 159).

palia of the episcopal office around their shoulders [three such figures appear, squeezed into the background, one with a beard, the others only partly visible, matching the gender unspecificity of "people," and allowing for her later claim that all virgins are daughters of Zion (206)].

And again I heard the voice. . . .

But beneath that splendor, which glowed like the dawn, I saw between Heaven and earth a thick darkness appear, the horror of which exceeded what human tongue can utter [omitted, perhaps in response to the double negative that follows]:

And again I heard the voice from Heaven saying, "If the Son of God had not suffered on the cross, this darkness would mean that no person could attain celestial glory" [i.e., without the darkness, the image of Ecclesia/Trinity attains celestial glory].

And where the splendor shone, which was mixed with purple and blue, it encircled the woman's image with strong odor. But another splendor, like a white cloud, decently enveloped that image from the navel down, to the point at which it had not yet grown further [Ecclesia is oddly truncated at about knee-level]. And these three splendors around that image shone afar, showing that within her many steps and ladders were well and properly placed [the figure has a white skirt with irregular panels like a mountainous landscape, rather than regular steps and ladders; these forms refer back to Book I, vision 2, where among the elements of the world, earth "displayed terrible terrors"—a very subtle reference to the horror of darkness that was otherwise omitted here].[30]

---

[30] *Scivias*, trans. Hart and Bishop, pp. 201ff.; and *Hildegardis Scivias*, ed. Führkötter and Carlevaris, pp. 174–76:

Post haec uidi quod praefatam muliebrem imaginem quidam splendor albus ut nix et tamquam crystallus perlucidus a uertice usque ad guttur eius circumfulserat. Sed a gutture usque ad umbilicum eius quidam alius splendor rubei coloris eam circumdederat, qui de gutture usque ad ubera illius uelut aurora rutilabat, sed ab uberibus usque ad umbilicum illius quasi purpura hyacintho intermixta fulgebat. Et ubi ipse uelut aurora rutilabat, claritatem suam sursum ad secreta caeli extendit; in qua pulcherrima et puellaris imago nudo capite et subnigris capillis et rubra tunica quae circa pedes eius diffluebat induta apparuit.

Et audiui uocem. . . .

Et circa eandem puellam uidi maximam turbam hominum lucidiorem sole stantem, qui omnes miro modo auro et gemmis ornati erant, ita quod etiam quidam illorum in capitibus suis uelati candidis uelaminibus aurea zona circumornatis fuerunt; supra quorum uertices similitudo gloriae ineffabilis Trinitatis, uelut mihi superius typice demonstrata est, quasi in sphaera in ipsis uelaminibus uelut sculpta apparuit, et in frontibus ipsorum agnus Dei, ac in collo

To summarize the pictorial interpretations of the text that go beyond it in privileging the feminine: The gigantic female image (like a feminine King Kong with Fay) both appropriates the symbol of the Trinity and subverts the patriarchal image of Abraham with the blessed in his bosom, while fore-grounding female virgins among the saved. In echoing the orans posture of the humble figure in Book I.1, She appears to have grown to replace the Majesty of God by towering into the heavens herself. And there the two fore-ground figures, Fear of God full of eyes and the headless "blessedness of poverty of spirit," surely mirror Hildegard herself, who is both the seer and the passive receiver, even when blinded, of the vision of God (fig. 14). Indeed, these diminutive and the gigantic figures also complement each other in that the head of one and the lower part of the other are hidden from view. Yet the fragmentation and distortion of the human form is not in the least threatening; like the light and dark heads paired in the windows in the first vision, these incomplete figures are not decapitated or deformed humans but convenient pictograms.

The second vision of Book I has often been treated in terms of its departure from standard scriptural exegesis of the Fall (fig. 15).[31] Eve is

---

eorum species hominis, et in dextra aure cherubin et in sinistra alia species angelica, ita quod et de ipsa similitudine gloriae supernae Trinitatis ad has species quasi aureus radius se extenderet. Sed inter hos quidam alii apparuerunt, qui infulas in capitibus suis et pallia episcopalis officii circa umeros habebant.

Et iterum audiui uocem. . . .

Sed sub eodem splendore ubi ipse uelut aurora rutilabat uidi inter caelum et terram densissimas tenebras apparere, quae tanti horroris erant ultra quam humana lingua effari possit.

Et rursum audiui uocem de caelo dicentem: "Si Filius Dei in cruce passus non esset, istae tenebrae nullo modo permitterent hominem ad supernam claritatem peruenire."

Vbi autem idem splendor quasi purpura hyacintho intermixta fulgebat, fortiter praedictam muliebrem imaginem constringens ardebat. Sed alius splendor ut candida nubes eandem imaginem ab umbilico et deorsum, quousque ultra nondum creuerat, honeste circumdederat. Et hi tres splendores circa ipsam imaginem se late diffundentes plurimos gradus et scalas in ea bene et decenter ordinatas ostendebant.

[31] See, for example, Newman, *Sister of Wisdom*, pp. 107–20, who claimed "Hildegard distanced herself from the Augustinian tradition, with its potential for antifeminism."

represented as a cloud combining water and air, instead of water and earth as in the standard Aristotelian works on the microcosm;[32] and Adam, positioned near fire and earth, is a beautiful being as yet without genitalia, thus also conforming to Hildegard's view, expressed elsewhere, that sex was not necessary for regeneration until after the Fall.[33] Indeed, Eve does not need Adam to procreate, since the stars that fill her are the future generations of human beings. The fact that some of these original ideas of Hildegard's are transposed into this illustration from other writings of hers is a good indication that she must have been the designer of the image. The *Scivias* narrative itself is almost defiant, in allowing Lucifer to trick Eve into telling the truth about the proscribed fruit and play to Adam's lust for Eve. Yet the full impact of this non-canonical recounting, I believe, is felt in the exclusions from the image; in contrast to the standard iconography, represented here in the Temptation and Fall panel on the Hildesheim bronze doors of about 1015, there is no sensual nude Eve (holding one apple as if it is her breast), no proffering of the fruit to Adam, no phallic serpent echoing her twisting posture (fig. 16). Instead, in the *Scivias* a single earth-bound androgynous form stands for humanity and/or Adam, but woman is literally vaporized into the heavens.[34]

This same composition illustrates another highly original aspect of many of the illuminations, one that has received some attention for its medical implications.[35] It constitutes another important area in which the pictures have to fill a silence in the text, and do so in a consistent yet very eccentric

---

[32]Allen, *The Concept of Woman*, p. 296.

[33]Allen, *The Concept of Woman*, pp. 299 and 516 n. 175.

[34]Once more the illustrator made the figure specifically male in the Hart and Bishop edition (p. 71).

[35]Singer, in "The Pathological Basis of the Visions" (in his *From Magic to Science*), was the first to claim that "the medical reader or the sufferer from migraine will, we think, easily recognize the symptoms of 'scintillating scotoma' in several of her visions." He, however, allowed full value to the theological and philosopical force of her writings. Oliver W. Sacks, *Migraine: Understanding a Common Disorder* (Berkeley and Los Angeles: University of California Press, 1985), pp. 57, 106–08, relied largely on Singer's analysis; he gives useful definitions of common aspects of migraine aura (pp. 248–49).

way. The vision begins by referring to "a great multitude of very bright living lamps, which received fiery brilliance and acquired an unclouded splendor."[36] Typically, these metaphors of light are dynamic, and there is nothing to suggest the large gold and red mullets that we see in the painting, though the smaller white stars are quite conventional. Jagged-edged lights that become increasingly brilliant are part of my own experience of premigraine auras, and are common to many of my husband's patients.[37] Such phosphenes hover in front of other objects in one's vision and stay in the center of vision as one's eyes move, so that they seem to multiply. Closing one's eyes reverses them, so a dark rim (steel-gray is often mentioned by Hildegard) becomes seeringly bright silver, like a shattered mirror; opening my eyes again catches colors from the surround in the mirror splinters, even though few people experience color in the scintillating scotomas. Next, for Hildegard, "A pit of great breadth and depth appeared, with a mouth like the mouth of a well, emitting fiery smoke with great stench, from which a loathsome cloud spread out."[38] The pictorial form is unpredictable from this, reaching up a jagged edge like a great wing. The impression of fiery smoke, shimmering like heat waves, typically making a patterned carpet seem to smoke, is also within general experience of migraine aura; so too is scotoma, which appears like a gaping black hole in one's vision, a jagged-edged and growing visual field deficit. In this and other cases I claim that the silences in the text were filled, in the pictures, by someone with an equal knowledge of these auras—presumably therefore the same person. Hildegard's biography certainly supports the view that she herself suffered from migraine; onset just before puberty, and heightened activity in her

---

[36]*Scivias*, trans. Hart and Bishop, p. 73; and *Hildegardis Scivias*, ed. Führkötter and Carlevaris, p. 13: "maximam multitudinem uiuentium lampadarum multam claritatem habentium, quae igneum fulgorem accipientes ita serenissimum splendorem adeptae sunt."

[37]For his work with headache see Verne S. Caviness, Jr., and J. Patrick O'Brien, "Headache," *New England Journal of Medicine* 302 (1980): 446–50.

[38]Hart and Bishop, trans., *Scivias*, p. 73; and Führkötter and Carlevaris, eds., *Hildegardis Scivias*, p. 13: "Et ecce lacus multae latitudinis et profunditatis apparuit, os uelut os putei habens et igneum fumum cum multo foetore emittens, de quo etiam taeterrima nebula se extendens."

early forties as she describes it, is the normal pattern of migraine, which is predominantly a female (and genetically determined) "disorder."

The third vision of Book I, with flame-like blinding lights, is another scintillating scotoma, but in the retelling/redrawing it was ordered into the structure of the cosmos (fig. 17). Nonetheless, the harsh contrasts of light and dark, the discomforting asymmetries of the core with its tongue-like protrusion between light and dark, and its shimmering stars are almost enough to trigger a migraine. One very notable technique developed in the *Scivias* manuscript is the application of tiny white dots to jagged black contours, serving to destabilize the outline and cause an unpleasant vibration; even when I am without symptoms, I am physically distressed when looking at this image.

One more such case is worth analyzing. The description of the first vision in Book Three inverts the usual order: whereas most visions begin with abstract forms, and Hildegard sees figures in them gradually, and then meanings, this begins with the image and description of the Majesty seated above a cloud and a great circle of gold (fig. 2, left); all of this clearly fills the frame:

> and it shone with a terrifying radiance the color of stone, steel and fire, which extended everywhere, from the Heights of Heaven to the depth of the abyss, so that I could see no end to it. [A second frame is therefore needed for the continuation, on the facing folio, fig. 2, right.]
>
> And then I saw a great star, splendid and beautiful, come forth from the One seated on the throne. And with that star came a multitude of shining sparks, which followed the star toward the South, looking on the One seated on the throne like a stranger; they turned away from Him and stared toward the North instead of contemplating Him. But, in the very act of turning away their gaze, they were all extinguished and were changed into black cinders.[39]

---

[39]*Scivias*, trans. Hart and Bishop, p. 309; and *Hildegardis Scivias*, ed. Führkötter and Carlevaris, p. 328:

> ex se reddens splendorem ualde terribilem, scilicet lapidei, chalybeii et ignei coloris, undique secundum amplitudinem suam sursum in altitudinem caeli et deorsum in profundum abyssi ita se extendentem, ut nullum finem eius uidere possem.
>
> Vidi etiam tunc de secreto eiusdem sedentis in throno stellam magnam multi splendoris ac decoris prodire, et cum ea plurimam multitudinem candentium scintillarum quae cum eadem stella omnes confluentes ad austrum inspiciebant

The light-dark reversal again matches the experience of migraine aura, and the picture ingeniously captures the gyrating motion of the stars, and their falling into an ocean (they were eventually precipitated into an abyss in the vision—the kinetic dynamism of the narrative account is replaced by fragmentation in the image, so that the elements seem to be undergoing kaleidoscopic changes). In its separate frame, this image is among the most unusual of the sequence.

These examples are not meant to imply that Hildegard's visions can be reduced to one kind of physiological state, and certainly not to a "pathological" cause. Yet in many cases, migraine auras may have formed a point of departure; this would fit her claim that the visions occurred with her eyes open, and that the sensible world did not disappear from view.[40] Her struggle to find meanings in the visions fits her textualization, which often adds figures at the first stage, and goes back systematically to explain each component, and then expands into further exegesis.

The "author portrait" that illustrates the preface to the Rupertsberg *Scivias* can help us understand the design process, although like all images it is open to different interpretations. I will argue that Hildegard, holding a stylus and a stack of wax tablets, is ready to record the visions, whereas Volmar, bodily removed in an antechamber and his ear turned as if listening to her intently, has his book open ready to record her words. The alternative is to suppose that Volmar is later making a fair copy of her text, but that interpretation scarcely accounts for his attentiveness to her.[41]

---

ipsum sedentem in throno quasi alienum, seque ab eo auertentes magis inhiabant ad aquilonem quam eum inspicere uellent. Sed statim in ipsa auersione inspectionis suae omnes exstinctae sunt, sic uersae in nigredinem carbonum.

[40]In 1175, at the age of seventy-seven, Hildegard responded to Guibert of Gembloux's questioning about her visionary experiences in a letter, quoted here from Newman, *Sister of Wisdom*, p. 6: "And because I see them this way in my soul, I observe them in accord with the shifting of clouds and other created things. I do not hear them with my outward ears, nor do I perceive them by the thoughts of my own heart or by any combination of my five senses, but in my soul alone, while my outward eyes are open. So I have never fallen prey to ecstasy in the visions, but I see them wide awake, day and night. And I am constantly fettered by sickness, and often in the grip of pain so intense that it threatens to kill me."

[41]Richard H. and Mary A. Rouse, "Wax Tablets," *Language & Communication* 9 (1989): 179–80; and "Sept Siècles de littérature manuscrite," in *La Naissance du texte*, ed. Louis Hay

According to the description she gave Guibert, the preface she wrote to *Scivias,* and the author portrait in the Rupertsberg manuscript, Hildegard saw her visions in a waking state (fig. 18). The light striking her brain and eyes, like the Pentecostal flames striking the Virgin and disciples in a Psalter that belonged to an earlier English visionary, Christina of Markyate, lends authority to the messages she receives (fig. 19).[42] The tablets also recall contemporary images of the prophet Moses with the Law.[43] A wide margin of hagiography, or of justificatory self-imaging, must be allowed for in this construction of author-ity. Yet the tale that is told of the genesis of the text and pictures is consistent and plausible. According to her preface, Hildegard was asked by the Divinity "Dic et scribe quae vides et audis"—"speak and write what you see and hear" as it is literally translated. If she were to follow those instructions, however, she would simultaneously have to cross the verbal register from aural to written (to write what she heard) and transpose the visual register to the cognitive in oral verbal expression (to speak what she saw). In fact, although the completed text provides a description of each vision, it would not be sufficient to provide the forms and colors of the illuminations. How much more simple to sketch the composition of her

---

(Paris: José Corti, 1989), pp. 91–92. I am extremely grateful to the Rouses for sending me copies of their articles, even though I contest their interpretation of the Hildegard portrait. In my view it is significantly different from the fourteenth-century Manesse Codex "portrait" of the poet Reinmar von Zweter in which they more plausibly see a scribe taking dictation on wax tablets and a young woman later making a fair copy on a scroll ("Wax Tablets," p. 180, fig. 3). Hildegard and Volmar more closely resemble the famous Ottonian "portrait" of Pope Gregory and Peter the Deacon from his *Registrum,* also mentioned by them with "unambiguous" textual evidence that Peter acted as stenographer to his patron (pp. 183, 189 n. 22); the comparison is also made in Madeline H. Caviness, "Anchoress, Abbess, and Queen: Donors and Patrons or Intercessors and Matrons?" in *Women's Literary and Artistic Patronage in the Middle Ages,* ed. June Hall McCash (Athens: University of Georgia Press, 1996), pp. 115–17, figs. 9 and 10.

[42]The so-called St. Alban's Psalter, Hildesheim, Cathedral Treasury, generally dated ca. 1121; see Ursula Nilgen, "Psalter der Christina von Markyate (sogennanter Albani-Psalter)," in *Der Schatz von St. Godehard* (exhibition catalogue) (Hildesheim: Diözesan-Museum Bernward, 1988), no. 69, pp. 152–65.

[43]As pointed out by Rouse and Rouse in "Wax Tablets" (p. 229), citing Ruth Mellinkoff, "Round-topped Tablets of the Law," *Journal of Jewish Art* 1 (1974), figs. 1, 3, 16, 17.

visions on her tablets; she could more or less simultaneously repeat the voices, perhaps adding a supplementary description, for Volmar to write down. The verb *scribere* connoted not the composition of a text but its transcription, which is hardly appropriate for an author in the process of composing.[44] A looser translation would fit better here, more in keeping with the idea of making marks with a stylus, impressing or inscribing, as sometimes phrased in Latin.[45] Such use would be more appropriate also for Hildegard's phrase in the famous letter to Guibert of Gembloux, written late in her life, in which she uses a single verb for "writing the words and visions that are there revealed to me."[46] Furthermore, a few texts indicate that wax tablets were not used exclusively for writing in the Middle Ages; a plan of the Holy Sepulcher is reported to have been drawn on wax tablets by a pilgrim ca. 700, and Hildegard's contemporary Gerald of Wales

[44]M. T. Clanchy, *From Memory to Written Record: England, 1066–1307* (Cambridge, Mass.: Harvard University Press, 1979), p. 218, has pointed out that the verb *dictitare* was used for writing in the sense of composing, whereas *scriptitare* meant transcribing into a fair copy on parchment. He also quotes the use by Oderic Vitalis of *legere vel dictare*, not *legere vel scribere*, for reading and writing. Much has been made of Hildegard's textual drafts on tablets, but the process of generating a fair copy is not greatly altered if we suppose her scribes' drafts were corrected in various stages; see Albert Derolez, "The Genesis of Hildegard of Bingen's 'Liber divinorum operum': The Codicological Evidence," in *Neerlandica Manuscripta: Essays Presented to G. I. Lieftinck*, ed. J. P. Gumbert and M. J. M. de Haan (Amsterdam: Van Gendt, 1972), pp. 23–33; and "Deux notes concernant Hildegarde de Bingen," *Scriptorium* 27 (1973): 291–95 (*à propos* the *Scivias* portrait).

[45]Early uses of *scribo* included scratching and engraving with a sharp pointed instrument, hence writing, drawing, and designing, as in Pliny; also depicting; see Charlton T. Lewis and Charles Short, *A Latin Dictionary*, rev. ed. (Oxford: Clarendon, 1958), pp. 1647–48. In the British Isles about 1125 "to brand" is among its uses, and *scriptitatio* is used for scribbling about 1165; see Ronald Edward Latham, *Revised Medieval Latin Word-List from British and Irish Sources* (London: Oxford University Press for the British Academy, 1965), p. 426. Richard H. and Mary A. Rouse, "The Vocabulary of Wax Tablets," in *Vocabulaire du livre et de l'écriture au moyen âge: actes de la table ronde, Paris, 24–26 septembre 1987*, ed. Olga Weijers (Turnhout: Brepols, 1989), pp. 227–28, cite a variety of such terms.

[46]The letter is quoted extensively in translation by Newman, *Sister of Wisdom*, pp. 6–7; she frequently stresses seeing the visions with her eyes open and claims to "see, know, and hear all at once."

supposed that the Irish Gospels of St. Briget were made from designs drawn on tablets by angels.[47] Also in the second half of the twelfth century, Peter of Celle explained the second Commandment (against graven images) as preventing "that tablet of the inward imagination, at the moment it should enter into contemplation, being found decorated with imaginary images," for if statues restricted vision and thought, and "stole consent, consent engraved the pleasing forms on the tablets of the imagination."[48]

I therefore propose amending the Hart-Bishop translation of her preface as follows:

> O fragile human, ashes of ashes, and filth of filth! Say and *jot down* what you see and hear. But since you are timid in speaking, and simple in expounding, and untaught in *the use of the stylus, dictate* and *inscribe* these things not by a human mouth, and not by the understanding of human invention, and not by the requirements of human composition, but as you see and hear them.[49]

A deliberate avoidance of compositional correction has already been noticed in the cosmic designs, and it would apply also to the architectural configurations.

Two more aspects of the pictures may be explained if they came into being in this way. The first is the large number that occupy a tall rectangular frame, filling a column of the text, or nearly so (figs. 2, 5, 14, 15). Yet as remarked before, there is no regular module, and some turn horizontally across the top or bottom of a page. Such compositions would

---

[47] Jonathan J. G. Alexander, *Medieval Illuminators and Their Methods of Work* (New Haven and London: Yale University Press, 1992), p. 35, with bibliography.

[48] *Peter of Celle, Selected Works,* trans. Hugh Feiss (Kalamazoo: Cistercian Publications, 1987), p. 161. In the original *De conscientia* the terms are *tabuli internae imaginationis* (tablets of the imagination), *imagines* (images), and *insculpsit* (engraved); see Jean Leclercq, *La Spiritualité de Pierre de Celle 1115–1183* (Paris: J. Vrin, 1946), p. 208.

[49] *Scivias,* trans. Hart and Bishop, p. 59; *Hildegardis Scivias,* ed. Führkötter and Carlevaris, p. 3: "O homo fragilis, et cinis cineris, et putredo putredinis, dic et scribe quae uides et audis. Sed quia timida es ad loquendum et simplex ad exponendum et indocta ad scribendum ea, dic et scribe illa non secundum os hominis nec secundum intellectum humanae adinuentionis nec secundum uoluntatem humanae compositionis, sed secundum id quod ea in caelestibus desuper in mirabilibus Dei uides et audis."

easily be adapted from the narrow tablets indicated in the author portrait, and commonly referred to in twelfth-century records;[50] many pictures of square format are subdivided vertically, as if two sketches have been juxtaposed (fig. 10).[51] In the cases when migraine aura was the immediate point of departure, there would have been plenty of time to make one or several compositional sketches. Letters could indicate colors, as we know they were used in drawings in manuscripts and in designs for stained glass;[52] few colors are in fact verbalized in addition to brilliance, whiteness, and darkness—red, blue, purple, color of iron, subdued color (the virtual lack of colors is in keeping with migraine auras). These compositional sketches would next be transferred to parchment leaves, since wax is easily damaged—and the tablets of course were reusable if the surface was rubbed or heated to smooth it.

Transfer to parchment would explain another characteristic of many of the compositions, especially in Book III. Single leaves could be turned and worked on from different directions, a manipulation that was especially useful to render some of the visions in which elements veered around. Figures could easily be drawn emanating from towers facing four ways, or two (fig. 20). In one demonstrated case, the leaves on which Villard de Honnecourt collected various designs in the thirteenth century—such as notations of architectural elements, statuary, furniture, etc.—were so turned before being bound into an album (fig. 21).[53] I postulate that at the next

---

[50]Rouse and Rouse, "Wax Tablets," p. 186, have suggested that these constraints may have influenced literary form.

[51]Clanchy, *From Memory to Written Record*, pp. 88, 91, 116, 183; he claims wax tablets for notations were "the most important equipment of the twelfth-century writer . . . not the parchment book depicted in conventional portraits of scribes."

[52]Patricia Stirnemann, "Nouvelles pratiques en matière d'enluminure au temps de Philippe Auguste," in *La France de Philippe Auguste: Le temps des mutations*, Actes du Colloque international, ed. Robert Henri Bautier (Paris: C.N.R.S., 1982), pp. 955–80. Theophilus, *De Diuersis Artibus: The Various Arts,* ed. and trans. C. R. Dodwell (London: Thoman Nelson and Sons, 1961), p. 48 (the designs for glass were made on gessoed tabletops).

[53]Paris, Bibliothèque Nationale, MS fr. 19093: Hans Hahnloser, *Villard de Honnecourt: Kritische Gesamtausgabe des Bauhüttenbuches ms. fr. 19093 der Pariser Nationalbibliothek*, 2nd ed. (Graz: Akademische Druck- und Verlagsanstalt, 1972), pls. 17, 18, 26, 28, 35, 54.

step, making a fair copy to be illuminated on text pages for a sumptuous copy of the *Scivias,* Hildegard's injunction against regularizing the compositions was respected, and I suspect she watched over the painters very closely. She is surely as much the author of these pictorial ideas as she is of the words that she also did not physically write.

Given the important complementary role the Rupertsberg set of pictures played in relation to the text, and my conclusion that they were generated at the same time, the question must be posed why they were not canonically integrated into the text copies. Unique illuminated manuscripts did, of course, exist—such as Herrad of Landsberg's *Hortus Deliciarum,* which remained during the Middle Ages in her house for the instruction of the nuns; yet its text was not circulated independently of the pictures, as happened with the *Scivias.* As in other cases of copying, the iconographic model could have been followed even with reduced means; the Salem manuscript, for instance, could have conserved Hildegard's compositions in tinted line drawings, without the expense of gold and silver.[54] The lacuna is even more surprising in light of Hildegard's immediate reputation; however, it is likely the text began to circulate soon after its completion in 1151, and the pictures may have remained longer in loose-leaf form. There is no evidence that the pictures were examined by the papal council that encouraged Hildegard to continue her work on the text; theology in twelfth-century Cistercian circles was as logo-centric as most of the academic discourses that inform medieval studies today.

In the paper upon which this chapter is based I argued that the pictures were more subversive than the text and were, therefore, at risk in an investigation. For instance, decisions were frequently made to represent neutrally gendered terms by fully female figures.[55] Newman's work, of course, has

---

[54]A classic case of copying an entire iconographic model is that of the Utrecht Psalter, the ninth-century triple psalter with an extensive cycle of literal illustrations at every psalm; three copies were made in Canterbury, spanning the mid-eleventh to the late-twelfth centuries, in bistre drawing, colored outline, and finally in full color with gold grounds (London, British Library, Harl. MS 603; Eadwine Psalter; Paris, Bibliothèque Nationale, MS lat. 8846).

[55]One century later, a commentator on the Dominican treatise on sexuality, *De secretis mulierum,* advises that the default gender should be masculine: "The question arises whether

amply shown that Sapiential theology allowed for the feminine as a life-giving principle; Bynum has also contributed to this exploration, finding that these ideas were especially current among Cistercians.[56] A problem arises only when these metaphors are translated into specific visual forms; it has essentially to do with the difference between text and image, word and icon.[57] To allude to the deity in non-gendered, or even female, terms in a text that purports not to argue truths logically but to reveal them metaphorically, is one thing. To create an iconic image of a female Majesty—such as the Ecclesia holding the virgins in her bosom (fig. 7), the feminized figure of the Trinity (fig. 13), and several others in the Ruperts-berg *Scivias*—could run the risk of being "misunderstood," of leading directly to Goddess worship if they were repeated in more public images. These autonomous figures depart markedly from the *Sapientia* who serves as caryatid to Christ in the Stammheim Missal (fig. 6). Barbara Newman, in her response to my paper, commented that the illuminator of the Salem *Scivias* interpreted the figure of the Knowledge of God (*Scientia Dei*) in Book III vision 4 as a holy man with angels and other heavenly beings (only three of whom are women) addressing prophets and patriarchs, whereas in the Rupertsberg recension a woman is adored by angels and turns toward a group of young women (figs. 22, 23).[58] Newman also

---

a hermaphrodite ought to be called a man or a woman. One might answer that he can be called either name because he has either sex, but this is incorrect; he should be called by the name of a man alone. The reason for this is that when a determination must be made about something, the worthier alternative should be chosen" (*Women's Secrets: A Translation of Pseudo-Albertus Magnus's De Secretis Mulierum with Commentaries*, trans. Helen Rodnite Lemay [Albany: State University of New York Press, 1992], p. 117).

[56]Caroline Walker Bynum, *Jesus as Mother: Studies in the Spirituality of the High Middle Ages* (Berkeley and Los Angeles: University of California Press, 1982).

[57]In her texts, for instance, Hildegard frequently distances herself from the authoritative crit-icism she offers of the condition of a male-dominated world, by stressing her weakness as a woman, attributing the world's decline to feminization; see Barbara Newman, "Divine Power Made Perfect in Weakness: St. Hildegard on the Frail Sex," in *Medieval Religious Women*, vol. 2, *Peaceweavers*, ed. Lillian Thomas Shank and John A. Nichols (Kalamazoo: Cistercian Publications, 1987), pp. 103–21. Her images do not attempt this rhetorical posture.

[58]Barbara Newman was the respondent in the session "Translation and Gender" organized by Jeanette Beer at the 28th International Congress on Medieval Studies, Kalamazoo,

pointed out that traces of the female *Sapientia* figure persist into the four-teenth century, in the Holy Spirit of the Trinity as painted on the vaults of Orschaling Church in Bavaria.[59] Yet both context and style influence our reception of such figures; by 1200, the powerful majestic cult image of the Virgin as *Sedes Sapientiae,* as abstracted power of thought holding the Child on her throne/lap, was being refeminized as the queen of heaven in elegant sweeping garments, with the emotive affect of ideal motherhood.[60] If the Rupertsberg pictures were too esoteric to have a broad appeal, that very same quality could lead to (mis)interpretations that place patriarchy in question; Hildegard's Goddesses are nowhere shown as Mother of God, but her women are shown capable of procreation without men.[61]

Michigan, 1993; she generously responded to a later draft as well, and shared unpublished material with me. See *Scivias,* trans. Hart and Bishop, pp. 357–58 and 364 (with fairly accurate copy of the Rupertsberg composition, p. 356); and von Oechelhaeuser, *Die Miniaturen,* pp. 97–98, pl. 16.

[59]I am grateful for a pre-publication copy of the section dealing with "The Alternative Trinity" from Barbara Newman, *From Virile Woman to WomanChrist: Studies in Medieval Religion and Literature* (Philadelphia: University of Pennsylvania Press, 1995), pp. 198–209, and for references to Evamaria Ciolina, *Der Freskenzyklus von Urschalling: Geschichte und Ikonographie* (Munich: Kommissionsbuchhandling R. Wolfle, 1980), p. 122; and Leopold Kretzenbacher, "Zwei eigenwillige bayerisce Dreifaltigkeits-Darstellungen," *Bayerisches Jahr-buch für Volkskunde* (1992): 130–31. The preponderance of female saints in the vault paintings (Sts. Agnes, Ursula, Agatha, Margaret, Apollonia, Helen, Elizabeth of Thuringia, and Hedwig) suggests that this tiny church served a female community.

[60]Ilene H. Forsyth, *The Throne of Wisdom: Wood Sculptures of the Madonna in Romanesque France* (Princeton: Princeton University Press, 1972), figs. 5–11 or any of 28–174, with 182–84. The "feminizing" tendency is even more pronounced in the paintings and statues of the Gothic period.

[61]Marilyn R. Mumford, "A Feminist Prolegomenon for the Study of Hildegard of Bingen," in *Gender, Culture, and the Arts: Women, The Arts, and Society,* ed. Ronald Dot-terer and Susan Bowers (Selinsgrove, Pa.: Susquehanna University Press, 1993), pp. 44–53, has emphasized the possibility of more radical interpretations of Hildegard's imagery, such as the egg-shaped universe (my fig. 17), which she sees as a vagina with clitoris and uterus.

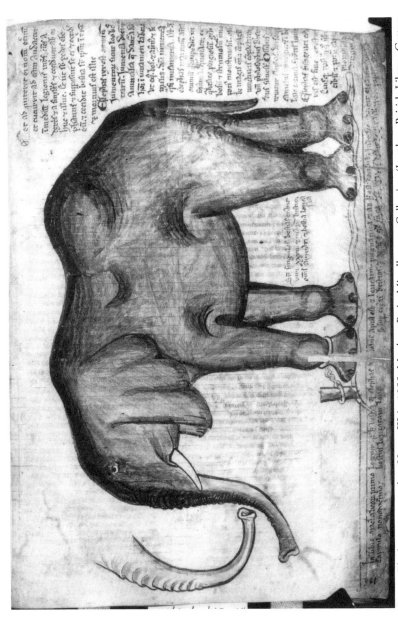

Fig. 1. Elephant presented to Henry III in 1255, Matthew Paris, Miscellaneous Collection (London, British Library Cotton MS Nero D.1, fol. 169v; by permission of the British Library).

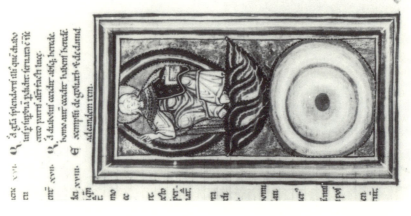

Fig. 2. Rupertsberg *Scivias* (formerly Wies-baden, Hessisches Landesbibliothek, MS 1, fols. 122v–23) Book III, vision 1 (Rheinisches Bildarchiv).

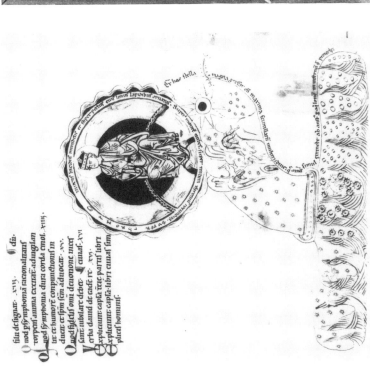

Fig. 3. (left) Salem *Scivias*, ca. 1200 (Heidelberg, Universitätsbibliothek Cod. Salem X, 16, fol. 111), Book III, vision 1 (by permission of the Universitätsbibliothek Heidelberg).

Fig. 4. (right) The River of Life flowing out of the Throne, with St. John and the angel, Bamberg Apocalypse: Bamberg, Staatsbibliothek MS 140 (formerly A II 42), fol. 57 (Foto Marburg/Art Resource, NY).

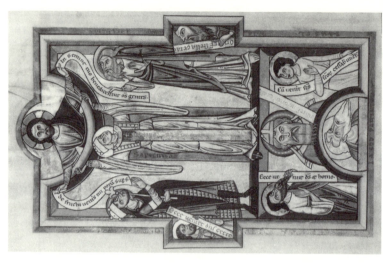

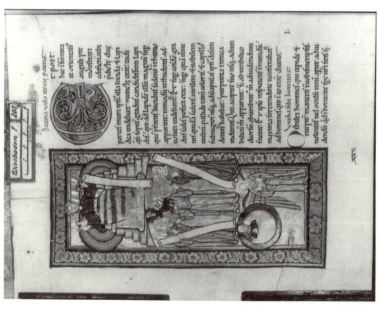

Fig. 5. (left) Rupertsberg *Scivias* (formerly Wiesbaden, Hessisches Landesbibliothek, MS 1, fol. 203v) Book III, vision 10 (Rheinisches Bildarchiv).
Fig. 6. (right) Sapientia, with the patriarchs and prophets, holds up a mandorla with Christ, Stammheim Missal made for the Benedictine Abbey of St. Michael's Hildesheim about 1160, collection of the Freiherr von Fürstenberg, fol. 11 (with permission of the owner).

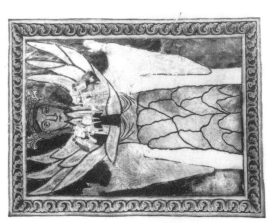

Fig. 7. (left) Rupertsberg *Scivias* (formerly Wiesbaden, Hessisches Landesbibliothek, MS 1, fol. 66) Book II, vision 5 (Rheinisches Bildarchiv). Fig. 8. (center) Josepha Knips, copy of the Rupertsberg *Scivias*, 1927–33 (Eibingen, Abtei St. Hildegard, Cod. 1), Book II, vision 5 (after Führkötter, 1977).
Fig. 9. (right) Gustave Klimt, *Pallas Athene*, 1898 (Vienna, Historisches Museum der Stadt Wien, inv. no. 100680; Erich Lessing/Art Resource, NY).

Fig. 10. (left) Rupertsberg *Scivias* (formerly Wiesbaden, Hessisches Landesbibliothek, MS 1, fol. 214v) Book III, vision 11 (Rheinisches Bildarchiv).
Fig. 11. (right) Josepha Knips, copy of the Rupertsberg *Scivias* 1923–27 (Eibingen, Abtei St. Hildegard, Cod. 1) Book III, vision 11 (after Führköter, 1977).

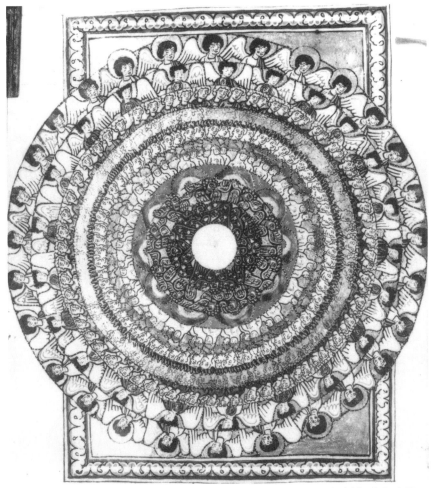

Fig. 12. Rupertsberg *Scivias* (formerly Wiesbaden, Hessisches Landesbibliothek, MS 1, fol. 38) Book I, vision 6 (Rheinisches Bildarchiv).

Fig. 13. Rupertsberg *Scivias* (formerly Wiesbaden, Hessisches Landesbibliothek, MS 1, fol. 47) Book II, vision 2 (Rheinisches Bildarchiv).

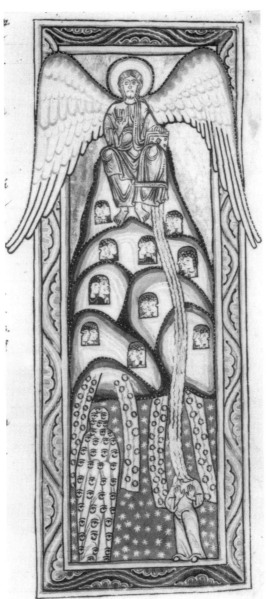

Fig. 14. Rupertsberg *Scivias* (formerly Wiesbaden, Hessisches Landesbibliothek, MS 1, fol. 2) Book I, vision 1 (Rheinisches Bildarchiv).

Fig. 15. Rupertsberg *Scivias* (formerly Wiesbaden, Hessisches Landesbibliothek, MS 1, fol. 4) Book I, vision 2 (Rheinisches Bildarchiv).

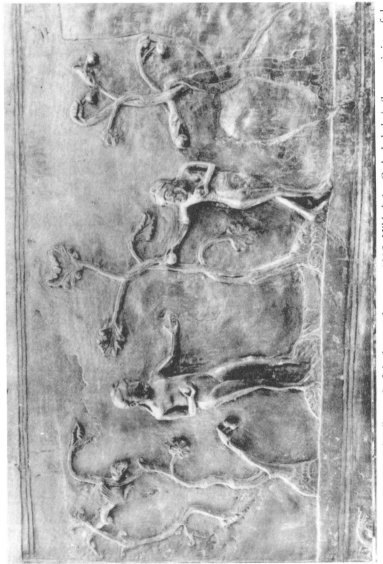

Fig. 16. Temptation and Fall, panel of the bronze doors, ca. 1015, Hildesheim Cathedral choir (by permission of the Dom- und Diözesanmuseum, Hildesheim).

Fig. 17. Rupertsberg *Scivias* (formerly Wiesbaden, Hessisches Landesbibliothek, MS 1, fol. 14) Book I, vision 3 (Rheinisches Bildarchiv).

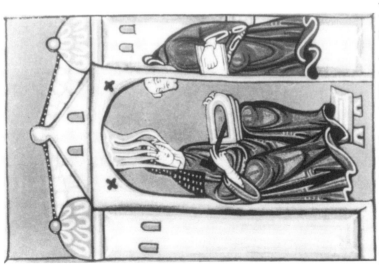

Fig. 18. (left) Rupertsberg *Scivias* (formerly Wiesbaden, Hessisches Landesbibliothek, MS 1, fol. 1) author portrait (Rheinisches Bildarchiv). Fig. 19. (right) Pentecost, Psalter of Christina of Markyate (so-called Albani-Psalter), Hildesheim, Dombibliothek MS God. 1, p. 55 (property of the parish of St. Godehard, reproduced by permission of the Dombibliothek).

Fig. 20. Rupertsberg *Scivias* (formerly Wiesbaden, Hessisches Landesbibliothek, MS 1, fol. 138v) Book III, vision 3 (Rheinisches Bildarchiv).

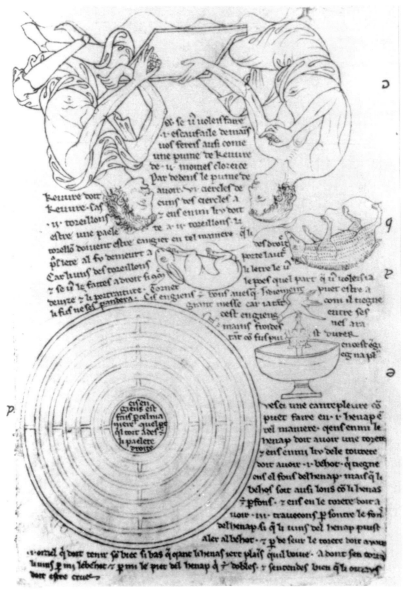

Fig. 21. Handwarmer and tantalus cup, boar and hare, men at gaming board, Villard de Honnecourt, Album, Paris, Bibliothèque Nationale MS fr. 19093, p. 9 (Bibl. Nat. Paris phot.).

Fig. 22. The figure of the Knowledge of God (*Scientia Dei*) adored by angels, Rupertsberg *Scivias* (formerly Wiesbaden, Hessisches Landesbibliothek, MS 1, fol. 146), Book III, vision 4 (Rheinisches Bildarchiv).

Fig. 23. *Scientia Dei,* Salem *Scivias,* ca. 1200 (Heidelberg, Universitätsbibliothek Cod. Salem X, 16, fol. 176), Book III, vision 4 (left half of page), with vision 10 (right half) (with permission).

Scientific Translation and Translator's Glossing in Four Medieval French Translators

Peter F. Dembowski

This chapter treats a type of redactorial and authorial activity that I call here "faute de mieux," translator's glossing. The term *gloss* is now, in biblical, classical, and medieval studies, often equated with commentary, but that important intellectual activity will not be treated here, even if the word *gloss* was used in connection with it.[1] By "glossing" I mean the sorts of translator's interventions added not so much to explicate a given doctrine of the translated text in general as to make more transparent the organization of the work and facilitate the understanding of a given passage, or a given term in particular. Translator's glossing thus includes several devices, some not immediately associated in our modern minds with glossing, but all of which play an important role in making the Latin source-text more accessible in its Old or Middle French garb. All such devices underscore the "service" aspect of the translation. They all make sure that the reader is constantly aware that he is reading a translated text, thereby allowing the translator to share with the reader the difficulties of the translating process.

The most obvious use of translator glossing is to be found in those sections of prefatory statements which refer specifically to the translating process. For example, in Jean de Meun's dedicatory preface addressed to

---

[1] Oresme systematically used the word *glose* for the longer commentaries (his own or translated from the traditional sources) or for shorter translator's interventions. For the importance of medieval commentaries even in the domain of the belletristic, see *Medieval Literary Theory and Criticism, c. 1100–c. 1375: The Commentary-Tradition*, ed. Alastair J. Minnis and A. Brian Scott (Oxford: Clarendon, 1988).

Philippe IV, after giving his name and listing all his works Jean states that he presents his royal patron with:

> Boece de Consolacion que j'ai translaté de latin en françois. Ja soit ce que tu [= Philippe IV] entendes bien le latin, mais toutevoies est de moult plus legiers a entendre le françois que le latin. Et por ce que tu me deis—lequel dit je tieng pour commandement—que je preisse plainement la sentence de l'aucteur sens trop ensuivre les paroles du latin, je l'ai fait a mon petit pooir si comme ta debonnaireté le me commanda. Or pri touz ceulz qui cest livre verront, s'il leur semble en aucuns lieus que je me soie trop eslongniés des paroles de l'aucteur ou que je aie mis aucuns fois plus de paroles que li aucteur n'i met ou aucune fois mains, que il le me pardoingnent. Car se je eusse espons mot a mot le latin par le françois, li livres fust trop occurs aus gens lais et li clers, neis moiennement letré, ne peussent pas legierement entendre le latin par le françois. (*De consolatione philosophiae* [hereafter *CP*], p. 168)[2]
>
> [Boethius's *De consolatione philosophiae* which I have translated from Latin into French. Although you certainly understand Latin, it is nevertheless very much easier to understand the French than the Latin. And because you told me—which I consider an order—to take the full meaning of the author without excessively following the words of the Latin, I have done this to the best of my ability as your graciousness commanded me. Now I beg the pardon of all those who, seeing this book, will think in some places that I have departed too much from the author's words or have sometimes put more, sometimes fewer, words than the author puts. For if I had expounded the Latin by the French word by word, the book would have been too obscure to laymen, and the clerics of even average learning would not easily have understood the Latin from the French.]

Some one hundred years later, Oresme will share with his readers essentially the same translator's anxieties. Oresme is more specific. In his own *Proheme* to *Le Livre de Ethiques d'Aristote* [hereafter *LE*],[3] in the section rubricated "Excusacion et commendacion de ceste oeuvre," Oresme

---

[2]Louis Venceslas Dedeck-Héry, ed., "Boethius' *De Consolatione* by Jean de Meun," *Mediæval Studies* 14 (1952): 165–275.

[3]Maistre Nicole Oresme, *Le Livre de Ethiques d'Aristote*, ed. Albert Douglas Menut, Published from the Text of MS. 2902, Bibliothèque Royale de Belgique (New York: Stechert, 1940).

begins by pointing to the inherent difficulties of translating Aristotle from Greek to Latin, and then continues:

> Et comme il soit ainsi que latin est a present plus parfait et plus habondant langage que françois, par plus forte raison l'en ne pourroit translater proprement tout latin en françois. Si comme entre innumbrables examples puet apparoir de ceste tres commune proposicion: *homo est animal*; car *homo* signifie homme et femme et nul mot de françois ne signifie equipeillennent [= "equipollently"]. Et *animal* signifie toute chose qui a ame sensitive et sent quant l'en la touche. Et il n'est nul mot en françois qui ce signifie preciseement. Et pour ce, ceste proposicion est vraye: *mulier est homo*, et ceste est fausse: "femme est homme." Semblablement ceste proposicion est vraye: *homo est animal*, et ceste est fausse: "homme est beste." Et ainsi est il de pluseurs noms et verbes, et mesmement de aucuns sincathegoremes,[4] si comme pluseurs preposicions et autres, qui tres souvent sont es livres dessus diz, que l'en ne puet bien translater en françois. (p. 100)

[And since, as it happens, Latin is at present a more perfect and a richer language than French, all the more reason therefore that one could not translate properly all Latin into French. As is apparent in the following common proposition (from among countless examples: *homo est animal*, because *homo* means both man and woman, and no single French word has an equivalent meaning. And *animal* signifies any thing that has a sensible soul and feels when it is touched. And there is no single French word that has this precise meaning. Therefore the following proposition: *mulier est homo*, is true, and the following: *woman is man*, is false. Similarly, the proposition: *homo est animal* is true, but *man is an animal* is false. And this applies to numerous nouns and verbs, and even to some syncategorems, such as numerous prepositions and other forms, which figure very often in the above mentioned books, and are not translatable into French.]

Oresme seems to be more optimistic than Jean de Meun, for he ends his *Proheme* not only with a necessary and skillful compliment to his royal patron but also with an echo of the *translatio studii* topos. Citing Cicero's opinion that "les choses pesantes et de grant auctorité sont delectables et bien aggreables as genz ou langage de leur païs," he concludes:

---

[4]Neither Oresme nor the modern editor glosses this obvious hellenism, cf. συγκατηγόρημα "that which in a sentence is not subject nor predicate," Liddell, Scott, Jones, *Greek-English Lexicon*, 9th ed. Supplement, 136. The term is taken from Priscian.

Or est il ainsi que pour le temps de lors, grec estoit en resgart de latin quant as Romains si comme est maintenant latin en regart de françois quant a nous. Et estoient pour le temps les estudians introduiz en grec et a Romme et ailleurs, et les sciences communelment bailliees en grec; et en ce paÿs le langage commun et maternel, c'estoit latin. Donques puis je bien encore conclurre que la consideracion et le propos de nostre bon roy Charles est a recommender, qui fait les bons livres et excellens translater en françois. (p. 101)
[And thus in those times for the Romans, Greek was in relation to Latin what Latin is for us in relation to French. And at that time the students in Rome and elsewhere were introduced to Greek, and the sciences were usually presented in Greek; while the common mother language in that country was Latin. And therefore I can conclude that the project of our good King Charles, who has good and outstanding books translated into French, is to be recommended.]

A second category of specific translator's glosses comprises redactorial interventions: statements not present in the source-text in which the translator acts as a conscientious editor, offering section or chapter headings. In the Old French *Decretum Gratiani* [hereafter *DG*][5] these headings are offered as rubrics. They greatly augment the referential purpose of the book (i.e., they facilitate finding the specific rule of canon law). The first part of *DG* consists of 101 *Distinctiones* (marked in the MS in Roman numerals), each of which is divided into several canons. While the *Distinctiones* do not bear any titles, most of the individual canons are preceded by an explicatory rubric. Thus, for example, the twenty-first *Distinctio* consists of nine canons, introduced as follows:

> *D'ou touz clers sont dit* [Where the name cleric comes from];
> *Comment ordre de provoire fu commanciee et par qui* [How and by whom the order of priests was initiated];

---

[5] Leena Löfstedt has given us an excellent edition of the first part of the thirteenth-century (anonymous?) *Gratiani Decretum: La traduction en ancien français du Decret de Gratien*, vol. 1, *Distinctiones* (Helsinki: Societas Scientiarum Fennica, 1992), and plans to publish volumes 2, *Causæ* 1–14 and 3, *De consecratione*, plus introduction and commentary. According to the editor ("La Loi canonique, les Platagenêt et S. Thomas Becket," *Medioevo Romanzo* 15 [1990]: 1), the original translation of *Gratiani Decretum* goes back to "vers 1200, peut-être même plus tôt."

Comment l'iglise de Rome fu establie [How the Church of Rome was
   established];

Li plus bas ne puet assoudre le plus hault [The lower cannot absolve
   the higher];

Empty space left for a rubric;

Li greingneur beneissent les meneurs [The greater bless the lesser];

Nus ne doit estre jugié par plus bas de lui [No one must be judged by
   a lower]; this canon contains an additional rubric: *Nus ne doit
   jugier l'apostoile* [No one must judge the Pope];

Comment Egnacius fu jugiez par les segonz [How Ignatius was judged
   by the others]; and

Que nus ne juge greigneur de soi [Let no one judge a person higher
   than himself]. (*DG*, pp. 42–45)

The absence of a rubric in the fifth canon is not extraordinary. It is
quite possible that in this work the rubric-glosses were written not by the
translator himself but by his co-worker, the rubricator. The scribe of this
redaction of *DG* has left a space for such rubric-glosses in several places,
without doubt to be filled by the rubricator-glossator. It would be
interesting to speculate about why certain rubrics were not inscribed. In the
case of the fifth canon above, there is no apparent reason for any difficulty
in summing up the canon, which simply illustrates the preceding one.

But the translator of *DG* has left untranslated the Latin *incipit* by which
the individual canons have been known. Throughout the Middle Ages
individual canons were referred to by their *incipit* rather than by their
number (numbering of canons was introduced by modern editors). Thus
in the twenty-first *Distinctio*, the first French introductory rubric is immediately followed by *Cleros,* the second by *In Nouo,* the third by *Quamvis,*
etc. From the point of view of the history of translations, it is interesting
to note that the Latin of these forms is not very good: "Les *incipit* latins
sont souvent mal transmis; ils présentent un nombre d'erreurs plus élevé
que le texte; il est probable que les copistes de notre texte maîtrisaient mal
le latin" (*DG*, p. 2) [The Latin *incipit*s are often badly transmitted; they
present a higher number of errors than the text; it is probable that the
copyists of our text had a poor command of Latin].

It is perhaps due to the discursive nature of Boethius that *CP* does not contain any such redactorial glosses while the Aristotelian translations by Oresme are full of them. In his translation of the first and third Books of the pseudo-Aristotelian *Le Livre de Yconomique* [hereafter *LY*],[6] Oresme divides the short *opusculum* into brief chapters that are carefully glossed, that is to say, rubricated. *LY* opens with a brief and very helpful incipit:

> Cy commence le livre appellé *Yconomique,* lequel composa Aristote et ouquel il determine de gouvernement de maison. Et contient .ii. petis livres parcialz. Ou premier il determine generalment de toutes les parties de maison et de toutes les communications qui sunt en maison. Et contient .vii. chapitres. (*LY*, p. 807)
> [Here begins the book called *Economics*, which Aristotle wrote and in which he sets forth the rules for household management. And it contains two short, separate books. In the first, he examines broadly all the parts of the household and all the interrelated divisions of a household. And it contains seven chapters.]

Each of those chapters is supplied by a title-rubric-gloss as, for example, "Le premier chapitre est le proheme, ou il[7] met son intention et declare aucunes choses qui sunt a son propos" (*LY*, p. 807) [The first chapter is the introduction, in which he states the purpose of his investigations and clarifies certain matters pertinent to his project]; and "Ou quart chapitre il met enseignemens pour le mari ou resgart de sa femme" (*LY*, p. 816) [In the fourth chapter he sets down instructions for the husband concerning his wife]. Oresme systematically makes his own smaller subdivisions,[8] not only

---

[6]"Maistre Nicole Oresme: *Le Livre de Yconomique* d'Aristote," ed. Albert Douglas Menut, *Transactions of the American Philosophical Society,* n.s., 47, nr. 5, 785–852. The projected edition of Oresme's *Politiques* announced by Menut (see *LY*, p. 783) has not, as far as I could ascertain, ever appeared.

[7]Oresme uses this *il* in his headings and his other glosses to refer to the author whom he translates and comments, i.e., Aristotle.

[8]We know that, in *DC* and *LE*, Oresme follows the traditional divisions into Books. We also know that Oresme himself divided the subject matter in *LY* into brief chapters. I believe that the subdivisions of the ten Books of *LE* and the four Books of *DC* into small chapters were also largely done by him, but it is not easy to ascertain this fact. The textual history of those works is most complex. Let us simply compare in that respect modern authoritative editions with the translations done by Oresme. Book 1 of W. K. C. Guthrie's

in *LY* but also in *LE* and *Du Ciel* (hereafter *DC*). Each chapter, without exception, is introduced by a title-gloss: "Ou .xiiii.ᵉ chapitre il determine en general de ce qu'il est appellé juste" (*LE*, p. 300) [In the fourteenth chapter he defines in general what is called just]; or "Ou secont chapitre il commence a parler des vertus intellectueles et premierement en general" (*LE*, p. 332) [In the second chapter he begins to speak about the intellectual virtues, and, at first, in general terms].

There are two additional redactorial interventions that should be mentioned here. Oresme systematically makes cross references to his own subdivisions or chapters. He does this chiefly in the traditional glosses (*stricto sensu:* commentaries), which he translates together with the main Aristotelian text. Thus we find such formulaic cross references as: "Car si comme il appert par le .viii.ᵉ chapitre du tiers de *Politiques*" (*LY*, p. 807) [For, as is demonstrated in the eighth chapter of the third book of *Politics*]; and "Si comme il appert par le .xxvi.ᵉ chapitre du .vii.ᵉ de *Politiques* et par le .xvi.ᵉ chapitre du premier d'*Ethiques*" (*LY*, p. 830) [As is shown in *Politics* VII, 12 (1332a 20ff.) and in *Ethics* I, 16] (*LY*, p. 807). In *LE*, gloss references are often made to the other parts of the same treatise. Thus, the phrase "il nous convient essayer . . . a comprendre ceste chose et a savoir que ce est" [we should try . . . to understand this matter and to know what it is] is glossed "Ce sera par especial ou premier et .x.ᵉ de *Ethiques*" (*LE*, p. 105) [This will be treated particularly in the first and the tenth book of *Ethics*]. Or, in his chapter 18 (Bk. 1), Oresme translates "nous loons un homme tousjours en raportant a autre chose et ou resgart de aucune habilité a autre chose bonne et vertueuse" [we praise a man always in relation to another thing and concerning some capacity (to do) other, good and virtuous thing] and adds a gloss both explicative and referential: "C'est une raison; car loenge est de choses ordenee a autre bien meilleur et felicité

---

edition of Aristotle's *On the Heavens* (Cambridge, Mass.: Harvard University Press, 1939) contains twelve chapters, and Book 2 contains fourteen chapters, whereas in *DC* the numbers are thirty-six and thirty-one, respectively. Similarly, Book 1 of H. Rackham's edition of Aristotle's *The Nicomachean Ethics* (Cambridge, Mass.: Harvard University Press, 1926) contains thirteen chapters or sections, and Book 2 contains nine, whereas *LE* has twenty-one and twelve, respectively.

n'est pas ordenee a autre plus grant bien, si comme il fu dit au .viii.ᵉ chapitre et est yci supposé" (*LE*, p. 139) [This is right; because praise concerns a matter tending to other, better good, whereas happiness does not tend to other, greater good, as it was said in the eighth chapter and it is supposed here].[9]

In *DC*, this use of such cross references becomes, if anything, even more frequent. Thus, for example, when Aristotle repeats that "de tout corps naturel est aucun propre movement; et des mouvemens les uns sont simples, les autres sont mixtes" [there is some proper movement of each natural body; and among the movements certain are simple and others are mixed], the translator-glossator offers a reference: "Tout ce fu declairié ou tiers chapitre du premier livre" (*DC*, p. 618) [All this was clarified in the third chapter of the first book]. When the source text speaks only in vague terms about "les raisons qui ont esté devant mises sont contre eulz" [the reasons which have been marshaled are against them], the referential gloss explains immediately: "Ou tiers chapitre et en le .viii.ᵉ" (*DC*, p. 628) [In the third and the eighth chapters].

In *LE*, the care taken to furnish more precise cross references is evident occasionally also in the glossed chapter headings: "Ou .xvii.ᵉ chapitre il traicte la seconde question du .xv.ᵉ chapitre, c'est assavoir se fortune puet oster ou muer felicité aprés la mort" (*LE*, p. 137) [In the seventeenth chapter he treats the second question of the fifteenth chapter, that is to say, whether fortune can remove or change happiness after death (of a second party)]; and "Ou .xxii.ᵉ chapitre il respont a la seconde question proposee

---

[9]It is important to note that when Oresme makes frequent reference to works other than his own translations, they are far less precise: "ce est assavoir, ou secunt livre de *l'Ame* et ou *Livre de Generation et corruption* et ou secunt livre de la *Generation de bestes*" (*LY*, p. 811) [For example, in *On the Soul* II [4, 415a 28], in *Generation and corruption* [I, 4, 319b 5ff.], and in the *Generation of animals* II [1, 731b 18ff.] (*LE*, p. 110); "Il note contre Platon, qui disoit que felicité est une ydee separee" (*LE*, p. 110) [He observes it against Plato, who said that happiness is a separate idea]; "Et les intelligences qui les mouvent sont plusseurs selonc Aver[r]oïs et appert ou .xii.ᵉ de *Metaphisique*" (*DC*, p. 148) [And the intelligences that move them are several, according to Averroës, and the matter is treated in the Twelfth Book of the *Metaphysics*].

au .xix.ᵉ chapitre" (*LE*, p. 326) [In the twenty-second chapter he answers the second question proposed in the nineteenth chapter]. But this particular practice is followed neither in *LY* nor in *DC*.

The chapter divisions with their descriptive headings as well as the cross references to the pre-established chapters are very important contributions made by the "service"[10] translator to the coherence and unity of the translations. This coherence is enhanced by the inclusion of tables of contents that list all the chapter headings. Yet, important as they are for easier consultation, the tables are not necessarily the work of the translator. We know that the text of *DG* was copied by two different scribes, but the long table of contents (six folios) was written by yet a different and considerably later hand. In *LY* and *LE* the tables of chapter headings (identical with the chapter headings found in the text) are placed at the beginning of each Book. They have been suppressed by the modern editor (cf. *LY*, p. 848, and *LE*, p. 103), but in the difficult, fragmentary and perhaps incomplete *DC*,[11] Oresme (or, less probably, the redactor of the base MS)[12] supplies not one but two tables of contents. Each Book is preceded by a list in which chapter headings are repeated in a slightly different form than appears in the text. Furthermore, at the end of this treatise there is a table of "things worthy of note." Oresme clearly explains this redactorial device: "En ces .iiii. livres sont choses bien notables desquelles pluseurs peuent estre trouvees par l'intitulation des chapitres et par la table qui s'ensuit ici, laquelle ne pourroit bonnement estre ordonee selon l'ordre des lettres de l'a b c" (*DC*, p. 732) [In these three books there are some very noteworthy things, several of which can be found by the chapter titles and by the table which follows here—the latter could not be

---

[10]For this use of the term *service translation* see my article "Learned Latin Treatises in French: Inspiration, Plagiarism, and Translation," *Viator* 17 (1986): 255–66.

[11]A modern specialist of Aristotle believes that *De Cælo* was originally composed of four more or less independent monographs, left unfinished at the death of the Philosopher, and that the present form of the treatise is the result of posthumous editorial work by various "redactors." See Aristotle, *Du Ciel*, ed. Paul Moraux (Paris: Les Belles Lettres, 1965), pp. viii–xxviii.

[12]I say "less probably" because all six surviving manuscripts have a *Table des choses notables*.

simply arranged according to the order of the alphabet]. Unlike the tables preceding each Book that list the chapters in their order of appearance in the treatise, this one is a good attempt to sum up analytically the content of Aristotle's text, as well as present the gist of the traditional commentaries. Again, the principle of cross-referencing is fully observed. Thus, for example, we read at the the beginning of the table (*DC,* p. 732):

> Ou premier livre [In the first book];
> De la Trinité divine, ou premier chapitre et ou .x.^e chapitre du quart [On the Holy Trinity, in the first chapter and the tenth chapter of the fourth book];
> De mixtion de mouvemens et comment de pluseurs mouvemens drois peust estre fait mouvement circulaire, et de pluseurs circulaires mouvement drois, ou tiers chapitre [Concerning mixing of movements and how a circular movement can be made from several straight movements, and from several circular movements a straight movement, in the third chapter]; and
> Comment aer peut monter et eaue descendre naturelement du centre siques au ciel et du ciel siques au centre, ou quart chapitre; et de ce plus a plain ou sixte chapitre du quart [How air can naturally go upward and water go downward from the center, that is to say, into the sky, and from the sky into the center, in the fourth chapter; and concerning this more plainly in the sixth chapter of the fourth book].

As we have seen, the preamble to this *table des choses bien notables* contains a germ of the idea of the alphabetical *index rerum*, which has now become part and parcel of any serious book on a scientific matter.

In *LE,* Oresme gives us another alphabetical list, which is one of the earliest, if not *the* earliest, examples of this device. At the close of his *LE,* he appends *La Table des moz divers et estranges,*[13] the character and purpose of which he explains as follows:

> Pour ceste science plus clerement entendre, je vueil de habondant exposer aucuns moz selon l'ordre de l'a.b.c., lesquelz par aventure sembleroient obscurs a aucuns qui ne sont pas excercitéz en ceste science; ja soit que il n'y ait rien obscur, ce me semble, quant a ceuls qui seroient .i. peu acoustumés a lire en cest livre. Car presque tous telz moz sont dedenz exposés ou en texte ou en glose. Et pour ce en

---

[13]We know that Oresme has drawn a list of a *Table de fors* [= "difficult"] *mos* in his *Livre de Politiques.* See below, n. 26.

laisse je pluseurs, car il n'est mestier de les exposer ailleurs ne autrement que ilz sont exposés en leurs lieux. (*LE*, p. 541)

[In order to understand this science more clearly, I wish to explain abundantly some words according to the order of a b c, which words could perchance seem obscure to those who are not trained in that science, even if there is nothing obscure in them, so it seems to me, for those who would be somewhat accustomed to read in this book, because almost all these words are explained herein, either in the text or in the gloss. And for this reason, I leave some of them, because there is no need to explain them elsewhere and in any other way than they are explained in their places.]

He offers an alphabetical list of fifty-four words (pp. 541–47), each followed by a definition and by an indication of the place at which the term was used. Thus, to take but one item: "*Synesie* est une partie ou une maniere de prudence quant est a bien jugier. Et de ce fu dit au .xii.ᵉ chapitre du sixte" (*LE*, p. 546) [Synesis is an aspect or a kind of prudence concerning good judgement. And this was exposed in the twelfth chapter of the sixth book]. These alphabetized glossed terms can be placed in three classes:

1. Greek neologisms: *architectonique, bomolochos, chaymes, demo-cratie, demos, demotique, discoles, epyekeye, eubulie, eutrapeles, gnomé, iconomie, oligarchie, phylautos, tymocracie*;
2. Latin neologisms: *actif, active, adultre* (elsewhere in the text, for example, p. 299, *adultere*), *contingent, excercitative, faccion, factive, illegal, legal, passif, predicat, prodigalité, prodig(u)e, rectitude, synesie, vacacion*; and
3. Latinisms, not necessarily introduced by Oresme, but used by him in a specialized sense: *civilité, conferent, continent, difference, diffinicion, justice equal, justice legal, obligacion legal, obligacion moral, object, passion*.

In addition, Oresme lists and glosses two French words to which he gave specialized meanings: *gerre* [for *genre*, literal translation of Lat. *genus*)[14] and

---

[14]This term is defined in the article *difference*: "C'est un mot commun. Mais aucunes fois il est pris en especial pour chascune partie de diffinicion exceptee la premiere qui est

puissance: "est un mot commun, . . . il est pris souvent en ceste science pour la puissance naturelle d'ame" [*power* is a common word, . . . it is taken often in this science to mean natural power of the soul], and he further explains that *puissance* can be *sensitive, intellective, cognoscitive, appetitive,* etc. (*LE*, p. 546).

Our four translators are also glossators in the strictest sense of the word: they explain and/or paraphrase the difficult terms or passages. The Text of *DG* has some marginal glosses (see *DG*, p. 1). Jean de Meun is responsible for some glosses that, in the base MS, are composed in a way that allows us to distinguish between Boethius's text and the gloss. In that MS "certain glosses, [are] embodied into the text . . . without logical connection while in other MSS they are already transformed and adapted to the text" (*CP*, p. 166, n. 3). This fact has allowed the modern editor to distinguish many of these glosses from the main body of the text. They are printed in italics. Obviously Jean de Meun practices a traditional form of explanatory, textual glossing. Thus, while translating the description of Lady Philosophy's vestment: "Harum in extremo margine Π, in supremo vero Θ legebatur intextum" [Π will be read woven in the extreme edge of them, and in the upper edge, in fact, the letter Θ], Jean also glosses: "Ou derrenier oule de ces robes et *ou plus bas* lisoit l'en tissue une letre grezesche, *tele* Π *qui senefioit la vie active,* et *pardesus* ou plus haut oule *une autre lettre, tele* Θ *qui senefioit la vie contemplative*" (*CP*, p. 172) [In the extreme edge of these robes one read, *at the bottom,* a Greek woven letter, to wit Π, *which signified the active life* and at upper edge *another letter,* to wit Θ *which signified the contemplative life*]. This is, of course, not a purely linguistic gloss. The two Greek letters can surely appear enigmatic to an uninitiated reader. In fact a modern editor of Boethius explains in a modern gloss (in

---

appellee gerre; si comme qui diroit ainsi: 'beste a quatre piéz qui peut hennir.' C'est la diffinicion de cheval. Et est cest mot 'beste,' c'est le gerre. Et cest mots 'a .iiii. piéz,' c'est la difference; et 'qui peut hennir,' c'est l'autre difference" (*LE*, p. 543) [It is a common word. Nevertheless sometimes it is taken in a special sense for each part of definition except the first which is called genus, thus supposed that someone would say "animal with four legs which can neigh." This is the definition of the horse. This word "animal" is the genus. And this word "with four legs" is the difference; and "which can neigh" is another difference].

a footnote) the same thing that Jean did in his "hidden" gloss.[15] It is unlikely that this particular gloss was authored by Jean himself. He probably found it in a gloss of his Latin source text. But there are other glosses in his text that seem more transparently his; as such they are, properly speaking, "translator's" glosses. When Boethius muses about the future and past times, Jean adds a gloss to ensure that his translated passage will be easily grasped: "car les futurs, *ce sont les temps a venir*, encores ne les a elle pas; les préteriz, *ce sont les temps trespasséz*, elle ne les a mais" (*CP*, p. 271) [because the future, *that is, the times to come*, it does not have; the preterites *that is, the times past*, it no longer has]. The expression "la passion du corps" [the suffering of the body] is perhaps too abstract, so the translator glosses "*c'est li sens du corps*" (*CP*, p. 268) [that is, the feeling of the body]. Quite often the Latin is too succinct, thus the expression "existimatio bona . . . deserat infelices" is first rendered as: "bonne presompcion . . . delaisse les maleurés" [good esteem . . . deserts the unfortunate one] and then is followed by a necessary gloss: "*c'est a dire que nulz ne croit que pouvres homs soit preusdom*" (*CP*, p. 181) [that is to say that nobody believes that a poor man is a worthy man]. Similarly, the too succinct and certainly abstract *fœdera rerum* is rendered literally: "les aliancez des chosez" [the accords of things] and then glossed: "*c'est les conjonctions de dieu et de homme*" (*CP*, p. 263) [that is, the conjunction of God and man].

What Jean de Meun does quite often, but in a more or less sporadic fashion, Oresme will do more systematically. An even more important difference between the two translators is that Jean does not make any graphic distinction between the text and the gloss. We very often can surmise what was in the text and what was added by the translator both because we have a well-preserved tradition of the Latin text and, more

---

[15]This explanation comes most probably from Boethius himself, who in his commentary on Porphyry's commentary on Aristotle's *Categories* explains: "Philosophia genus; species vero ejus due: una quæ Θεωρητικά dicitur; altera quæ Πρακτικά, id est speculativa et activa"; see *La Consolation philosophique de Boece*, ed. and trans. Louis J. de Mirandol (Paris: Hachette, 1861), p. 334 [Philosophy is the genus, but there are two species of it: one which is called Theory, the other Practice, that is, speculative and active philosophy].

important, because Jean frequently adds his own little glossing markers such as *c'est, ce sont, c'est a dire que,* etc. In contrast, Oresme explicitly distinguishes between the Aristotelian text and the gloss. The MSS of *LY, LE,* and *DC* almost always make this distiction. In the base MS of *LY,* the former is written in *lettre de cour,* the latter in small *bâtarde.* In *LE,* the gloss is placed "at top, bottom and on both sides, like frame around the text, as in manuscripts of works on civil and canon law of 13th and 14th centuries"[16] (*LE,* p. 46). In *DC,* the text and gloss of the basic MS follow one another, but the first is indicated by *Tiexte,* the second by *Glose.*

It would be difficult to underestimate the importance of the clear separation of text and gloss practiced by Oresme.[17] It meant that for serious texts the free recasting and paraphrasing translation or, rather, adaptations, no longer were the only option in the popularizing vernacularizations. Nevertheless, there remains a problem for students of learned translations, for while we can determine fairly easily what is text and what is gloss, it is more difficult to determine which are traditional gloss-commentaries translated by Oresme, which are his glosses, and particularly which are his translator's glosses.

Because of their different natures, each of Oresme's works must be treated individually in respect to the translator's glossing. *LY* has been translated from the Latin text of a pseudo-Aristotelian *Economics* found in a William of Moerbeke version. This text does not have any comments, but Oresme supplies some of the typical translator's glosses. Thus, for example, he renders the Lat. *georgica* as *la cure georgique* [georgic operation] followed first by a "hidden gloss": "ce est a dire, de cultiver la terre" [that is to say, cultivation of the land], and then by a proper gloss: "Elle est dicte *georgique* de *ge* en grec, que est terre; et de *orge,* que est culture ou labour" [Called *georgic* from *ge* in Greek, meaning land; and *orge,* meaning cultivation or tilling of the soil] (*LY,* p. 810). Finally the enthusiastic glossator adds a

---

[16]It is interesting to note that the traditional Talmudic commentaries follow similar graphic arrangements.

[17]Oresme's principle of separation was well understood by the copyists. Out of six surviving MSS of *DC* all but one distinguish graphically between the text and the gloss.

cultural cross reference: "Et selon ce, un livre de Virgile est appellé *Georgiques*" [Thus a book by Virgil is called the *Georgics*] (*LY*, p. 810). Even when the source text seems linguistically transparent but is perhaps too succinct: "As hommes la premiere cure doit estre a chescun de sa femme ou espouse"[18] [The first concern of every man must be his wife or spouse] (*LY*, p. 811), Oresme does not hesitate to gloss by elaborating: "Car apres le seigneur, la femme est la premiere comme compaigne. Secundement sunt les enfans et tiercement les serfs et les possessions" [Because next to the master, the wife as his companion holds first place. The children come second, and the slaves and possessions third] (*LY*, p. 811). Such a gloss as this lies somewhere between a translator's intervention and a gloss *tout court*, and represents a typical glossing activity in *LY*.

While most of the glosses in *LY* can probably be ascribed to Oresme, the situation in *LE* is quite different. We know that he essentially followed the Latin text of the so-called *Vetus translatio*.[19] Thomas Aquinas wrote an extensive commentary on this version. Oresme also mentions in his glosses *l'autre translacion,* usually called *Translatio arabica* and which is associated with Averroës.[20] Both of these versions were heavily commentated, and most of the glosses in *LE* come from the traditional commentaries contained in both versions. The modern editor describes the translator's contribution to glossing as follows:

> In the case of the *Ethics*, Oresme's additions to the text can hardly be called a commentary, for only rarely do his explanations take on the dimensions of a discussion of the text. Yet his contribution considerably exceeds that of mere

---

[18]Here the Latin *uxor* is rendered by a French binomial *femme ou espouse*. Such use of binomial synonyms, while extremely common in translations, is not necessarily a symptom of the "glossing mentality" of the translators. The tendency to use such doublets existed also outside translations. See my "Les Binômes synonymiques en ancien français," *Kwartalnik Neofilologiczny* 23 (1976): 81–90.

[19]The "first Latin translation of all ten books of the *Ethics* from a Greek original, made about 1245 by Robert Grosseteste, bishop of Lincoln" (*LE*, p. 39).

[20]"Translated at Toledo in 1240 by Hermannus Allemanus, from a paraphrase of the *Ethics* contained in the *Intermediate Commentary* by Averroes" (*LE*, p. 39).

glossator. The nature of his elucidations in the *Ethics* makes it clear that here, at least, he was primarily concerned with translations and only secondarily with interpretation. (*LE*, pp. 40–41)

Thus in *LE*, Oresme's own glosses belong, to a large extent, to the very category which interests us most. Translator's glosses can be distinguished from various "editorial" glosses (very frequent in *LE*), which we discussed earlier, and from the broader interpretative comments. Most of Oresme's translator's glosses appear when the target text does not seem clear enough. Thus a philosophical expression "Car bonne vie est a peu celle chose que est bonne operacion" [Because good life is approximately that which is good operation] is rendered more transparent by a gloss: "La chose n'est pas reputee vivre qui n'a operacion" (*LE*, p. 125) [That which does not imply good operation is not considered to be alive]. For the social or literary historian the two following examples are interesting. In the first, Oresme elegantly translates "brothel keepers" [πορνοβοσκοί] as "Et telz sont ceulz qui se paissent ou mangüent du gaaing des folles femmes incontinentes et touz telz gens" [And such are those who sustain themselves by feeding on the gains of the immoral and incontinent women and all such people] and proceeds to explain "all such people": "Comme gouliardois et aucuns jugleurs et aucuns cabusëeurs" (*LE*, p. 240) [like goliards and some jugglers and some impostors]. In the second, he glosses the word *tragedie*[21] as: "Sont ditiez, comme rommans qui parlent et traictent de aucuns grans faiz notables" (*LE*, p. 137) [They are poems such as romances which speak and treat great and worthy deeds]. Also interesting for us is Oresme's elucidation of the word *comedy*. He glosses the sentence "Et ce peut asséz apparoir par les comedies des anciens et par celles que l'en fait a present" [And this can be seen in the comedies of the ancients and by those that are made now] with: "Il entent ici par comedies aucuns gieux, comme sont ceulz ou .i. homme represente Saint Pol, l'autre Judas, l'autre un hermite, et dit chascun son personnage et en ont aucuns roulles et rimes. Et aucunes fois en telz giex l'en dit de laides paroles, ordres, injurieuses et deshonestes"

---

[21]"This is apparently the first use of 'tragedie' in French" (*LE*, p. 138).

(*LE*, p. 271) [He means here by comedies the plays, as are those in which one man represents St. Paul, another Judas, another a hermit, and each speaks his personage, and they perform roles and verses. In such plays, immoral, dirty, injurious and dishonest words are sometimes said]. (This last sentence neatly sums up for us the history of morality plays and of their reception.)

Crucial for our understanding of his role as translator-glossator are Oresme's remarks in *LE* in which he elucidates the meaning, and sometimes the etymology, of the Greek terms that he has found in his Latin source.[22] In such glosses the translator shares, so to speak, with the reader the difficulties of his art and science. Thus, after "Et celuy qui a superhabundance ou excés en paour n'a pas nom imposé" [And the one who has a superabundance or excess of fear has no name imposed], he hastens to gloss: "En langage grec, car en françois l'en le apelle couart" [in the Greek language, for in French he is called coward]. Similarly, in the same paragraph, he translates "Et celui qui superhabunde ou excede en oser, il est fol hardi ou trop hardi" [And he who superabounds or who has excess of daring, he is madly bold or too bold], and then he explains (awkwardly): "Il a nom approprié en grec et en latin. Mais en françois, hardy ne signifie pas mal qui ne adjousteroit en disant fol hardy ou trop hardy" (*LE*, p. 165) [He has an appropriate name in Greek and in Latin. But in French bold does not signify fault unless one adds madly bold or too bold]. Oresme glosses *eutrapeles*: "En grec 'eu' c'est bon ou bien 'trapeles' c'est tournant, siques 'eutrapeles' est celui qui scet bien a point tourner les faiz et les

---

[22]We have already seen his etymological gloss of *georgique* in *LY*. In the same text Oresme also explains that *monarchie* comes "de *monos* en grec, que est un; et de *archos*, qu'est prince ou seigneur et est cellui que l'en appelle en latin *paterfamilias*" [from *monos* in Greek, which is one; and from *archos*, which is prince or master, and he is the one called *paterfamilias* in Latin]. Similarly, he tells us that *ethique* comes "de *ethos* en grec, qu'est meurs ou acoustumance; et de *ycos*, qu'est science" [from *ethos* in Greek, which means mores or custom, and from *ycos*, which means science]. He concludes this gloss with another interesting, false etymology, this time of *yconomique* (which, incidentally, explains his curious spelling of economics): "de *ycon* en grec, que est ymage ou signe; et de *nomos*, qu'est regle" [from *ycon* in Greek, which means image or sign; and from *nomos*, which means rule] (*LY*, p. 807).

paroles a solaz et a esbatement. Et par aventure, de ce vint ce que l'en dit en françoys d'un homme qu'il est bon tripelin" (*LE*, pp. 167–68) [In Greek "eu" is good, "trapeles" turning, thus "eutrapeles" is one who can turn deeds and words for solace and for pleasure. Perhaps this is the reason that in French one says of a man that he is a good "tripelin"]. Elsewhere (p. 270), he repeats this gloss almost *verbatim*, but gives *trupelin* instead of *tripelin*. Oresme offers us here an early example of what will become a venerable tradition of the *fausse étymologie savante*, for it is highly unlikely that Oresme's *tripelin* or *trupelin* could be a borrowing from Greek.[23]

If in *LE* Oresme was primarily concerned with translations and only secondarily with interpretation, this situation was reversed in *DC*. His *Livre du ciel et du monde*, also known as *Du Ciel*, is a careful and well-glossed translation of *De Coelo*.[24] Oresme's contribution to the explicatory scientific glossing of this text is important enough to warrant a whole chapter in Menut's Introduction entitled: "Brief Summary of Oresme's Commentary" (*DC*, pp. 16–31).

But even if in *DC* Oresme as commentator-glossator offers an enormous mass of work, his role as translator-glossator is not negligible. He is conscious of the difficulties of translation, and this awareness can be seen in his brief prologue when he anounces the fact that "ci commence le livre

---

[23]Menut believes that the word "is derived from *tripe*, which fathered the still common *tripaille*" (*LE*, p. 168). This etymology also presents some semantic difficulties. The word is unattested elsewhere: Frédéric Godefroy, *Dictionnaire de l'ancienne langue française et de tous ses dialectes du IXe au XVe siècles*, 10 vols. (Paris: F. Vieweg, 1880–1902; repr. New York: Kraus, 1961), 8: 400, cites our *trupelin*. The term might come from *trepler, tripeler* "to dance, to agitate" (see Walther von Wartburg et al., *Französisches Etymologisches Wörterbuch* [*FEW*], 26 vols. [Bonn, Leipzig, and then Basel, 1928–83], 17: 367, and Godefroy, *Dictionnaire*, 8: 43).

[24]Which in turn is a Latin translation of Aristotle's Περί οὐρανοῦ. Oresme followed chiefly the text translated from the Greek, the so-called *nova translatio* begun by Robert of Lincoln in ca. 1250 and completed by William of Moerbecke in ca. 1265, but he also occasionally used the so-called *translatio Scotti* (Michael Scot's translation from the Arabic ca. 1230). According to the modern editor of *DC*, the French translator systematically consulted Averroës's *Middle Commentary*, which in the medieval MSS usually accompanied the *translatio Scotti*.

d'Aristote appelé *Du Ciel et du monde"* [Here begins the book of Aristotle called *On the Heavens and the World*], which, following the order of Charles V, he "propose translater et exposer en françoys" [proposes to translate and to explain in French]. He then offers a good translator's gloss for the title:

> Et est cest livre ainsi intitulé quar il traite du ciel et des elemens du monde, en prenant cest nom *monde* pour les .iiii. elemens contenus dedens le ciel et souz le ciel, quar autrement et communelment en cest livre, cest nom est prins pour toute la masse du ciel et des .iiii. elemens ensemble. Et est cest mot prins ailleurs en pluseurs autres significations qui ne sont propres a cest propos. (*DC*, p. 38)
> [Here begins the book of Aristotle called *On the Heavens and the World*. And this book is titled thus because it treats the heavens and the elements of the world, taking this word *world* to mean the four elements contained in the heavens and below the heavens, because otherwise, and commonly in this book, this name stands for all the mass of the heavens and for the four elements. And this word is taken elsewhere to have several other meanings which are not proper to this subject.]

This warning about the polyvalence of the word *monde* is followed by the glossing of such difficult technical terms as *magnitude, continu, divisible, ligne, longuitude, latitude, spissitude* [thickness], etc. (*DC*, pp. 44–48). Here again these glosses fall somewhere between scientific elucidation and purely linguistic translator's gloss.

But the text is sprinkled with glosses that address the problem of language in general and the translator's language in particular. Thus, for example, explaining that one does not use the term *all* to mean *both* (*ambes .ii.*), Oresme glosses tautologically: "Quar en grec et, par aventure, presque en tout autre language, l'en ne disoit pas de .i. ne de .ii., il y sont touz, mais l'en le disoit de .iii. et des nombres ensuianz" (*DC*, p. 52) [Because in Greek, and perhaps in any other language, one did not speak about one or two as being all, but one did say it about three and the following numbers]. As lexicographers know, tautology is inevitable in elucidation of a term. Oresme glosses thus the phrase "environ le milieu": "Ce est entor un point appellé centre qui est ou milieu du cercle" (*DC*, p. 60) [That is, around the point called the center, which is in the middle of the circle]. When the Latin Aristotelian text speaks about *ingenitum*, our translator-glossator explains: "Et *ingenitum* en ceste maniere peut estre appellé *ingenerable*" [And *ingenitum* in that sense can be called *ingenerate*], but when Aristotle adds a distinction: "Item, *ingenitum* est dit d'une chose qui peut estre et n'est pas" [Item, *ingenitum* is said to be the thing which can be but is not], Oresme becomes both a good theologian and a conscientious glossator with: "Si comme Antecrist et en ceste maniere *ingenitum* c'est *non-engendré*" (*DC*, p. 188) [Like Antichrist, and in this meaning *ingenitum* signifies *non-generated*].

But just as in *LE*, the most interesting translator's glosses in *DC* are those in which Oresme deals directly with the "foreignness" of his source texts. Oresme returns to the terminological difficulties that he addressed in his prologue, when he glosses *ciel*: "Aristotle met ycy une distinction qui avoit lieu en language grec, mais elle n'a pas du tout lieu en latin ne en françoys, quar les Grecs appeloient tout le monde et le ciel par un nom et nous n'appelons pas le monde ciel" (*DC*, p. 156, see also p. 158) [Aristotle makes here a distinction which existed in the Greek language, but which exists neither in Latin nor in French, because the Greeks called all the world and the heavens by one name and we do not call the heavens world]. The term hemisphere (*hemispere*) is first explained etymologically: "En grec, *hemi* c'est 'demi' et *hemispere*, c'est 'demie-espere,' et est la moitié du ciel que est desus nous et celle qui est desouz est un autre hemispere" (*DC*, p. 324) [In Greek *hemi* is "half" and hemisphere is "half-sphere", and it is the half of the heavens which is above us, and the one which is below us is another hemisphere], and then it is followed by a traditional explicative gloss. In a similar way Oresme glosses the term *estoilles*: "Il entent par *estoilles* generalment le soleil et la lune les autres estoilles. Et ce segnefie en latin *astrum*" (*DC*, p. 430) [By *stars*, he means generally the sun, the moon and other stars. And in Latin it means *astrum*]. Sometime later, also in Book II, Oresme refines the semantically troubling points of *estoilles*:

> Et est a savoir que ce nom *stella* ou *stelle* en latin signifie seulement les estoilles, mes *astrum* ou *astra* signifie generaument estoilles et lune et soleil. Et pour ce, comme je dis au commencement en ce chapitre, et apres, l'en doit entendre par *estoilles* generaument les choses desus dites. (*DC*, p. 452)
> [That is to say that this name *stella* or *stelle* in Latin signifies only the stars, but *astrum* or *astra* signifies generally stars and sun and moon. And because of it, as

I said at the beginning of this chapter and afterwards, one must understand by *stars* generally the things said above.]

A last example is probably the most typical of Oresme's translator's glossing: After having translated Aristotle's view about two kinds of rotating movements: "Et de corps sperique par soy .ii. mouvemens peuent estre: un est circumgiracion et l'autre volutacion ou titubacion" [This spherical body can by itself have two movements: one is *circumgyration*, the other *volutation* or *titubation*], he offers the necessary gloss:[25]

> Le premier est quant tel corps est meu environ son centre, si comme un bacin qui tourne sus un bastonnet, et est dit en françois tournier ou virer, de *girari*; et ainsi sont meus les cielz epicicles dedens le ciel. L'autre mouvement est comme d'une roe de charete que l'en maine par chemin et est dit en françois roeler ou comme une pelote roele. (*DC*, p. 448)
> [The first one is when such a body is moved around its center, like a basin rotating on the stick, and in French one says *turner* or *virer* from *girari*; thus are moved in the heavens the epicycles in the heavens. The other movement is like the movement of the wheel of a cart which is led on the road and it is expressed in French by *rouler*, as a ball rolls.]

Not only does this gloss offer us a very good illustration of what is meant by *circumgiration* and by *volutacion et titubacion* by proper comparisons with simple everyday phenomena, but the glossator also shares with us his linguistic consciousness by etymologically linking the common verb *virer* to the abstract *giracion*.[26]

Three obvious conclusions can be drawn from this brief examination of translator's glosses. The first and the most important is that various redactorial and explicative glosses made by the translator significantly contribute to the quality of the "service" translations. This point was well

---

[25] I say "necessary" because (*circum*)*giration*, *volutacion*, and *titubacion* do not seem to be easily grasped by a non-Latinist. We know that the last word was garbled in four MSS.

[26] The fact that modern etymologists derive *virer* from *vibrare* and not from the Late Latin descendents of *gyrus* (cf. *FEW*, 14: 384ff.) does not diminish the role of Oresme as a pioneer of the etymologically minded gloss.

noted by the first modern French translator of Aristotle's *Politics*, Jules Barthélemy-St.-Hilaire,[27] who, some 160 years ago, praised Oresme's *Livre de Politiques* for, among other things, the translator's judicious use of redactorial glosses in achieving clarity in presentation and organization of this text. I believe that I have demonstrated that Barthélemy-St.-Hilaire's opinion concerning the *Livre de Politiques* can be applied very well to all of Oresme's translations.

Second, I wish to underscore that this clarity *toute française* is due above all to the neat distinction between the text and the gloss. This distinction (which we have noted also in *DC*) has permitted the translator to offer French texts that both respect and *serve* Gratian or Aristotle.

Third, the examination of a translator's glossing demonstrates that my distinction between the "borrowing" and the "service" translation holds true even in these careful scientific translations. For while the text of Aristotle is respected, and translated to enhance this respect in the reader of the French translation, the commentary-glosses often contain the "borrowed" translated passages from Averroës, Albertus Magnus, Aquinas, and others. Except for Averroës, who is frequently mentioned in *DC*, Oresme acknowledges only occasionally this or that author of the glosses that he cites. Most of the time he "borrows" from the common fount of glossing tradition and passes off many translated passages as his own. Ultimately, only an exhaustive study of the whole commentary tradition will permit us to distinguish between glosses adapted by Oresme (and other scientific translators) and his own contributions as a glossator. Meanwhile, we can safely assume that the shorter and more strictly textual-linguistic glosses that serve to elucidate the translation problems are his own. And they certainly are a precious contribution to the early art and science of translation.

---

[27] *Politique d'Aristote*, trans. Jules Barthélemy-St.-Hilaire, 2 vols. (Paris: Imprimerie Royale, 1837). See esp. pp. xci–xcii.

La traduction du latin au français dans les encyclopédies médiévales à partir de l'exemple de la traduction des *Otia imperialia* de Gervais de Tilbury par Jean de Vignay et Jean d'Antioche[1]

Claude Buridant

Les commentaires consacrés à l'activité traductrice de Jean de Vignay, qu'il s'agisse d'introductions aux éditions ou de monographies, font, de lui, dans l'ensemble, un médiocre "latimier" dont les défauts majeurs seraient les suivants: il connaît mal le latin, et ses traductions ne sont pas exemptes de contresens; il traduit lourdement et gauchement en suivant pas à pas ses modèles.

Cependant, une évolution allant dans le sens d'un affinement, d'une plus grande liberté, s'observerait depuis ses oeuvres de jeunesse jusqu'à ses dernières oeuvres, évolution soulignée en particulier par C. Knowles dans l'ensemble de ses articles, ou dans ses éditions de Jean de Vignay, et par L. Löfstedt. Mais aussi par B. Dunn-Lardeau,[2] examinant sa traduction de la *Legenda aurea* en se référant au Prologue où il dit que sa tâche est de "faire connaître les vies, les Passions et les moeurs des saints aux gens qui ne sont pas lettrés," c'est-à-dire qui ne savent pas le latin. Ce qui n'empêche pas Jean Rychner de porter un jugement sévère sur l'une des dernières

---

[1]La révision du texte de cette communication doit beaucoup à D. Gerner, qui l'a soumis à une relecture attentive. Je lui adresse ici mes vifs remerciements.

[2]Brenda Dunn-Lardeau, *Texte latin et branches vernaculaires*, Actes du Colloque International sur la *Legenda Aurea* (Montréal: Bellarmin et Paris: Vrin, 1986).

traductions de Jean de Vignay, celle des *Echecs moralisés,* dont il dénonce le "charabia" au regard des traductions parallèles du *Solatium ludi scachorum* de Jacques de Cessoles par Jean Fréron, de l'ordre des Frères Prêcheurs de Paris, remarquable de maîtrise et de concision, et par un anonyme lorrain.[3]

D'autre part, il est réputé pour avoir introduit, à la faveur de ses traductions, nombre de néologismes transposés du latin: sur le plan lexical, son apport serait loin d'être négligeable, comme l'ont souligné L. Löfstedt, D. Trotter et ma propre contribution à l'analyse de la traduction des *Choses de chevalerie.*[4]

L'on peut d'autant mieux apprécier ses caractéristiques de traducteur que l'on peut comparer ses oeuvres, dans plusieurs cas, à d'autres traductions parallèles. C'est le cas du *De re militari* de Végèce, traduit également par Jean de Meun; de la traduction de la *Legenda aurea;* du *Solatium ludi scachorum* de Jacques de Cessoles, dont on vient de rappeler qu'il avait fait l'objet de deux autres traductions; des *Otia imperialia* de Gervais de Tilbury, traduits avant Jean de Vignay par Jean d'Antioche.

Cette appréciation peut aussi s'appuyer sur les propres déclarations de principe de notre traducteur, qui se trouvent dans sa traduction de Végèce et dans *Les Enseingnemens de Theodore Paliologue,* et que commente D. Trotter dans l'introduction à son édition des *Merveilles de la terre d'outremer,*[5] reprenant les grandes lignes d'un article antérieur consacré à cette seconde traduction. Jean de Vignay s'y déclare partisan de la

---

[3]Jean Rychner, "Les traductions françaises de la *Moralisatio super Ludum Scaccorum* de Jacques de Cessoles, étude comparée des traductions en tant que telles," dans *Recueil de travaux offert à M. Clovis Brunel,* 2 vols. (Paris: Société de l'École des Chartes, 1955), 2: 480–93.

[4]Voir Claude Buridant, "Jean de Meun et Jean de Vignay, traducteurs de l'*Epitoma rei militari* de Végèce. Contribution à l'histoire de la traduction au Moyen Age," dans *Études de langue et de littérature françaises offertes à André Lanly* (Nancy: Université Nancy II, 1980), pp. 51–69; Flavius Vegetius Renatus, *Li livres Flave Vegece de la chose de chevalerie* (Helsinki: Suomalainen Tiedeakatemia, 1982); et Jean de Vignay, *Les Merveilles de la Terre d'Outremer: traduction du XIV siècle du récit de voyage d'Odoric de Pordenone,* éd. D. A. Trotter (Exeter: University of Exeter, 1990).

[5]Voir *Les Merveilles,* éd. Trotter, pp. xxiii–xxx.

traduction littérale ("en ensivant la pure verité de la letre," "la verité pure sivre selonc la letre"), en se rattachant à une tradition solidement établie illustrée par nombre de prologues, remontant en dernier lieu à saint Jérôme, encore que les professions de foi des prologues soient loin d'être respectées généralement . . . au pied de la lettre.

Cette conception s'opposerait à une conception plus "moderne" dont Jean d'Antioche serait précisément un représentant. Qu'on se réfère à la postface de sa traduction de la *Rhétorique* de Cicéron (1282), traduction du *De inventione* et de la *Rhétorique ad Herennium* (attribuée alors à Cicéron); il y réclame du "fidus interpres" qu'il soit aussi un "expositor" et un "orator," comme le souligne R. Baehr en faisant de Jean d'Antioche un véritable précurseur de la théorie de la traduction illustrée plus tard par Nicole Oresme, qui subordonne le principe du *verbum e verbo* à l'éclaircissement du *sens*.[6]

Jean d'Antioche accorde aussi, dans ce prologue, une importance particulière aux problèmes de syntaxe:

> Mais il ne pot mie porsiure l'auctor en la maniere dou parler, car la maniere dou parler au latin n'est pas semblable generaument a cele dou françois, ne les proprietez des paroles ne les raisons d'ordener les araisonemenz et les diz dou latin ne sont pas semblables a celes dou françois, et ce est comunaument en toute langue.

---

[6]Wo die Aufgabe es erfordert, muss also der "fidus interpres" auch "expositor" und "orator" sein: il covint au translateor de ceste science de translater aucune fois parole por parole, et aucune fois et plus sovent sentence por sentence et aucune fois por la grant oscurté de la sentence li convint il sozjoindre et acreistre; . . . nul translateor o interpreteor ne porroit jamais bien translater d'une lengue a autre s'il ne s'enformast a la maniere et as proprietez de cele lengue en qui il translate.

Damit hat am Ausgang des 13. Jahrhunderts Johan d'Antioche nach langer Vorherrschaft des Ideals der Wortwörtlichkeit als erster Franzose der übersetzung den Weg gewiesen, dem sie unter allmählich wirksam werdenden Einfluss Italiens von der Mitte des 14. Jahrhunderts an im Rahmen einer kräftig aufblühenden übersetzungsliteratur in Theorie und Praxis folgen wird. Voir Rudolf Baehr, "Rolle und Bild der Übersetzung im Spiegel literarischer Texte des 12. und 13. Jahrhunderts im Frankreich," dans *Europäische Mehrsprachigkeit: Festschrift zum 70. Geburtstag von Mario Wandruszka*, éd. Wolfgang Pöckl (Tübingen: Niemeyer, 1981), p. 348.

"Le français diffère du latin tant au niveau du lexique . . . qu'au niveau de l'agencement des phrases. C'est là une constatation que nous retrouverons chez plusieurs traducteurs."[7] Mais surtout, Jean d'Antioche poursuit le raisonnement en l'étendant à toutes les langues. La difficulté de traduire n'est donc pas analysée par lui comme venant d'une carence particulière du français, mais bien comme résultant de la différence entre les langues, chacune ayant en quelque sorte son génie propre . . . le latin et le français sur un pied d'égalité.

> Si les deux langues sont différentes, ce n'est pas que l'une soit inférieure à l'autre, mais plutôt qu'il est dans la nature même des langues de diverger de la sorte. C'est là une idée que l'on rencontre très peu souvent au moyen âge cette idée de la nature différente de chaque langue conduisant évidemment à la conclusion, chez Jean d'Antioche, que la traduction mot à mot est impossible.[8]

Jean de Vignay et Jean d'Antioche représenteraient, en somme, deux conceptions différentes et quasi opposées de la traduction à la fin du XIIIe siècle et au début du XIVe siècle. Jean de Vignay représenterait une conception étroite, "rigoriste," où la traduction *verbum e verbo* reste moulée et calquée sur le latin; Jean d'Antioche représenterait une conception plus large intégrant le *verbum e verbo* dans la transposition *sensus de sensu,* le latin et le français ayant chacun leur "génie" propre. Mais s'observerait, dans l'oeuvre de Jean de Vignay, une évolution de la conception de la traduction, allant du rigorisme étroit à une plus grande liberté d'adaptation à un public non lettré, sans qu'il réussisse toutefois à se défaire du calque scrupuleux de la syntaxe latine.

Si les chercheurs ont généralement condamné la traduction—calque illustrée par Jean de Vignay, ce type de traduction a pourtant bien été acceptée et appréciée par les contemporains, comme le remarque D. Trotter à propos de la traduction des *Merveilles de la terre d'outremer.*[9] Une preuve

---

[7]Serge Lusignan, *Parler vulgairement: Les intellectuels et la langue française aux XIIIe et XIVe siècles,* 2nd éd. (Paris et Montréal: Vrin et les Presses de l'Université de Montréal, 1987), p. 144.

[8]Ibid.

[9]*Les Merveilles,* éd. Trotter, p. xxx.

du succès de ce type de traduction nous est donnée par l'appréciation portée dans son prologue par un compilateur du XVᵉ siècle, copiste du manuscrit Paris BN français 1170, s'amusant à fondre en une seule les deux traductions du *Jeu des Echecs* par Jean Fréron et Jean de Vignay: "La traduction de Vignay lui 'semble plus clere en langaige, et aussi elle contient aucunes histoires belles et notables, combien qu'elles ne soient pas en latin'."[10] Ce jugement porté au XVᵉ siècle nous invite à nous méfier de l'anachronisme: il faut sans doute nuancer les appréciations négatives trop souvent portées au XXᵉ siècle sur les traductions de Jean de Vignay; les contemporains y trouvaient certainement leur provende.

Le récent article de M. Gosman sur la traduction du *Speculum historiale* par Jean de Vignay contient des observations nuancées qui affinent les jugements tranchés portés par les critiques sur Jean de Vignay, à partir d'une fine analyse de la notion d' "équivalence":

> Jean is a loyal translator in the sense that he does not, as the anonymous translator of the *Roman d'Alexandre en prose* did, rework his source text in order to obtain a real medievalization. . . . The whole Alexander passage in the Vatican manuscript is FUNCTIONALLY "equivalent" to the text Vincent committed to parchment. Jean respects the signification of the source text and its way of expression: *res et verba ponderantur*. . . .
>
> The essence of "equivalence" is, though this may sound paradoxical, "plural": every angle of incidence has its own "equivalence." GLOBAL "equivalence" does not exist. Jean's text shows that the FUNCTIONAL "equivalence" covers FORMAL, PRAGMATIC (on the macro-level as well as on the micro-level) and the SEMANTIC "equivalences," each of which exhibits [graduated levels] of perfection.[11]

Un des enseignements de l'étude de M. Gosman est aussi de souligner: les différences sensibles qui s'observent chez Jean de Vignay selon la nature du texte qu'il a à traduire;[12] la difficulté qu'éprouve Jean de Vignay à rendre

---

[10]Rychner, "Les traductions françaises," p. 489.

[11]Martin Gosman, "The Life of Alexander the Great in Jean de Vignay's *Miroir Historial*: The Problem of Textual *Equivalence*," dans *Vincent of Beauvais and Alexander the Great: Studies on the* Speculum maius *and Its Translations into Medieval Vernaculars*, éd. W. J. Aerts, Edme R. Smits, et J. B. Voorbij (Groningen: Forsten, 1986), pp. 85–99.

[12]Gosman, "Life of Alexander the Great," p. 86.

la spécificité des *realia* classiques, et, corollairement, la relative pauvreté de son lexique, qui réduit considérablement les nuances des correspondants latins: "[As opposed] to the usual tendency in informative texts the *Miroir* offers a relative number of semantic shifts, in a negative way; his lexical range is more limited [than of the ST-author's]."[13]

Les observations de M. Gosman sur la pratique de Jean de Vignay rejoignent celles de J.-P. Bordier, éditeur et commentateur des différentes traductions françaises médiévales de la *Vie de sainte Pélagie.*[14] Jean de Vignay a été en effet amené à traduire deux fois la *Vie de sainte Pélagie,* une première fois à partir de la version du *Speculum Historiale* de Vincent de Beauvais, insérant au livre XII, ch. 96 et 97 l'*Abbreviatio* de la *Vie* par le dominicain Jean de Mailly; une seconde fois, plus tard, dans sa traduction de la *Legenda aurea* de Jacques de Voragine. La comparaison entre les deux traductions est des plus instructives. La première présente une syntaxe latine compliquée et profuse calquée sur celle du modèle, comme dans la phrase d'introduction,[15] que l'on compare à la phrase correspondante de la traduction anonyme de l'*Abbreviatio* dans le *Légendier français dans l'ordre de l'année liturgique,* où l'on a affaire à des structures narratives égrenant les événements et s'appuyant sur des patrons de phrases typiques (*Il avint . . . et vint . . . et estoit bele . . . et avoit avec li . . . Quant . . . , il*).[16] Menant

---

[13]Ibid., p. 97; voir aussi p. 95: "C'est le lieu de parler alors de "partial semantic 'equivalence'."

[14]J.-P. Bordier, "La vie de sainte Pélagie en ancien et en moyen français," dans *Pélagie la pénitente: Métamorphoses d'une légende,* éd. Pierre Petitmengin, tome 2, *La Survie dans les littératures européennes* (Paris: Études Augustiniennes, 1984).

[15]Adonc en Anthioche, si comme pour aucune cause .viij. evesques voisins se furent assemblez entre eulz et l'evesque d'Eleopoleos, qui maintenant est dicte Damiete, preeschast au peuple, soudenement en apert devant touz une fame, arestante soi illec, de souveraine beauté et de tres bel aornement resplendissante, trespassa devant eulz en tres grant compaignee de jouvenceaus et de pucelles, lequiex ele menoit aprés soi par si grant amour et noblesce que en quelconques lieu que ele alast ele raemplissoit l'air par odeur de diverses flaireurs de aromates. Laquele quant les evesques la virent passer le chief nu, il se tornerent arriere de li ausi comme d'un tres grant pechié. Voir Bordier, "La vie de sainte Pélagie," pp. 190–91.

[16]Il avint que .viij. evesque des citez dou païs furent asamblé pour une cause en Anthioiche, desquielx li evesques de Damiete commença a preechier au pueple, et vint

systématiquement la comparaison entre les deux versions, J.-P. Bordier peut conclure: "Devant les problèmes posés par la syntaxe, on distingue nettement deux attitudes, selon que les traducteurs choisissent de calquer ou non les tournures du latin. L'opposition apparaît clairement si on compare les deux versions, *JM* et *MH* de l'abrégé de Jean de Mailly."[17]

La traduction de la *Vie de sainte Pélagie* de la *Légende Dorée* par Jean de Vignay est au contraire dépourvue de latinismes, et le récit y est d'une grande fluidité narrative, s'appuyant sur un égrenage des événements dans des séquences en *et*.[18] Et J.-P. Bordier de conclure, à partir d'une comparaison avec la traduction du pseudo Jean Beleth: "Ces deux passages font apparaître ce qu'une étude de tout le texte montrerait: c'est le ps.—Beleth qui use systématiquement du latinisme, Jean de Vignai l'évite et les autres versions adoptent des solutions intermédiaires."[19]

La comparaison entre les deux versions de la *Vie de sainte Pélagie* se révèle donc instructive: l'original du *Speculum* offre un latin plus

---

devant aus touz, lai ou il preschoit, une femme qui seoit sor .i. cheval et estoit bele a grant mervoille et bien aornee et avoit avec li une turbe de jovancés et de puceles qui aprés li aloient, car par tout ou elle aloit elle getoit si grant odeur qu'il sambloit que li ers fut touz plains d'espices. Quant li evesque la virent passer par devant aus a nue teste, il tornerent d'autre part lour visaiges ausi cum il feissent d'un tres grant pechié. Voir Bordier, "La vie de sainte Pélagie," p. 187.

[17]Bordier, "La vie de sainte Pélagie," pp. 217–18.

[18]Une fois que ele aloit par la ville a si grans cointises que il n'estoit sus li nule chose que l'en peust veoir, fors or et argent et pierres precieuses, et par tout la ou ele aloit ele raemplissoit l'aire de oudeur de diverses flaireurs, et aloit devant ele et aprés grant multitude de jouvenciaus et de puceles qui estoient aussi vestus de tres nobles vestimens, et un saint pere, qui avoit non Neron, evesque de Eleopoleos, qui est orendroit apelé Damiete, passoit par la cité et la vit, et donc commença a pleurer tres amerement pour ce que ele avoit greigneur cure de plaire au monde que il n'avoit de plaire a Dieu, et donc se lessa cheoir sus le pavement et feroit la tere de sa face et l'arousoit de lermes et disoit. . . . Voir Bordier, "La vie de sainte Pélagie," p. 203.

[19]L'hypothèse de J.-P. Bordier sur les collaborateurs éventuels de Jean de Vignay semble cependant peu crédible pour expliquer des différences dans la traduction d'un même texte. Abstraction faite des interventions de copistes, on a malgré tout le sentiment d'un style, d'une manière uniforme, personnelle, même dans le charabia; voir Bordier, "La vie de sainte Pélagie," p. 218.

hiérarchisé, plus complexe, que Jean de Vignay calque dans une traduction pas à pas. En revanche, dans la *Legenda Aurea,* la Vie de sainte Pélagie est écrite dans une trame narrative simple que Jean de Vignay peut aisément faire passer en français. La technique de traduction de Jean de Vignay varie donc sans doute moins en fonction de sa maturité et de son public qu'en fonction du type de texte qu'il a à traduire: les textes plus savants ou plus abstraits lui posent davantage de problèmes, qu'il s'agisse du *De re militari* de Végèce, du *Speculum historiale* ou des *Enseignemens* de Théodore Paléologue, et il s'y montre alors d'une fidélité pusillanime à un latin qu'il se borne à calquer. L'examen des traductions des *Otia imperialia* par Jean d'Antioche et Jean de Vignay devrait nous permettre en tout cas, à la faveur d'une comparaison systématique, d'affiner et de nuancer encore les caractéristiques des deux traducteurs.

Il faut d'abord dire quelques mots de l'original et des problèmes particuliers qu'il pose au traducteur: les *Otia imperialia,* écrits vers 1210 par Gervais de Tilbury pour la récréation de son protecteur, l'empereur germanique Othon IV, appartiennent à la fois au genre scientifique des encyclopédies et et à celui des récits merveilleux de voyage.[20] De plus, comme le relève D. Gerner dans ses notes,[21] cette encyclopédie est précédée d'une préface qui constitue un véritable opuscule sur les rapports entre le pouvoir temporel et le pouvoir spirituel. Jean de Vignay se trouve d'emblée confronté, dans cette préface, ainsi que dans les quelques premiers chapitres de l'ouvrage, à des pages difficiles à la syntaxe complexe où le raisonnement fait peu de part à la description. En tant que traité de philosophie théologique, en tant qu'encyclopédie, les *Otia* posent ainsi au traducteur, plus que d'autres textes, le problème de la transposition d'une syntaxe qui peut être relativement élaborée, mais aussi celui de l'adaptation du vocabulaire savant latin en français. En revanche, en tant que récits de

---

[20]Jacques Le Goff dans sa Préface à la traduction du Gervase de Tilbury, *Le Livre des merveilles: divertissement pour un empereur,* éd. Annie Duchesne (Paris: Les Belles Lettres, 1992), pp. xi, xiii.

[21]Dominique Gerner, *Les Oisivetez des Emperieres. Traduction des* Otia Imperialia *de Gervais de Tilbury par Jean de Vignay dans le manuscrit Rotschild n° 3085 de la Bibliothèque Nationale de Paris. Édition et Étude,* thèse dactylographiée (Strasbourg, 1995), 4: 7.

merveilles, ils invitent le traducteur à transposer un vocabulaire qui peut être "exotique" et à rendre des structures phrastiques caractéristiques de la narration. L'on a donc affaire à deux types de texte juxtaposés dont les difficultés de transposition sont très différentes pour un traducteur.

Il faut aussi noter que la traduction des ouvrages de type encyclopédique constitue, à la fin du XIIIe et au début du XIVe siècle, une entreprise nouvelle dans le lent mouvement de vulgarisation qui gagne les oeuvres de type scientifique, et qui a commencé par l'historiographie: Jean d'Antioche et son successeur, Jean de Vignay, ont donc à innover. La comparaison des deux traductions contemporaines des *Otia Imperialia* offre à la recherche une occasion de choix, semblable à celle que peut offrir, ainsi que le souligne J. Rychner, la comparaison des trois traductions des *Echecs moralisés*.[22]

Étant donné l'ampleur du sujet, nous ne ferons qu'indiquer quelques pistes. C'est par les traits qui se retrouvent dans la plupart des traductions contemporaines qu'il nous faut commencer, avant de traiter de leur originalité: les deux traducteurs ont, dans leur transposition, des contraintes communes de langue qui touchent plus particulièrement le lexique. Les traducteurs ont affaire, dans les parties philosophique et encyclopédique en particulier, à un énorme fond de termes abstraits qu'ils ont à transposer, et dont nous avons à apprécier les équivalents en fonction des ressources dont ils disposaient, qui ne peuvent être évaluées qu'à partir de minutieuses enquêtes. La description des éléments fondamentaux de la cosmogonie, ainsi, n'est pas sans poser des problèmes de transposition. Prenons, par exemple, les composés en *sub*:

> *sublunaris,* dans *sublunarem regionem* (L 884, 45)[23]: Jean d'Antioche le rend par une périphrase: *la region qui est dessoubz la lune* (JA I, I, 24), mais aussi par

---

[22]J. Rychner, "Les traductions françaises," pp. 481–82.

[23]Les références du texte latin et des deux traductions des *Otia* renovoient à l'édition de Leibniz (L), Gottfried W. von Leibniz, *Otia Imperialia ad Ottonem IV Imperatorem ex manuscriptis* (Hanovre, 1707), et aux thèses dactylographiées de Cinzia Pignatelli, *La traduction des* Otia Imperialia *de Gervais de Tilbury par Jean d'Antioche dans le manuscrit 9113 de la Bibliothèque Nationale de Paris. Édition et Étude* (Strasbourg, 1996) (JA), et D. Gerner pour Jean de Vignay (JV) (voir n. 21).

solunaire ailleurs (JA I, I, 13), alors que l'adjectif est sans doute volontairement évincé par Jean de Vignay, et à deux reprises: *une haute region* (JV I, 11 et 21);

subcoeleste, dans cette phrase: *Quasi coeleste vel subcoeleste militantis ecclesiae est, quae dum ad triumphandum properat, cursum suum dirigit ad id, quod est perfectum* (L 883, 12–13): Jean d'Antioche le rend par *le soubzcelestial* (JA I, Pr. II, 77), Jean de Vignay par *le subcelestiel* (JV, Pr., 63).

Pour la préfixation en *sub-*, c'est donc quatre possibilités qui sont exploitées par les deux auteurs: *qui est dessoubz, soubz/so* + base par Jean d'Antioche; élimination ou calque savant en *sub* dans *subcelestiel* par Jean de Vignay.

Un autre exemple concerne les adjectifs en *in-* + base + *bilis* qui n'ont que de parcimonieux équivalents francais au XIIIe siècle:

Super istud arbitror esse coelum Trinitatis, ubi sola Trinitas habitat non localiter, sed incircumscripte, & inenarrabili et inattingibili gloria (L 884, 30–32);

Par dessus le ciel empiré est le ciel de la Trinité, ou la sceue (?) deïté habite sans dissernacion de place et sans ce qu'elle se contiengne par aulcun lieu, car elle est en tout lieu, *et de ce ne doit on pas trop enquerre* (JA I, I, 16);

Et sus celui ciel m'est il avis que c'est le lieu de la Trinité ou la seule Trinité habite, non pas que ce soit illecques son propre lieu sanz ce qu'elle ne soit ailleurs et partout, mes pour ce que celui ciel est avironné et ennobli de sa tres grant gloire, si grande que nul ne la puet nombrer, considerer, pourpenser ne ataindre (JV I, I, 14).

A la traduction édulcorée de Jean d'Antioche répond chez Jean de Vignay une rafale de termes visant à cerner les sèmes de l'original *inenarrabilis* et *inattingibilis.*

Mais plus généralement, les deux traducteurs usent à l'envi de circonlocutions pour rendre les composés en *-in* + base + *bilis:*

imperscrutabilis:
cujus ratio nobis est imperscrutabilis (L 960, 21);
et pour nous ne savons la rayson pour quoy ce advient (JA III, Préf. 14);
pour ce que nous ne savons pas la cause et la reson pour coi il se meut (JV III, Préf. 10).
aquam . . . imperscrutabilem (L 983, 22);
et n'est homme vivant qui la peust faire asechier jusques au fons (JA III, LXVI, 2);
et nul n'i puet trouver fons (JV CXLII, 2).

imputrescibilis:
De carne imputrescibili macelli (L 963, 38);
de la char qui ne puet pourrir (JA III, XII);
absent chez JV.

inaccessibilis:
inaccessibilis in sua altitudine (L 974, 46);
elle est telle que on ne puet monter a sa haultesse (JA III, XLII, 2);
elle est si haute que nul n'i va (JV CXV, 1);
ambitus arduus et pro magna parte inaccessibilis ad ascensum (L 982, 20–21);
c'est une royte montaugne sans chemin qu'il y ay point (JA III, LXVI, 2);
et la circuité de cele montaigne est si haute et y a une partie qui n'est pas habitable
et n'i puet on monter (JV CXLII, 2).

inascensibilis:
mons est Atlas, inascensibilis propter sui celsitudinem (L 986, 2);
mont Athlas, qui est tant hault que par sa haultesse on n'y puet monter (JA III,
LXXIX, 1);
et n'i puet on aler pour sa hautesce (JV CLV, 1).

inexpugnabilis:
quam cum diu obsedisset, quia inexpugnabilis erat (L 1001, 34);
quant Moyses eut assegié longuement la cité de Merce et ne la pouoit prendre pour
ce qu'elle estoit moult forte et bien deffensable (JA III, CXI, 5);
et quant il ot sis longuement devant ces chastiaus, qui estoient fors a prendre (JV
CLXXXVII, 4).

ingustabilis:
de racemis ingustabilis (L 1004, 32);
absent chez JA;
des resins dont nul ne puet gouster (JV CC, titre).

C'est donc le recours aux circonlocutions qui s'impose en l'absence de
calques synthétiques. Il en va de même pour *infinitus, infructuosus, innu-
merus, inscrutatus, insolitus, inusitatus*.

On appréciera, dans cet autre exemple, les équivalents qui tentent de
rendre, chez les deux traducteurs, une série de termes abstraits, dont

inauditu:
Censemus enim, nova quadruplici ratione judicari, aut creatione, aut eventu, aut
raritate, aut inauditu (L 960, 14–15);

> car les choses sont tenues pour nouvelles par quatre raysons: par creation, par
> advenement des aventures, ou pour ce que peut adviengnent, ou aussy pour ce
> qu'elles ne furent oncques oÿes (JA III, Préf. 12);
> et nous disons les choses estre nouvelles en .iiij. manieres: ou pour ce que il sont
> criees et faites, ou pour ce que il aviennent par euls, ou pour ce que nous veons
> pou de tiex choses, ou pour ce que nous n'en avons point oï parler (JV LXXII, 8).

Une circonlocution rend *rareté*, mot abstrait non attesté encore, une autre
circonlocution transposant *inouïes*.

L. Löfstedt avait déjà noté, pour sa part, les équivalents en *non-* rendant
les substantifs ou adjectifs en *in-* dans la traduction du *De re militari* de
Végèce par Jean de Vignay. Cependant, ici, Jean de Vignay se distingue
dans ce domaine par la présence de quelques équivalents savants, au regard
de son concurrent, et c'est là, on le verra, l'une de ses caractéristiques. Ainsi
d'*incredible*:

> stupet auditor incertus, an sileat, an loquatur injuncta (L 982, 42);
> le paysant s'en esbaï de ce qu'il oÿ dire et ne savoit lequel faire, ou de le reveler ou
> de le celler, car il luy sembloit abusion de le croire (JA III, LXVI, 13);
> celui fu tout esbahi de ce que il oï, si ne sot que faire, de dire ces choses, pour ce
> que il estoient incredibles, ou de taire les (JV CXLII, 11).
> Non est mirandum aut incredibile (L 1003, 14);
> l'en ne se doit pas merveillier ne mescroire (JA III, CXVIII, 1);
> ce est chose a merveillier, et aussi conme incredible (JV CXCIV, 1).

Ou d'*invisible*:

> facies tamen ipsius mansionis sicut ipsorum daemonum vulgaribus est incognita et
> invisibilis (L 982, 23–24);
> mays on ne puet veoir les deables ne leur habitacle (JA III, LXVI, 3);
> et la porte de ce lieu ou il habitent est invisible et ne set on par ou il entrent (JV
> CXLII, 3).

On s'intéressera aussi à la façon de rendre les superlatifs synthétiques du
latin, qui ne sont conservés que dans un noyau résiduel (cf. *grandisme*,
saintisme, etc.). L'on relève à l'occasion des transpositions intéressantes chez
Jean d'Antioche:

l'itération lexicale dissociée: acutissimum visum (L 964, 48);
(une) bonne veue et aguë (JA III, XIII, 2).
La comparaison stéréotypée d'intensité dont I. Vogel a fait des relevés systéma-
tiques: salem albissimum (L 961, 39);
sel blanc comme cristal (JA III, II, 8).[24]

Une autre difficulté, d'un ordre différent, concerne la traduction des
étymologies, qui constituent le socle héréditaire de la cosmographie et de
la géographie, les références obligées enregistrées par les ouvrages lexicogra-
phiques, des descriptions encyclopédiques, que peuvent reprendre également
les récits de la Genèse. Les *Otia imperialia* de Gervais de Tilbury offrent
ainsi une véritable grille cosmographique qui repose sur l'étymologie:

empyreus = coelus mundus; firmamentum < firmus; mundus < semper movetur
sol < solus lucens; luna < luminum unam
terra < quia teritur; mare < amaritumine
dies < gr. daos = claritas; nox < gr. nux = obscuritas
Adam < interpretatur per litteras: quatuor orbis climata. Ut enim ait Augustinus,
Adam in quatuor literis Graecis, ex quibus constat, quatuor habet principia
verborum Graecorum, *anatole,* quod est Oriens, *dysis,* quod est occidens, *arctos,*
quod est septentrio, *mesembria,* quod est meridies, quasi subjiciantur ei quatuor
orbis climata. Unde in Historia seu Bibliotheca Versificata.

Ces éléments de cosmographie et de géographie apparaissent comme les
invariants d'un système de représentation du monde et comme les référents
de tous les essais d'encyclopédie depuis le haut moyen âge.

Les deux traducteurs peuvent respecter l'étymologie latine, dans des
équivalences évidentes par communauté de base:

firmamentum < firmitatem (L)
firmament > ferme (JA)
firmament < fermeté (JV)

Mais on constate une déperdition dans l'exemple de *mundus*:

---

[24]Irmgard Vogel, *Die affektive Intensivierung der Adjektiva mit Hilfe des Vergleichs im
Altfranzösischen* (Heidelberg: Winter, 1967).

mundus < motu - movetur (L)
monde < mouvement (JA)
monde < mouvable (JV)

Le souci de transposer terme à terme les étymologies, chez Jean de Vignay, se révèle à travers les exemples suivants, où la déperdition est au contraire très nette chez Jean d'Antioche:

in vere < omnia virent (L)
vair < prin temps d'esté (JA)
ver < le temps ou toutes choses verdissent (JV)
lune < luminum unam (L)
lune < clarté du ciel (JA)
lune < lumiere une (JV)

En ce qui concerne les noms abstraits, un premier relevé élémentaire permet les constatations suivantes. Jean de Vignay, latinisant, transpose la plupart de ces noms par des équivalents qui ne se retrouvent que très partiellement chez son prédécesseur:

mots en -*cion* correspondant pour la plupart aux mots latins en -*tio*:
actio (L 881, 36); *oeuvre* (JA I, Pr. II, 17); *accion* (JV, Pr. 17);
admiratio (L 978, 13); 0 (JA III, LXIII, 1); *amiracion* (JV CXLI, 1).

De même pour *conjuracion, consecration, contriction, direction, discrecion, dispensacion, disposition, dissolution, execution, oppression, proposicion* (erreur, sans doute, pour *proportion*) *relation, renovation.*
Mais on relève aussi pour:

solsticium (*solsticium facit hyemale* [L 888, 39]); il fait on arrestement que l'on appelle yvernal du soleil (JA I, V, 24); il fet illecques stacion d'iver (JV I, V, 21); *allegatio* (*vice allegationem* [L 993, 14]); ou lieu d'alleguement (JA III, XCVI, 17); ausi conme par maniere de objections (JV CLXXII, 5); *superscriptus* (*de nomine ejus superscripto C litteram capitalem abrasit* [L 977, 33]); 0 (JA III, LIII, 3); subscription (JV CXXIX, 2).

Un exemple particulièrement net témoigne de la différence esentielle qui sépare les traducteurs sur ce terrain:

Dum unctio sacerdotalis immutata semper et uniformis in capite perstitit, ad virgam pertinet directionis. De qua rex ille et propheta David: "Sedes tua; Deus, in seculum seculi, virga directionis, virga regni tui." (L 881, 44–46)

Mais l'oncion de prestre qui est premiere tient tousjours une mesure au chief sans changier, et appartient a la verge d'adressement. Et de ceste verge dit le roy et le prophete: "Beau sire Dieu, ton siege est au siecle du siecle, et la verge de ton royaume est verge de adressement." (JA I, Pr. II, 22–23)

Vraiement l'onction de prestrise n'est pas muable, mes est touzjours d'une forme et demore el chief et appartient a verge de direction, de laquele le prophete David dit: "Ton siege, sire Diex, est el siecle des siecles. La verge de direction est de ton regne, etc." (JV I, Pr., 22)

Un exemple permet d'apprécier ce qui sépare les deux traducteurs dans la transposition des noms abstraits, où Jean de Vignay pratique nettement le calque:

Quantum fuerit Salomonis ingenium, dum meditor, nullam subtilitatis ejus potentiam invenio, praeter sapientiam ex solo Dei munere, secreta quadam inspiratione venientem. Inter praeclara ejus artificia legimus. . . . (L 1000, 5–7)

Quant je bien me pense de l'engin et du sens Salmon, je ne treuve en luy soutiveté ne aultre puissance de parfons sens fors le sens que Dieu ly donna par une seule inspiracion divine. Entre les nobles oeuvres que Salmon fist. . . . (JA III, CIV, 1)

Quant je me pourpense combien l'enging de Salemon fu grant, je regarde que tele subtilleté ne si grant ne li pooit venir que du don de Dieu, qui li venoit par seule inspiracion. Et entre les autres soutis artefices que il faisoit. . . . (JV CLXXX, 1)

On y relève toute la palette des possibles: mot savant dans les deux cas (*inspiracion*); concurrence de doublets populaire/savant (*soutiveté/subtillleté*); concurrence de mot populaire/mot savant (*nobles euvres/artefices*).

On ne s'étonnera donc pas de trouver chez Jean de Vignay un ensemble de substantifs attestés pour la première fois ou chronologiquement très proches de premières attestations, néologismes, latinismes ou idiosyncrasies dûment identifiés au cours de recherches minutieuses et dont une enquête approfondie devra mesurer la vitalité et la diffusion.[25]

---

[25]Il s'agit d'apprécier la différence entre innovation, ponctuelle et éphémère, et néologisme, répétable et durable, selon la distinction établie par L. Deroy.

On relève ainsi dans les substantifs en *-tion: anematization* ("action d'anathématiser," à côté de *anathematizement*), *collection, dispensacion* (au sens d'"administration, office," qui est le sens latin, ou de "permission"), *levation, elusion, interprestation, interrupcion, perscripcion, prevaricacion, subscripcion*; dans les substantifs en *-té: confinité, emperialité (vostre -), groseté* (= épaisseur, d'un liquide), *infecondité, pluralité, temporalité, ventuosité*; des adjectifs en *-able*, comme devisable, honorable, mentable. (On relève aussi d'autres mots intéressants: les substantifs *antipodes, edefice, superfice, paripateticiens*, mais aussi des verbes comme *optinuer, suppediter.*)

Ici encore, tout n'est pas résolu pour autant par l'emploi des adjectifs en *-able* et de leurs substantifs correspondants: une bonne illustration des difficultés rencontrées par les traducteurs se trouve dans les équivalences qu'il leur faut trouver aux mots abstraits désignant les différents modes de l'éternité, pour lesquels le latin dispose de *aeternus* et de *sempiternus*. Un relevé des occurrences dans le Prologue et le premier chapitre de la *Prima Decisio* donne les résultats suivants:

> *sacerdos in aeternum* (L 882, 49–50); prestre perpetuel (JA I, Pr. II, 66); prestre en pardurableté (JV I, Pr., 57);
> *aeternum* (L 883, 9); pardurable (JA I, Pr. II, 76); perpetuel (JV I, Pr., 64);
> *sine fine* (L 883, 9); pardurable sans fin (JA I, Pr. II, 57); sanz fin des maintenant jusques em pardurableté (JV I, Pr., 64);
> *in aevum* (L Pr. 78); 0 (JA); pardurable (JV I, Pr., 78);
> *in aeternum* (L 883); 0 (JV); pardurableté (JV I, Pr., 78);
> *in aeternum* (L 884); pardurablement (JA I, I, 20); en pardurableté (JV I, 17).

L'équivalent favori et quasi-unique employé par Jean de Vignay est donc *pardurable/pardurableté*, que l'on retrouve aussi pour *inextinguibilis: lucerna inextinguibilis* (L IX, 46); *la lumiere pardurable* (LXXXIII, 1); non traduit par Jean d'Antioche.

Or, il est un passage où cette équivalence figée pose un problème, celui où est établie une distinction majeure, dans les *Otia,* entre l'éternité divine et celle des anges:

> Unde sicut Deus solus aeternus, ita mundus sempiternus, quia semper, id est, per omne tempus aeternus. Angeli quoque sempiterni, quia temporaliter aeterni. (L 884, 23–24),

ce que Jean de Vignay, ne disposant que du mot *pardurable* en face d'*aeternus* et de *sempiternus,* ne peut rendre que par une substitution explicative:

> Et tout aussi conme Dieu est pardurable et est sanz conmencement et sanz fin, aussi fist il le monde pardurable; mes il ot conmencement et ara fin, et pour ce est dit le monde pardurable, car il sera par tout le temps durable. Les angres sont autrement pardurables, quar il orent conmencement et n'aront ja fin. (JV I, 10)

On appréciera, en comparaison, la traduction de Jean d'Antioche qui oppose précisément *eternel* et *sempiternel:*

> Ainsy comme Dieu est seul eternel, c'est a dire sans commencement et sans fin, ainsy est le monde sempiternal, ce est a dire par tout le temps eternel, et les anges aussy sont sempiternal, car ilz sont selon le temps eternaux. (JA I, I, 11–12)

On rejoint ici les observations de M. Gosman, sur le caractère limité du lexique de Jean de Vignay face au latin.

Cependant, Jean de Vignay flanque à l'occasion ses transferts, d'équivalents faisant fonction de gloses, et ici encore l'on mesurera tout ce qui peut le séparer de Jean d'Antioche dans l'exemple de *curru: in curru igneo* (L 884, 45); en charrette de feu (JA I, I, 24); .i. curre, une charrete de feu (JV I, 21). D'un côté, une traduction directe*,* de l'autre un transfert appuyé précisément par cette traduction, qui lui sert de passeport. La glose appuie le transfert dans ces autres exemples: *coelum igneum* (L 887, 38) non traduit chez JA; .i. ciel foiun, c'est a dire semblable a feu (JV IV, 3).

On retrouve ici une constante de Jean de Vignay, que L. Löfstedt note dans la traduction du *De re militari* de Végèce, où des gloses explicatives flanquent les latinismes. Cette pratique est largement répandue dans toute cette traduction, qui permet à Jean de Vignay d'acclimater tout un ensemble de latinismes, et en particulier ceux se rapportant aux *realia* de l'Antiquité:

> *fustibales* (lat. *fustibali*), ce sont mangonel (IV, 22, 111, mais sans glose en III, 26, 98);
> *les contubernals, c'est les diseniers* (II, 13, 62) / les contubernes, ce sont disaines (II, 14, 63);

chacune centurie, c'est .c. homes, si com dit est (II, 14, 62);
li centurion, c'est centeniers ou chevetaines de cent (I, XXV, 53).

Ce cas est d'autant plus intéressant que pour les mêmes fonctions, Jean
d'Antioche, dans la traduction des *Otia*, fait une transposition directe:
tribunos, centurios (L 882); chevetains, connestable (JA, Pr. II, 52); non
traduit par JV. S'opposent, ici comme ailleurs, deux conceptions de la
traduction: une conception de la traduction comme équivalence, avec un
apport explicatif éventuel, et une conception de la traduction comme
transposition médiévalisante.

Un autre procédé d'acclimatation des mots savants est l'itération
lexicale: *dispositio* (L 887, 35); non traduit (JA); *en l'ordenance et en la
disposicion* (JV IV, 1), binôme avec mot savant épaulé d'un mot plus
populaire. Au regard de son prédécesseur, Jean de Vignay n'hésite pas à
employer, en équivalence du latin, les ressources que lui offre la
nominalisation: calque des participes présents: *rigor punientis* (L 881, 22);
rigueur de payne (JA I, Pr. II, 7); la rigueur du punissant. (JV Pr. 10); de
même pour la dérivation: *trementem verba domini* (L 882, 1): qui doubte
les parolles de Dieu (JA I, Pr. II, 30); le tremblable es paroles de Dieu.
(JV Pr. 28).

Un problème qui se pose aux traducteurs est aussi de rendre la riche
préfixation verbale du latin, et il est intéressant de noter ici les ressources
qu'ils exploitent. Chez Jean de Vignay, ces ressources sont de deux ordres:
recours, en équivalence du latin, au micro-système des particules séparées,
sur lesquelles j'ai attiré l'attention;[26] pour répondre à la préfixation verbale
du latin, Jean de Vignay emploie volontiers des verbes de large sémantisme,
assortis de particules adverbiales, au premier rang desquels *estre, mettre*:

estre: adesse, praeesse sont ainsi traduits par *estre devant, subesse* par *estre dessus.*
metre: praecedere est traduit par *estre mis avant. Praefere* (L 882, 25); *estre devant*
mis au prestre (JV Pr. 42); en face de *'metre avant du prestre'* chez Jean d'Antioche

---

[26]Claude Buridant, "Les particules séparées en ancien français," dans *Romanistique-
germanistique, une confrontation: Actes du colloque de Strasbourg,* éd. Claude Buridant
(Strasbourg: Presses Universitaires de Strasbourg, 1987).

(JA I, Pr. II, 47). *Praefici: devant mise. Praefere: metre avant. Pratermittere (praeter-missum): metre arriere.* (JV IV, 1)

Les particules séparées traduisent évidement sans problème leurs correspondants latins: *arma foras extulit* (L 882, 15); porta premierement les armes (JA I, Pr. II, 39); metre les armes fors (JV Pr. 36).

Chez Jean d'Antioche, le calque du préverbe entraîne un néologisme:

> Est in Aegypte ficus, cujus lignum in aquam projectum non supernatat, ut communis lignorum natura est aquis supernatare (L 962, 11–12); . . . il ne surnoye pas tant comme fait aultre fust (JA III, IV, 1); le fust . . . va au fons et ne noe point desus. (JV LXXVIII, 1)
> laudemus et superexaltemus (L 967, 51); sy devons loer et surexaulcer Dieu le pere tout puissant (JA III, XXIV, 13); laissé en latin chez JV (XCVII, 9).

Sur le plan syntaxique, les développements encyclopédiques touchant en particulier la cosmogonie et la théologie ne sont pas sans présenter des difficultés aux deux traducteurs. Se moulant étroitement sur l'original latin, en procédant syntagme par syntagme, comme un mauvais élève de version latine, Jean de Vignay, ici comme ailleurs, s'enferre assez souvent dans des phrases mal construites et non exemptes de contre-sens, au regard de Jean d'Antioche, dominant mieux la matière.

> Dum unctio sacerdotalis immutata semper et uniformis in capite persistit, ad virgam pertinet directionis. De qua rex ille et propheta David: Sedes tua, Deus, in seculum seculi, virga directionis, virga regni tui: Dilexisti justitiam et odisti iniquitatem. Propterea unxit te Deus oleo laetitiae prae consortibus tuis. Quoniam igitur ad sacerdotalem pertinet unctionem diligere justitiam et odire iniquitatem, jus suum cuique tribuendo; & contra aequitatem juris naturalis nihil proprium affectando, cum per iniquitatem quis hoc dixerit meum, illud tuum, ut c.XII. q. I. c. 2. De qua iniquitate, (quae est) quasi contra communionem legis naturalis aequitas depravata, dicit Dominus in evangelio: Facite vobis amicos de mammona iniquitatis, quasi de divitiis, contra aequitatem juris et communis naturalis congregatis. (L 881, 44–53)

> Mais l'oncion de prestre qui est premiere tient tousjours une mesure au chief sans changier, et appartient a la verge d'adressement. Et de ceste verge dit le roy et le prophete: "Beau sire Dieu, ton siege est au siecle du siecle, et la verge de ton royaume est verge de adressement. Tu aymes justice et hays iniquité, pour ce te

oingny Dieu ton dieu de huylle de leesse sur tous tes compaignons." A l'ontion de prestre doncques appartient justice et haïr iniquité, et de rendre a chascun son droit, et que l'en ne convoyte riens contre loyaulté. Et quant vient par iniquité que l'en dit: "Ceste chose est mienne, celle est a toy," et l'en s'encline a tort contre la loy naturelle, c'est mal fait. Et de telle iniquité dit Nostre Seigneur en l'Evangille: "Faictes amys de la monnoye d'iniquité," ainsi comme de richesses assemblees a tort et contre rayson. (JA I, Pr. II, 25–27)

Vraiement l'onction de prestrise n'est pas muable, mes est touzjours d'une forme et demore el chief et appartient a verge de direction, de laquele le prophete David dit: "Ton siege, sire Diex, est el siecle des siecles. La verge de direction est de ton regne, et cetera." Et pour ce que a prestrise appartient l'onction d'amer droiture et haïr iniquité en livrant a chascun son droit, et que el ne couvoite autre chose contre equité de droit naturel; et qui par iniquité dira: "Ce est mien et ce est tien," si conme la cause est en la douziesme question, el premier chapitre, de laquele iniquité aussi conme contre la communion de la foy et de la loy naturel, c'est equité trop mauvese, si conme Nostre Seigneur dit en l'Evangile: "Faites vous amis de la monnoie d'iniquité," aussi conme de richesces acquises contre la conmunion d'equité et de droit. (JV Pr. 22–26)

D'un côté, chez Jean d'Antioche, une traduction aérée, allégée des articulations du latin, chez son successeur, un calque avec une syntaxe maladroite, *de laquele* étant à rattacher à *Nostre Seigneur* en supprimant *si comme*. On pourrait citer encore bien d'autres phrases qui, chez Jean de Vignay, se terminent en queue de poisson en regard de correspondants plus clairs chez Jean d'Antioche, parce que dégagés du modèle latin. D'un côté une traduction ayant quelque hauteur, tirant l'essentiel, opérant une sélection, non sans édulcoration; de l'autre une traduction analytique, myope, qui conduit parfois à des non-sens.[27]

Dans les *Oisivetés des Empereurs,* l'étroit modelage de Jean de Vignay sur l'original latin, malgré sa myopie, peut cependant offrir des avantages par rapport à Jean d'Antioche, et en particulier celui de fournir de l'original une

---

[27]Ce sont bien des tendances que l'on retrouve dans d'autres traductions de Jean de Vignay, comme le signale L. Löfstedt pour la traduction du *De re militari*. Dans cette traduction, comme dans celle des *Otia*, nombreux sont les propositions infinitives et les ablatifs absolus calqués sur le latin.

équivalence précise, pour reprendre le terme de M. Gosman, là où Jean d'Antioche se contente d'une transcription approchée. En voici un exemple particulièrement net:

> Discrevit Deus tempora per dies, ut diximus, & annos, voluitque ad omnia sidera annum pertinere, dum diversis spatiis annos distinxit, nunc breves, nunc prolixos sideribus contribuens. Dicitur autem annus ab *am,* quod est *circum,* quia in se revolvitur. Hinc est, quod antiquiores ante usum literarum annum sub specie serpentis figurabant, cujus cauda ad os revolvebatur, sicut Janum bifrontem pingimus, quia caput incipientis anni & finem deficientis respicit. Est ergo *annus* circumvolutio siderum. . . . (L 888, 50–55)

> Comment Dieu ordonna le temps et la saison.
> Nostre Seigneur party le temps et devisa par jours et par ans, et voult que l'an appartenist a toutes les estoilles, quant il fist les ans longs et cours par diverses espaces, et les donna aux estoilles: et vault autant a dire comme "entour" ou "en tournoyant," car tousjours tourne et se revelope en luy mesme. Et pour ce que anciennement, avant que lectres venissent en usage, paingnoit l'on les moys de janvier en figure de serpent qui mengoit ou tenoit sa queue aux dens, et come nous le paingnons a present a deux cheres, pour ce qu'il regarde le chief de l'an qui y commence et aussy la fin de l'an qui y finist; et aussi pareillement n'est ce autre chose que tournaiement des estoilles. . . . (JA I, VI, 1–4)

> En quantes manieres l'an est devisé.
> Quant nostre Seigneur ot ces choses devant dites faites et ordenees, il crut et amonta les temps par jours, et les jours par ans, et voult que les anz appartenissent a toutes les estoiles quant il devisa les ans par diverses espaces, les unes espaces briés, et les autres lons, et est dit *annus* ab *an* en grec, qui vaut autant en latin conme environ, quar l'an est tornié par revolucion en soi faite et revient tousjourz au premier point. Et pour ce, anciennement, les gens figuroient l'an aussi conme un serpent qui est mis en rondesce et a sa queue retornee en sa bouche, aussi conme nous paignon et figuron maintenant a .ij. visages, car l'un regarde la fin de l'an passé et l'autre le conmencement de l'an a venir. Et est dit l'an proprement circonvolution, aussi conme tourniement des estoilles. (JV VI, 1–3)

Cependant, comme on l'a constaté pour la traduction de la *Legenda aurea,* dans la transposition de la troisième partie, où se succèdent les récits de "merveilles," les traducteurs éprouvent nettement moins de difficultés pour transposer, et le vocabulaire et la syntaxe du latin. Ainsi, alors que pour les développements philosophiques, Jean de Vignay calque péniblement la lourde syntaxe étagée du latin, il retrouve dans cette partie des patrons de phrase familiers de séquences narratives. La construction de la phrase française est relativement aplanie par rapport à la construction en hiérarchisée du latin, la multiplication de l'adverbe *si* thématisant soulignant les articulations de la séquence narrative.[28] La traduction de Jean d'Antioche va dans le même sens. Particulièrement révélatrice est cette transposition d'une scène de combat, où une série de propositions coordonnées effacent les participes en arrière plan du latin, greffés sur les actions principales:

> Exclamat miles ut alterum veniat, et ad vocem ex opposito miles aut instar militis celer occurit, peraeque, ut videbatur, armatus. Quid plura? ostensis clypeis, directis hastis equi occurrunt; equites impulsibus mutuis concutiuntur, et elusa jam alterius lancea ictuque evanescente per lubricum, Osbertus adversarium suum potenter impellit ad casum. (L 979, 48–51)

> Et quant il vindrent la, le chevalier se fist hiaumer, et lessa l'escuier, et entra dedenz cel lieu tout seul et s'escria que il vouloit joster. Et tantost .i. autre chevalier li acourut encontre, tost et hastivement, tout prest et tout armé. Et tantost il s'antrevindrent et donnerent si grant cop l'un a l'autre que la lance du chevalier de la montaingne rompi et la lance de Esber demoura entiere, et il l'empaint si fort que il gita l'autre chevalier a terre. (JV CXXXV, 7–8)

Jean d'Antioche traduit plus précisément en l'occurrence:

> Les deux chevaliers se veirent ou champ l'ung devant l'autre, ilz apprestent leurs escus et levent leurs lances et fierent les chevaulx des esperons et s'entrefierent de moult grant vertu contre les escus, mays la lance de l'adversaire Osbert ala glaçayant et ne lui fist nul mal. Osbert charga son coup et empoint son adversaire de grant puissance et l'abaty du cheval a terre. (JA III, LIX, 18–19)

Dans la transposition tendent aussi à s'imposer des articulations narratives en *quant . . . si/il,* qui répondent au souci stylistique, mais révélateur aussi d'une architectonique mentale, d'une véritable "Weltan-

---

[28]Suzanne Fleischman, "Discourse Pragmatics and the Grammar of Old French: A Functional Reinterpretation of *si* and the Personal Pronouns," *Romance Philology* 45/3 (1991): 251–83.

schauung," tendant à ne laisser aucun vide dans le récit,[29] de le suivre "en continu" dans une chaîne d'actions et de réactions en thème-rhème, comme l'a souligné B. Combettes.[30] On sait que ces cascades de séquences en *quant . . . si/il* sont particulièrement développées dans la *Conqueste de Constantinople* de Robert de Clari, où *quant* apparaît en moyenne toutes les dix lignes dans l'édition P. Lauer. Robert emploie la construction *quant . . . si* tout particulièrement pour récapituler une information préalablement assertée, thématique donc, avant d'introduire une nouvelle information.

Les phrase en *quant . . . si/il* tendent aussi à se multiplier dans les séquences narratives chez Jean de Vignay en équivalence du latin:

Verum infoecunditatem ipsius comperiens Archiepiscopus Arelatensis, sanctissimus vir, miraculis praeclarus, Caesarius, mare civitati suae subjacens adiit, et chirothecam suam vento marino repletam strinxit. Accedens itaque ad vallem, inutilem tunc habitam, in nomine Christi chirothecam, plenam vento, scopulo cuidam injecit, ventumque perpetuum jussit emittere. (L 972, 31–35)

Et quant l'arcevesque d'Arelate ot ouÿ et esprouvé sa maleurté et son infecondité, li qui estoit saint honme et resplendissoit en miracles, entra en la mer qui estoit desous sa cité et empli son gant du vent de la mer et puis l'enclost. Et quant il ot ce fet, il vint a cele valee et aporta le gant qui estoit plein de vent. Et quant il fu en cele valee, il jeta son gant en une ouverture d'une roche et li conmanda de par Jhesu Crist que il li feist venir vent pardurable. (JV, CVIII, 3–4)

Chez Jean d'Antioche, l'emploi de ce type de phrase est plus restreint. Sans compter que ces propositions en *quant . . . si/il* sont particulièrement propres à rendre les participes absolus du latin, ce qui est évidemment impossible dans des développements non narratifs.

Un phénomène des plus intéressants, bien que ténu, repérable chez Jean de Vignay, est l'apparition, dans les séquences narratives, de propositions

---

[29]Bernard Cerquiglini, Joël Foret, and Danielle Mukherjee, "Le récit saturé: l'enchaînement narratif dans la langue littéraire médiévale," *Cahiers de Recherche de Sciences des Textes et Documents*, 7/1 (1976): 45–64.

[30]Bernard Combettes, *Recherches sur l'ordre des éléments de la phrase en moyen français*, Doctorat d'État, Nancy, A.N.R.T., Université de Lille III, Lille (1988).

temporelles de perception jouant le rôle de liant, répondant éventuellement aux adverbes du latin comme *itaque, proinde*:

> Sane Lunensis, ut eis piratica, vita in usu erat, rapiendi animo accedentes spe sua frustrati miraculo divino tanti thesauri indigni judicati, dum fugiunt, ad fugiendum insecutionem parant, dum fugant et fugientem insequuntur navim, magis fugiuntur; sicque fit, quod dum insecutionem parant, navis fugit, stat cum subsistentibus, redit cum redeuntibus. Tanta novitate tanta vicinia ad Luccensem haec inaudita sed diu tentata retulit. Nec mora, sanctissimus Luccensis antistes Johannes navigia disponit, remos orationem aptat, psalmorumque usus, navigio navim, quam non persequitur, consequitur et cum debita veneratione recipit. Indignati Lunenses, quod Luccensibus insecuta ductum navis occurrit, quaestionem movent de acquitis, proponunt, quae ad sui commodum questus eis videntur accommoda. (L 968, 14–21)

> Et la coustume de ceus du pas estoit de rober et de prendre ce que il pouoient trouver, et *quant il virent cele nef,* il cuidierent que ce fust .i. tresor d'or et d'argent et la vodrent prendre, . . . mes la nef s'arrestoit quant eulz revenoient arriere, elle revenoit, car il n'estoient pas digne d'avoir si precieus tresor. Et *quant il virent qu'il ne la pooient prendre,* et nouvelle qui tost court fu tantost espandue par la terre, si que saint Jehan qui estoit evesque de Luques l'oï dire, et tantost il fist aprester sa navie et ala la, et fist ses avirons d'oroisons. Et la nef, que il ne vouloit pas prendre a force ne par couvoitise, le conmença a suivre, et il la reçut par grant reverence. *Et quant ceus de Lune le virent,* il furent trop dolent et distrent. . . . (JV XCVIII, 16–19)

Jean de Vignay retrouve ici spontanément, en équivalence du latin, des patrons de phrase et des enchaînements du "récit saturé" finement dégagés par Jean Rychner dans *L'Articulation des phrases narratives dans la Mort Artu* et par Cerquiglini, Foret, et Mukherjee.[31]

L'examen encore embryonnaire des deux traductions permet, au total, de tirer les conclusions suivantes. Pour la traduction de Jean de Vignay les développements encyclopédiques à la syntaxe complexe sont transcrits de manière étroite par un traducteur qui peine manifestement devant son

---

[31] Jean Rychner, *Formes et Structures de la prose française médiévale: L'Articulation des phrases narratives dans la Mort Artu* (Neuchatel: Faculté des Lettres de Neuchâtel et Genève: Droz, 1970); Cerquiglini, Foret, et Mukherjee, "Le récit saturé."

modèle, et qui s'y accroche scrupuleusement en le calquant, sur le plan lexical également; mais tout bien considéré, les calques lexicaux des termes abstraits tout particulièrement, sont source d'enrichissement et de renouvellement du lexique. "Latimier" étroit, qui n'a certes pas l'envergure qu'aura plus tard un Nicole Oresme, n'ayant pas une théorie vraiment élaborée de sa technique de traduction, Jean de Vignay participe néanmoins de cette large vague qui, à partir du 14e siècle, fait fructifier le lexique français provigné sur le latin. Les récits et anecdotes des *merveilles,* dont la syntaxe est plus linéaire, sont transposés avec beaucoup plus d'aisance. Jean de Vignay y applique sans difficulté majeure les structures phrastiques habituelles des récits en prose comme les chroniques, et y transpose le vocabulaire par des mots courants à son époque.

Dans l'ensemble de la traduction comme ailleurs, qu'il s'agisse du *Miroir Historial,* des *Choses de chevalerie* ou des *Enseignemens Theodore Paleologue,* Jean de Vignay cherche avant tout à donner du latin, comme l'a souligné M. Gosman, une équivalence fonctionnelle, soutenue par des apports explicatifs éventuels, avec tous les risques de mimétisme étroit que cela comporte. Jean d'Antioche, au contraire, est d'avantage un "transpositeur" qui rend son modèle en un vulgaire intelligible, avec tous les risques d'édulcoration que cela comporte, tout en médiévalisant volontiers.

Il reste que cet exposé n'est qu'une ébauche et ne fait que tracer des pistes. De nombreuses questions sont encore à approfondir concernant particulièrement Jean de Vignay: le type de traduction fonctionnellement équivalente qu'il propose, selon les termes de M. Gosman, vise quel public? Est-ce une traduction minimale, qui ne cherche qu'à *esponre* le texte latin, comme le suggère D. Trotter, une sorte de support pour la lecture? Serait-ce le fruit d'une oeuvre collective, comme le suggère J.-P. Bordier? Une étude systématique serait encore à mener sur la richesse lexicale du lexique de Jean de Vignay, intégrant les glossaires des éditions établies par Löfstedt, Knowles, et Bordier, et constituant une première base de données.[32]

---

[32]Leena Löfstedt, *Li Livres Flave Vegece*; Paleologi Theodoro, *Les Enseignemens de Théodore Paléologue,* éd. Christine Knowles (London: Modern Humanities Research Association, 1983); et Bordier, "La vie de sainte Pélagie."

Medieval Psalm Translation and Literality

Louis G. Kelly

Quoniam rex omnis terrae Dominus: psallite sapienter. (*Psalm* 46:9)
[Since the Lord is the king of all the earth, sing wisely.]

In his *Enarrationes in Psalmos,* one of the most influential of the Psalm commentaries, Augustine comments, "Let us not seek sound for the ear, but light for the heart."[1] *Sapienter* is a loaded word, referring directly to the relationship between God and the person singing the psalm. Avoiding the mystical problems this entails, we shall look at it from the point of view of a medieval commentator and translator from the Latin tradition. What factors entered into the task of vernacular Psalm translation in western Europe during the Middle Ages? How did they "sing wisely?"

The history of the Latin psalter is rather complex. The first group of versions, translated during the second century, was the *Vetus latina*, taken from the Greek of the Septuagint. Augustine commented on the version current in North Africa. Ironically for the subject of this paper, his text reads the synonymous *psallite intelligenter,* a first notable indication that ancient literality did not produce uniform texts. Though the *Vetus latina* survived in the patristic commentaries, there were three other Latin versions circulating and in use from the fifth century on: the Roman, the Gallican and the *Psalterium iuxta Hebraeos,* all of them from the pen of St. Jerome.[2]

---

[1]"Non quaeramus sonum auris, sed lumen cordis," Augustine, *Enarrationes in Psalmos*, 3 vols., CCSL 38–40 (Turnhout: Brepols, 1956), p. 534.12–13.

[2]See Jerome, "Tractatus in librum Psalmorum," *S. Hieronymi presbyterii Tractatus sive Homiliae in Psalmos, in Marci Evangelium aliaque varia argumenta*, ed. Germain Morin, CCSL 78 (Turnhout: Brepols, 1958), pp. 1–467; and *Libri Psalmorum. Versio antiqua gallica*, ed. Francisque Michel (Oxford: Oxford University Press, 1860).

The Roman was Jerome's first attempt at revising the *Vetus latina,* the Gallican his second. Last of all, in exasperation over the errors of the Septuagint, he took his "Hebrew Psalter" directly from the Hebrew text. In the centuries following, each one of these versions was used in various places in Europe as tradition demanded. Apart from the different source texts, the second variable affecting manner of translation is intentionality: the drive towards various types of translation, literal or otherwise, depends on the purpose envisaged for the target text. The Psalter still is one of the favorite books of the Bible for devotion and meditation, and it is doubtful whether a literal translation would leave room for anything but an intellectual response. In any case, under the guise of the famous theory of the four senses of Scripture, the Middle Ages was very much aware of the multiplicity of senses a text acquired through the response of the reader. Hence, in the light of a textual tradition that was anything but an example of literality and given the wide variety of responses one has to a religious text, is it possible for there to be such a thing as a "literal translation" of a book whose Latin tradition is as varied as that of the Psalter?

English versions begin with Caedmon and become frequent during the twelfth century. In French they begin about the twelfth century. It is interesting that the English use interlinear glosses before the French, and that French interlinear glosses seem to appear in England first, but such versions are not at issue here. This chapter, rather, is interested in those versions that were translated and published for the edification of the cleric and the layman who could read. The Psalms appeared in two types of publication. The first is the complete book of Psalms, "free-standing" psalters such as the fifteenth-century Metz Psalter and the various English psalters published by the Early English Text Society.[3] The second is fragmentary psalters in books of private devotion. The most important of these are the "Primers." These were vernacular versions of the Offices, usually containing the Little Office of Our Lady, the Office for the Dead,

---

[3] *Le Psautier de Metz: Texte du XIVe siècle,* ed. François Bonnardot (Paris: Vieweg, 1884). See also *The Earliest Complete English Prose Psalter,* ed. Karl D. Bülbring, EETS, o.s., 97 (London: K. Paul, 1891).

and the Penitential Psalms. The only one of these remaining in the modern breviary is the Office for the Dead.[4]

At least on the surface, the major thrust towards literality for a medieval translator was the deeply held conviction that English and French, indeed any vernacular, were incapable of carrying the weight of meaning generated by a sacred text. This argument was put forward in detail in 1408 at the Council of Oxford, convened to condemn the Lollards, the texts of which are printed in Deanesly's *The Lollard Bible*.[5] But the very sophisticated argumentation of the official case against translation hides a naïve Realism that identifies word and matter. More important to our case is the Lollard reply, which claims that while formal equivalence is not possible on the levels of vocabulary and grammar, functional equivalence is. These same arguments are taken up in the foreword to the *Psautier de Metz* (ca. 1450), which admits the problems inherent in translating into the vernaculars but promises a version that will be accurate when judged against both original text and the *gloze*. The attitude is that of Jerome, that God finds sound scholarship enough and that no matter what theologians may say, divine inspiration is not needed by a translator and, in consequence, is not on offer from God.

We have very little evidence on how vernacular translators worked. I think it is certain that the modern use of dictionaries was unheard-of. For the doctrinal questions the biblical translator had at his disposal an astonishing number of commentaries, beginning with the great commentaries by the Fathers, for example Hilary and Ambrose. But they also had access to Augustine's *Enarrationes in Psalmos* taken from the *Vetus latina,* as were the commentaries of Ambrose and Hilary of the early fourth century. At the end of the fourth century Jerome had commented both his Gallican and his Hebrew Psalter, and Psalm commentary remained an industry after the fall of the Roman Empire. There was also persistent critical input from the more sophisticated East, translated happily by such as Scotus Erigena during

---

[4]See *The Prymer; or, Lay folks' prayer book* (*with several facsimiles*), ed. Henry Littlehales and Edmund Bishop, EETS, o.s., 105 (London: K. Paul, 1895).

[5]Margaret Deanesly, *The Lollard Bible* (Cambridge: Cambridge University Press, 1920).

the early Middle Ages. Besides these patristic commentaries, the fourteenth-century translator had access to the *Glossa ordinaria*, to Peter Lombard's immense compilation of Psalm commentary in the mid-twelfth century,[6] and the great Scholastic and post-Scholastic commentaries of Nicholas of Lyra, Albertus Magnus, Aquinas, Denis the Carthusian, and many others. Most of these, in particular the *Glossa ordinaria* and the great thirteenth-century commentaries, were on the Gallican Psalter and took little note of any but the patristic commentaries. We can add to this the standard university courses in biblical theology and, an issue that still needs careful investigation, the use made of Jewish theologians by a number of important Christians, including members of the Schools of Chartres and St. Victor.

The contribution of the glosses was not confined to interpretation of symbolic passages or the elucidation of ambiguities. It was more the reinforcement of an attitude of mind by the melding of Jewish attitudes to Scripture and pagan rhetoric, particularly that of Cicero, which had never been forgotten but which began to enter vernacular languages through translators in the early fourteenth century. The Jewish contribution to Christian exegesis was the ancient sense that the temporal world had a divine world as its double, and that certain things and events here gave us a glimpse of the other. In particular, certain events in this world were anticipations or forerunners of even greater events in the future. The glossators mined their predecessors for all they were worth—some of the thirteenth-century resolutions of difficult passages were taken almost untouched from the patristic commentaries. For the ancient world, rhetoric had been one way to truth—the richness proper to words (*copia verborum*) being a guarantee of the speaker's grasp of the *copia rerum,* that is, the proper stock of facts. The whole business had been argued out for Christians by St. Augustine in the *De doctrina christiana.*

For Augustine as for Jerome, translation of the Scriptures was a theological act in which rhetoric came to the aid of doctrine. In essence, until the thirteenth century theology was an application of the interpretative

---

[6]Peter Lombard, *Commentaria in Psalmos,* in vol. 1 of *P. Lombardi magistri sententiarum, parisiensis episcopi Opera Omnia,* PL 191: 61–1295 (Paris: J.-P. Migne, 1854).

side of rhetoric to Scripture, it was truly the "science of the Book" in which the mysteries hidden under the text were revealed. The advent of dialectic in theology had little effect on biblical commentary, which kept largely to the Augustinian model, and none on translation. The translation model for the vernaculars avoided the extremely literalist routine of the earliest translators and took its cue from the early commentators, from Augustine in particular: behind the literal sense of Scripture lie the various mystical senses which refer the text on the page to the beliefs of the Church, to one's own progress to God, and to one's own problems in dealing with God. During the Middle Ages there was considerable controversy among Bible scholars on the rights of the literal sense versus the various mystical senses. The thirteenth-century scholastic commentators in the main insisted that the literal sense be preserved by any translator so that the other senses could be built from according to the intention of God, but many of the standard glosses, for example Peter Lombard's compilation which I am using here, were quite clear that the literal sense had the least priority for a Christian.

A translator will escape this tendency to slight the literal sense only if he aims at a word-for-word translation. But given the temper of his times, he will interpret in spite of himself. Hence medieval translators of all stripes ruthlessly assimilated ancient social realities and institutions to the world they knew. Further, any translator who treats his task as an aid to devotion is concerned with leading the reader into some of the byways of the mystical sense as he sees it through his own religious experience. Thus, in following the dictates of their religious sensibility, medieval translators were influenced by any glosses they had read. True, if they controlled themselves, they rarely repeated the gloss verbatim. Under these conditions the gloss will often appear in some form or other. And to ensure that their version gave light to the heart, they assimilated Jewish social realities to those of their own society, and often filled in other details.

To illustrate what I am talking about, take Psalm 7, which, according to tradition, David composed while he was on the run from Absalom. The Latin is the Gallican Psalter (see Appendix below); the French versions are from the Metz Psalter and the Douce Manuscript (Oxford), both about 1450; and the English versions are from a fourteenth-century free-standing psalter and from a fifteenth-century primer. All of these versions are meant for devotional reading, or even for recitation, private or public.

Let us begin with the Metz Psalter, whose preface is quite explicit on the difficulties of Psalm translation, the translator's reliance on glosses, and the devotional purpose of his translation. This fifteenth-century translation, a very popular one in France, to judge from the number of manuscripts in which it exists and the range of dialects of those manuscripts, is definitely a piece of rhetoric. It is meant to be read aloud and to stick in the mind afterwards. Of the four psalters in question, it is the one that pays the most attention to senses other than the literal: it is therefore the most affected by the gloss tradition. Yet actual quotations from the glosses are rare. In verse 8, for example, the Metz Psalter's *sinagogue et assembleie des peuples* reproduces Peter Lombard's *synagoga, id est congregatio.* But where the Devil is concerned, such echoes are tempting to reinforce the moral sense. Hence the lion of verse 2, a fearsome beast in the Old Testament, becomes the Devil for the Metz translator:

> Que aucune foiz per aventure li lyons d'enfer ne ravisse mon arme pour li tueir, pues que nuls ne la deffent ne secourt et ne la[7] welt sauveir.
> [That at no time the lion of Hell happen to snatch away my soul to kill it, since there is nobody to defend it or help it, and no one wants to save it.]

This was a chance hardly to be missed, for all glosses on the Latin text reference this verse to the Devil in I Peter 8–9, in which the Devil "goes about like a roaring lion, seeking whom he would devour." Our translator also has an obvious sense of the sinfulness of mankind. *Merito* (Ps 7:5) [deservedly] is translated *je weil bien* [I fully accept]. Though this abasement before one's own sins is not merited by the Latin, it is built from Peter Lombard's gloss on *merito:*

> id est, si hoc malum quod sustineo, mihi per praeteritam culpam quod commiserim contra Absalon contigit.

---

[7]Manuscript: *lai* [people]. In the light of the Latin and other Middle French versions, the pronoun *la* seems the better reading.

[that is, if this evil which I am suffering, has come to me through some fault I committed against Absalom in the past.]

Apart from this there is the choice of doctrinally significant French words to slant the meanings of the Latin original:

sauve moi et me delivre de touz ceulz qui me persecutent et me font grevance.
(Ps 7:2)
[Save me and deliver me from all those who persecute me and do me harm.]

Salvum me fac [make me safe] and *persequentibus* [my pursuers] are relatively neutral in Latin, but the Christians gave them specifically religious senses. These are picked up by the French translator: *Sauve* for *salvum me fac* and *qui persecutent* for *persequentibus* are definitely religious words that reflect the glossators' insistence on interpreting David's situation at the hands of Absalom as a figure of what the ordinary Christian goes through at the hands of the Devil. Something similar happens in the following:

Et toute ma gloire ramenoisse et faice retourneir en pourre et en pouciere. (Ps 7:6)
[And may he gather up all my glory and turn it back to powder and dust.]

The Latin word *deducat* means simply "to drag down." One wonders whether *faice retourneir* is an echo of the religious commonplace that we all return to dust. And take the liturgy of Ash Wednesday:

Memento homo quia pulvis es et in pulverem reverteris.
[Remember Man, that thou art dust, and into dust thou shalt return.]

In all, this is a version that takes the mystical meaning of the psalm more seriously than the literal, and translates in consequence.

The Douce psalter is much less overtly influenced by the glosses. True, it does slant the meaning of *convertere* (Ps 7:13) in the religious direction of the gloss:

Si vus ne serrez convertit, sa espede crollerat.
[If you are not converted, he will brandish his sword.]

In this it is at one with Metz:

> Se vous n'estes convertis a li. . . .
> [If you are not converted to him. . . .]

But in general it attempts to remain relatively neutral as far as interpretation is concerned, even where the gloss has spoken. In Psalm 7:2 *persequentibus* is the neutral *parsuanz,* and the lion remains a lion:

> Que alquune fiede ne ravisset sicume leuns la meie aneme, dementres que n'est chi reaimet ne chi salf facet.
> [That no enemy snatch my soul away like a lion, as there is nobody to redeem it or make it safe.]

This translator lacks the sense of the sinfulness of mankind demonstrated by Metz: *merito* (Ps 7:5) is translated *par desserte.* And the version is overtly conscious of its own society. For example, it consistently translates the Latin *iniquitas* by *felunie,* a good feudal word meaning lack of loyalty to an overlord. Similarly, *nequitia* (Ps 7:10) becomes *ordeet* [filth]. Is this an expression of feudal disgust for the vices unworthy of a knight? *Ord* is a common word of abuse when referring to the lower orders.

There are also a number of interpretations that show either irony or a willingness to go for the most usual meaning of the Latin: "Si je rendis au *guerredunanz* a mei males choses" (Ps 7:5) [if I render evil to the man who gives me my just deserts] where *retribuentibus* is taken in its usual sense of giving back, often referring to a duty or debt. And *in finibus inimicorum meorum* of Psalm 7:7 [in the territory of my foes] is translated *devises de mes enemis* [plans of my foes]. Though *finis* does mean "purpose," this reading is odd considering both the context and its equally normal meaning of "territory," which appears in the other versions. But it is not impossible that the translator's choice of this sense does reflect the Christian use of *inimicus* for the Devil, and Satan's reputation for cunning. This version also gets a high color without the obsessive rhetoric of Metz, for example, *Astetei enfante torceunerie*[8] (Ps 7:15) [behold he brings forth cruelty], where the

---

[8]Metz: "Vezci il enfante iniustice et fauceteit" [Behold he brings forth injustice and falsity].

relatively neutral *iniustitiam* of the Latin becomes "cruelty" in the French. In all, this version has different priorities from Metz: it is one which takes the side of the literal sense.

To a very large extent we find the same sort of behavior in the English psalters, which would, I expect, have been claimed to be literal by their translators, but which do attempt to be contemporary. Both versions take the lion of Psalm 7:2 to be a lion and leave the reader to sense the common identification of the animal with Satan, if they know it. The only approach to direct influence of the gloss is Psalm 7:13. There, like the French versions, the Primer version has: "If ye ben not convertid, he schal florische his swerd; he hath bent his bow and maad it redi." But the older version reflects the etymological sense of the Latin *convertere,* and at the same time manages to get the Christian sense by a nicely rhythmic paraphrase: "But yif ye be not styred from ivel, he shal shew hys vengeance; he made his menaces, and he dyted them." However, with *shew hys vengeance,* the older version reproduces an explanation from the gloss in lieu of translating directly:

"gladium suum vibrabit," id est, manifestum vindictam exeret.
["will brandish his sword," that is, will make his revenge obvious.]

These are the only clear cases of direct influence of the glosses in the English. Likewise, as a whole, the English psalters have few echoes of feudal society, for example, in the fourteenth-century psalter: "That the enemi ne rauis nought my soule as a lion, ther-whyles that ther nys non to *ransoun* it, ne to mak it sauf" (Ps 7:2). Ransom was a feature of medieval warfare. But the Primer takes the word *redimat* etymologically: "Lest eny tyme he, as a lioun, ravysche my soule, the while non is that ayenbieth, nether to make saaf." "Ayenbieth" is, like the Latin, "to buy back," and both acquired the religious sense of "redeem." Among the other puzzles of what influenced what is the subjunctive of the Primer: "The wickidnesse of synneris be endid" (Ps 7:10). Is this reading carelessness? Or does it reflect the Hebrew Psalter, which has *consumatur,* rather than the Gallican *consumetur?*

Even where there is no cultural or exegetical imperative, the English psalters tend to interpret rather freely. The fourteenth-century version tends to fill in all that is implied in religious teaching. In verse 2, for instance, the Latin *libera me* becomes *deliver me fram alle yvel*. Similarly the arrows of verse 14 are not only burning, but *brynnand in pynes*. The Primer is a good deal less venturesome than the older psalter. But even it has its attempts to visualize Hebrew reality in a medieval fashion. The most spectacular such rethinking is verse 17, where the Hebrew parallelism between *caput* and *verticem* is interpreted as a progression of God's anger, so that not only does the wrath of God descend on the sinner's head but also *verticem* (crown of the head) becomes *necke*:

> His sorewe schal be turned into his heed, & his wickednesse schal come doun into his necke. (Ps 7:17)

Though this is in direct defiance of the gloss, the translator might have been reading *cervicem*; it all depends on the clarity of his Latin manuscript. Did the translator suffer from that commonest of all academic afflictions, chronic neck pain?

The Bible would not be the Bible without interpretation problems. The Latin is quite clear that God is the subject of Psalm 7:12–13, and not too clear about what happens next. Augustine has God preparing the punishment of the sinner in Psalm 7:14 and then fudges the issue in the rest of the psalm. The later glosses in general agree that it is the enemy of the psalmist who is the subject of Psalm 7:15–17, but they disagree over who is the subject of Psalm 7:14. The idea of God preparing evil makes them most uncomfortable, and Jerome states bluntly in his commentary on the Gallican Psalter that it is the Devil who is subject here. Regarding Psalm 7:14, both French versions and the English Primer sit on the fence. The earlier English translator makes it clear that in his view God is the subject of Psalm 7:14, by a direct change of subject in Psalm 7:15: "Lo, the sinner doth unright-fulnesse; he conceived sorow, and childed wickednesse." This, at least, agrees with Peter Lombard:

> ex homine est causa damnationis . . . quae concepit a diabolo.
> [from Man is the cause of damnation, which he took from the Devil.]

And as if that was not enough, the pit of the next verse becomes: "He opened *helle* & dalf it, and fel into the diche that he made." All very biblical, where the translator conflates the pit or lake of the original with Gehenna, the ravine outside Jerusalem used as a rubbish-tip. Because it was normally on fire, Christ often used Gehenna as a figure for Hell.

One must admit that the history of the text stacked the cards against literal translation. Following the best traditions of preaching on the Psalms, these versions are allusive in the best sense of the term: they refer to other parts of the Bible, to liturgical piety, to popular piety where this was approved, and, where it was useful, to the society of the time. In essence we have a restrained use of the glosses, at least in this psalm. The translators keep the initiative. The Metz Psalter demonstrates a strong tendency both to prefer mystical senses when they could be squeezed into the text, and to be rhetorical. I doubt whether this combination would have been seen as contradictory. Indeed, the popularity of the Metz translation in the French-speaking world is its own guarantee of quality. But where Metz can be accused of writing commentary into the text, the others, while retaining the color of their times and at times being independent to the point of mistranslation, tend to adopt the attitude of the scholastic commentators who preferred a close translation, all other things being equal. They are also far less rhetorical than Metz. By this means the literal sense was obvious, and in the way the original did, the target text allowed the reader to "find light for the heart."

In their various ways all of these translators avoided strict literality, and it was a principled avoidance, for their lexical choices show a pastoral responsibility for their readers. This responsibility might be reflected in flashes of mystical insight, which heightened a doctrinal point or concretized a new social reality. This was the obvious affirmation of the responsibility of the translator to ensure that he and his readers "sing wisely."

Appendix

Psalm 7 (Gallican Text)

1. PSALMUS DAVID QUEM CANTAVIT DOMINO PRO VERBIS CHUSI
FILII IEMINI [2]Domine Deus meus in te speravi, salvum me fac ex
omnibus persequentibus me et libera me, [3]nequando rapiat ut leo
animam meam, dum non est qui redimat neque qui salvum faciat.
[4]Domine Deus meus, si feci istud, si est iniquitas in manibus meis,
[5]si reddidi retribuentibus mihi mala, decidam merito ab inimicis
meis inanis. [6]Persequatur inimicus animam meam et comprehendat
et conculcet in terra vitam meam, et gloriam meam in pulverem
deducat. [7]Exsurge, Domine, in ira tua, exaltare in finibus
inimicorum meorum, et exsurge Domine Deus meus in praecepto
quod mandasti. [8]Et synagogus populorum tuorum circumdabit te.
Et propter hanc in altum regredere. [9]Dominus iudicat populos.
Iudica me Domine secundum iustitiam meam, et secundum inno-
centiam meam super me. [10]Consummetur nequitia peccatorum et
diriges iustum, et scrutans corda et renes Deus. [11]Iustum adiutorium
meum a Deo, qui salvos facit rectos corde. [12]Deus iudex iustus,
fortis, et patiens; numquid irascitur per singulos dies? [13]Nisi
conversi fueritis, gladium suum vibrabit. Arcum suum tetendit et
paravit illum, [14]et in eo paravit vasa mortis, sagittas suas ardentibus
effecit. [15]Ecce parturiit iniustitiam, et concepit dolorem et peperit
iniquitatem. [16]Lacum aperuit et effodit eum. Et incidet in foveam
quam fecit. [17]Convertetur dolor eius in caput eius et in verticem
ipsius iniquitas eius descendet. [18]Confitebor Domino secundum
iustitiam eius, et psallam nomini Domini altissimi.

Toward a Social Genealogy of Translation Theory: Classical Property Law and Lollard Property Reform

Rita Copeland

The classical models of translation derived from Cicero and Horace had, and still have, a very long legacy, not only theoretical but also political. The notions of access to language and text that they so influentially articulated are premised on systems of ownership and property rights; and of course underlying their arguments are Rome's cultural-imperial claims to dominance as a new world power. It should not be surprising, therefore, that later resignifications of ancient theories of translation were also political transformations of the function of translation. In the hands of Lollard translators, the classical models of translation are converted to mean their very opposite, not only as theoretical but also as social paradigms. I offer here a preliminary reading of some of the better known primary sources to propose that we can transfer translation debates to the plane of social-economic debates about private property and communality.

I begin with Cicero because his *De optimo genere oratorum,* with its famous formula "non verbum pro verbo," inaugurates the western European debate about translation. The *De optimo genere oratorum* is an introduction to Cicero's own translations of Demosthenes and Aeschines, which he has undertaken in order to provide a "regula" or rule against which Roman orators can judge a Latin standard of Atticism. The aim of this undertaking, as Cicero expresses it, is to lay possession to a norm of Atticism for Latinity:

> nec converti ut interpres, sed ut orator, sententiis isdem et earum formis tamquam figuris, verbis ad nostram consuetudinem aptis. In quibus non verbum pro verbo necesse habui reddere, sed genus omne verborum vimque servavi. Non enim ea me

adnumerare lectori putavi oportere, sed tamquam appendere. Hic labor meus hoc assequetur, ut nostri homines quid ab illis exigant, qui se Atticos volunt, et ad quam eos quasi formulam dicendi revocent intellegant. (5.14–15)

[And I did not translate them as an interpreter, but as an orator, keeping the same ideas and the forms, or the "figures" of thought, but in language which conforms to our usage. And in so doing, I did not hold it necessary to render word for word, but I preserved the general style and force of the language. For I did not think I ought to count them out to the reader, but rather to weigh them out. The result of my labor will be that our Romans will know what to demand from those who claim to be Atticists and to what standard of speech they are to be held.][1]

Anticipating the question "Why should I read this translation of yours rather than the Greek original?" he counters that Romans accept Latinized drama on its own terms, and so should accept his own translations of Greek orators as sufficient models of Atticism (6.18).

As Cicero's language of commercial exchange suggests, however, we should read his efforts against the much broader question of property. In his enormous study *The Class Struggle in the Ancient Greek World,* G. E. M. de Ste. Croix observes that property rights are "a peculiarly sacred subject in the eyes of the Roman governing class," and that Roman civil law is an elaborate system for regulating property rights among citizens and their families.[2] Cicero is particularly obsessed with the inviolability of private property. In the *De officiis,* for example, he wonders what greater mischief there could be than an equal distribution of property, and asserts that states were established above all with the aim of preserving property rights (2.73).[3] Roman law discriminates on grounds of social status, and the administration of the civil law came to institutionalize the predisposition in favor of the propertied classes by "attaching greater weight to evidence

---

[1]Text and translation (the latter with minor changes here) from Cicero, *De inventione; De optimo genere oratorum; Topica,* ed. and trans. Harry M. Hubbell (1949; Cambridge, Mass.: Harvard University Press, 1976), pp. 364–65.

[2]G. E. M. de Ste. Croix, *The Class Struggle in the Ancient Greek World: From the Archaic Age to the Arab Conquests* (Ithaca: Cornell University Press, 1981), p. 329.

[3]See Ste. Croix, *The Class Struggle,* pp. 329, 426.

given by members of the upper classes."[4]

I have argued elsewhere that the familiar themes of Cicero's translation theory in the *De optimo genere oratorum* and other texts should be understood in terms of an aggressive cultural agenda in which Roman writers can displace their Greek sources.[5] But I would further suggest here that the idea of possessing the text, translating it, "not word for word" but "in language that conforms to our usage" so that Romans will have their own standard of Atticism, argues converting the text as property to new ownership: translating as an *orator* rather than as a mere *interpres*, translating *against* the language of the original ("non verbum pro verbo"), establishes the translator's new proprietary claims. Certainly Cicero's rejection of literal translation, which "counts out" Greek to Latin words like coins, in favor of a conversion of value by weight, suggests a transference and securing of property. In the *Tusculan Disputations* Cicero says that he has "often translated from the Greek poets . . . that Latin eloquence might not lack any embellishment in this kind of discussion" (2.11.26).[6] Cicero arrogates for his own translations a certain inviolate foundational status: it is to his Latinized eloquence that future students will look for a Latin stylistic rule.

Horace more explicitly advances the notion of textual appropriation as property rights: this is certainly how his ancient commentators understood the force of the well-known lines in *Ars poetica*:

> Difficile est proprie communia dicere. . . .
> Publica materies privati iuris erit, si
> non circa vilem patulumque moraberis orbem
> nec verbo verbum curabis reddere fidus
> interpres. (120–34)
> [It is difficult to treat *communia* in a way that is *proprie*. . . . Public material will

---

[4]Ste. Croix, *The Class Struggle*, p. 330.

[5]Rita Copeland, *Rhetoric, Hermeneutics, and Translation in the Middle Ages: Academic Traditions and Vernacular Texts* (Cambridge: Cambridge University Press, 1991), pp. 29–36.

[6]*Tusculan Disputations*, ed. and trans. John E. King (Cambridge, Mass.: Harvard University Press, 1945).

be under (your) private jurisdiction if you don't linger on the vulgar, well trodden path, nor try to render word for word like a *fidus interpres*.][7]

The first line, "difficile est proprie communia dicere," has proved one of the most controversial lines in Latin literature.[8] Horace's own language—the distinction between "public material" and "private jurisdiction"—suggests that the term *communia* must be read in the light of property law. The Pseudo-Acronian scholiasts glossed the word *communia* as *intacta,* that is, "untouched" or "untried," and cast its meaning in legalistic terms: "in the same way that a house or a field without an owner is common (*communis*), and when occupied becomes personal property (*proprius*), so something that has not been given expression by anyone is common."[9] In this legal sense of "common" as opposed to "owned," *communia* means not "owned by all" but, rather, "claimed by none," in the sense of something new or unclaimed. *Publica materies,* on the other hand, suggests something already owned by all, "public property."[10] The Porphyrian scholia of late antiquity offer a slight adjustment on this, equating *communia* with *publica materies,* reading both in the sense of common or public property, that is, traditional subjects, as opposed to what is *privati iuris*, one's own material.[11] Whether one accepts *communia* as "new" unclaimed matter or as publicly owned and hence familiar material, it is clear that such textual transactions take their definition from civil institutions of property rights.

In Horace, as in Cicero, the practice of literal translation, word for word like an *interpres*, seems to be tantamount to an abdication of rights of ownership: for Cicero, the right of Romans to appropriate Greek sources,

---

[7]Text from Horace, *Satires, Epistles, and Ars poetica,* ed. and trans. H. Rushton Fairclough (1929; Cambridge, Mass.: Harvard University Press, 1978). The translation is my own.

[8]*The "Ars poetica,"* vol. 2 of *Horace on Poetry,* ed. C. O. Brink, 3 vols. (Cambridge: Cambridge University Press, 1963), pp. 204 and 432–40.

[9]*Pseudacronis scholia in Horatium vetustiora*, ed. Otto Keller, vol. 2 (Leipzig: Teubner, 1904), p. 330.

[10]See Brink, ed., *The "Ars poetica,"* pp. 204–10.

[11]*Scholia in Horatium codicum Parisinorum latinorum 7972, 7974, 7971*, ed. Hendrik J. Botschuyver (Amsterdam: Bottenburg, 1935), p. 432.

for Horace the ambitious claims of the individual poet to territorial sovereignty over publicly owned materials. In the same way that Roman civil law exists to regulate and preserve rights of property for citizens, Roman translation theory seems to emerge as a system to regulate textual ownership. In translation theory, the economic-political role of patrician ownership is identified with the practice of rhetorical appropriation (Cicero notes that he translates as an *orator*); the *interpres* or grammatical exegete, who humbly expounds the text word for word, occupies the inferior civil-legal position of non-propertied classes.

In this preliminary genealogy of translation as property law, I wish only to touch briefly on Jerome. Of course, Jerome is a key figure in transmission of ancient translation theory to the Middle Ages, as well as in the christianization of translation theory, and I will return to him later in my discussion. Jerome's contribution cannot be understood apart from institutionalized patristic attitudes towards property ownership which, according to Ste. Croix, did not retain the most radical eschatological orientation of the evangelists, and which largely preferred the notion of charity to that of personal or communal renunciation of property.[12] Jerome and early medieval theorists substitute a notion of reconstituting originary meaning beyond language for the Roman objective of claiming rights to the original text.[13] Regarding these questions, however, I want to skip forward one thousand years to Lollard debates on translation, because those debates crystallize themselves around reformist Christian (and especially apostolic) notions of property, in ways that I do not believe we find in earlier medieval or patristic contexts.

The Prologue to the *Wycliffite Bible* echoes ancient models of word and sense, via, of course, the transmissional authority of Jerome:

> First it is to knowe that the beste translating is, out of Latyn into English, to translate aftir the sentence and not oneli aftir the wordis, so that the sentence be as opin either openere in English as in Latyn, and go not fer fro the lettre; and

---

[12]See Ste. Croix, *The Class Struggle*, pp. 425–41, esp. 435.

[13]See Copeland, *Rhetoric, Hermeneutics, and Translation* (pp. 42–55), for a discussion of the ideas of Jerome and other early medieval writers about "possession" of the translated text.

if the lettre mai not be suid in the translating, let the sentence euere be hool and open, for the wordis owen to serve to the entent and sentence, and ellis the wordis ben superflue either false. . . .

At the bigynnyng I purposide with Goddis helpe to make the sentence as trewe and open in English as it is in Latyn, either more trewe and more open than it is in Latyn. And I preie for charite and for comoun profyt of cristene soulis that if ony wiys man fynde ony defaute of the truthe of translacioun, let him sette in the trewe sentence and opin of holi writ.

. . . And the noumbre of translatouris out of Greek into Latyn passith mannis knowing. . . . Therfore Grosted seith that it was Goddis wille that diuerse men translatiden, and that diuerse translacions be in the chirche, for where oon seid derkli, oon either mo seiden openli. Lord God, sithen at the bigynnyng of feith so manie men translatiden in Latyn and to greet profyt of Latyn men, lat oo symple creature of God translate into English for profyt of English men![14]

This sets forth a number of issues, some of which can be traced back to classical theory and its Christian modifications, and some of which are new with the Lollards. Literal translation is inadequate on its own, although not for the same reasons that classical theorists eschew it: whereas in classical theory counting out the words like coins yields up insufficient profit for the enterprising translator, here, for the Lollard translator, rendering mere words makes for an economy of superfluity, an unnatural economy of false interest. On the other hand, the text also echoes Jerome's notion that Scripture's words are imbued with mystery, that its meanings are contained almost diacritically in its letters and verbal forms, and that the translator thus has a responsibility to the very letter of the text (so that, for Jerome, translating Scripture is different in kind from academic translation).[15] Thus, as the Prologue says, it is good to "go not fer fro the lettre." Most significantly, the Prologue introduces the notion of an "open" translation— "open" to understanding of the "sentence," but also "open" to collective

---

[14]Text from Josiah Forshall and Frederic Madden, eds., *The Holy Bible, containing the Old and New Testaments, with the Apocryphal books, in the earliest English versions made from the Latin Vulgate by John Wycliffe and his Followers*, 4 vols. (Oxford: Oxford University Press, 1850), 1: 57–59.

[15]See Jerome, Ep. 57 to Pammachius, ed. with a commentary by G. J. M. Bartelink, *Liber de optimo genere interpretandi (Epistula 57)* (Leiden: Brill, 1980), p. 13.

efforts at "opening" its textual difficulties. Here the Prologue cites Grosseteste to authorize the idea that diverse translations are a good thing, because someone will get it right ("where oon seid derkli, oon either mo seiden openli"); but I think that the idea of textual and translative collectivity here is the product of peculiarly Lollard notions of redistribution of wealth. More than any earlier medieval translation theory, Lollard translation theory and the official responses to it invite contextualization in a tangible social-economic program.

Wyclif's own ideas on dominion and temporalities are founded on apostolic reformism. In his treatise *On Civil Dominion* he directs his attacks (as later Lollards would do) at the wealth of churchmen: as Anne Hudson summarizes his views, "Christ and the apostles taught that Christians should be subject to temporal powers, that the clergy's business was with spiritual matters and that they should neither possess more earthly goods than were necessary for the immediate survival nor wield power of any kind over secular authorities."[16] It is, of course, to the laity, and especially to the government of England, that Wyclif looks to be the instrument of ecclesiastical reform. Among other things, Wyclif offers a very academic and theoretical proof of communal ownership of all goods, arguing that to be in a state of grace is to hold dominion over all God's world; but that since there are many individuals who might be in a state of grace, they can all own everything only if they hold everything in common.[17] But this remains only a theoretical possibility, since the just are not to be understood as human individuals in this life. Indeed, as Hudson has pointed out, Wyclif is not a communist, and Lollard theory in general does not advance the radical idea of communal ownership of goods.[18]

---

[16]Anne Hudson, ed., *Selections from English Wycliffite Writings* (Cambridge: Cambridge University Press, 1978), p. 5.

[17]John Wyclif, *Tractatus de civili dominio,* ed. Reginald L. Poole, 4 vols. (London: Trubner, 1885), 1: 96. I take my summary of this material from Anthony Kenny, *Wyclif* (Oxford: Oxford University Press, 1985), pp. 45–52.

[18]Anne Hudson, *The Premature Reformation: Wycliffite Texts and Lollard History* (Oxford: Clarendon, 1988), pp. 374–75.

But following Wyclif's ideas on the rightful dominion of secular rulers, who represent something like God's vicars on earth for jurisdiction over temporalities, Lollard polemic elaborated the radical implications of disendowment of the clergy and redistribution of its wealth under the governership of the king. The Lollard "Disendowment Bill" (which is not a bill in any parliamentary sense), probably from the first decade of the fifteenth century, offers an extraordinary analysis of the wealth that could accrue to the king if only he took possession of the temporal holdings of the English clergy:

> oure liege lorde the Kyng may have of the temperaltees by bisshopes, abbotes and priours, yoccupyed and wasted provdely within the rewme, xv erles and m^{1}vc (1500) knyhtes, vi m^{1}cc (6200) squyers and c houses of almesse mo thanne he hath now at this tyme, well mayntened and trevly by londes and tenementz susteyned. And euermore whanne alle this is perfourmed, oure lorde the Kyng may have euery yeer in clere to his tresour for defence of his rewme xx m^1 libri and more.[19]

Listing more than eighty abbeys and priories and their monetary value, the Disendowment Bill calculates a total gain for the crown of something between £200,000 and £300,000, not counting colleges, chantries, cathedrals, various churches, and more. The best part of this is what the king could do with this income:

> And thus in all the rewme may men have xv erles, [1500] knyhtes and squyers moo thenne be now sufficyauntly rentyd, and yitt therto xv unyuersitees and therto [1500] preestes and clerkes sufficiantly fondon be temperell almesse, yif yt lyke the Kyng and lordes to spenden hem in that vse, and the Kyng to his tresour [20,000] libri by yeer. And yitt c houses of almesse and euery houvs c marcis with londe to feden with alle the nedefull pore men and no coste to the tovne but only of the temperaltes morteysed [alienated] and wasted amonge provde worldely clerkes. . . .[20]

While this is not communitarian in any way, it offers a very practical program for the redistribution of wealth: the lines are hierarchical, since the

---

[19]Hudson, ed., *Selections from English Wycliffite Writings*, p. 135.
[20]Hudson, ed., *Selections from English Wycliffite Writings*, pp. 136–37.

king will have the power to dispose of the new properties as he sees fit, but the suggestion is that all social ills can be solved by an infusion of immoral private wealth into the coffers of a just secular government.

But the reason that it is still appropriate to read this as a proposal for a complete redistribution of wealth is that in Lollard eyes it really is just that: the Lollard political struggle is always with the established clergy and its claims to private ownership of temporal goods and ultimately of spiritual truth, and not with the government or the dominion of secular lords. Where "private" is a bad word in Lollard social thought, it is only the clergy that is guilty of private ownership (manifested, for example, in Lollard attacks on "private religion"), precisely because the clergy is supposed to be true to its apostolic origins and free of such temporal claims.

In the case of scriptural translation, the wealth of the text is similarly to be opened through redistribution in the vernacular; and the work of translation is to be distributed among the members of a newly enfranchised textual community. With Scripture as with private wealth, the Lollard struggle is entirely with the ecclesiastical establishment. Scripture must be reclaimed from the wrongful private possession of a Latinate clergy: in this battle over language, private and communal are recast as the opposition between a Latin elite (which imposes false linguistic claims on Scripture) and a vernacular public. This is also of a piece with Lollard attacks on the friars for hoarding books in their treasure chests.[21]

In its understanding of Scripture as wealth, Lollard thought is unreservedly communitarian: in invoking the classical distinction between literal and sense translation they "invest" it with a completely new purpose, to undo the idea of singular, appropriative ownership of the text, and to instate the idea of communal property through a collective project of vernacular translation. No single translator will "own" this vernacular textual property: where one translator renders "darkly" another may render more "openly," and this is to be achieved by translating according to sense and not only

---

[21] See Richard H. and Mary A. Rouse, "The Franciscans and Books: Lollard Accusations and the Franciscan Response," in *From Ockham to Wyclif*, ed. Anne Hudson and Michael Wilks (Oxford: Blackwell, 1987), pp. 369–84.

according to the letter. In other words, where classical theory releases the *translator* from scrupulous literalism so that the translator can assert new property rights over it, Lollard theory releases the *text* from the imprisonment of mere language so that it can be a newly collective property.

Interestingly, it is the official clergy that most radically inverts the classical model by invoking literalism as an argument for restricting the circulation of Scripture.[22] In the Oxford *Constitutions* of 1407–09, Archbishop Thomas Arundel argues that the meaning of Scripture is bound by its language: he determines that "it is dangerous to translate the text of Holy Scripture from one language into another, as St. Jerome says, since it is difficult in translations to preserve the same idiomatic meaning."[23] Arundel's reductive application of Jerome's views on translation makes an opportunistic case for linguistic determination of the text, in which the particularity of idiom ought to control the meaning. As Jerome had said, the rhetorical peculiarities of language present one of the greatest obstacles to idiomatic translation.[24] Arundel's construction of the issue, then, is that only translation of Scripture *verbum pro verbo* will serve the theological mysteries of Scripture, and since such translation is impossible, Scripture should not leave the protective guard of its clerical conservators.

In Arundel's arguments, the imperative to follow the letter of the text is actually the instrument of private dominion. Here only a hypothetical *fidus interpres* could legitimately contest the official clergy's textual rights to Scripture. We come full circle: while Arundel's arguments about the inviolability of the letter of the text are counter-Ciceronian, his motivations are actually consonant with the classical imperative to protect property.

---

[22]The arguments in this paragraph are based on material in my article "Rhetoric and the Politics of the Literal Sense in Medieval Literary Theory: Aquinas, Wyclif, and the Lollards," in *Interpretation: Medieval and Modern*, ed. Piero Boitani and Anna Torti, The J. A. W. Bennett Memorial Lectures, Perugia, 1992 (Cambridge: Brewer, 1993), pp. 1–23, esp. 17–18.

[23]Text in *Concilia Magnae Britanniae et Hiberniae*, ed. David Wilkins, 4 vols. (London: Sumptibus R. Gosling, 1737), 3: 317.

[24]Jerome, Preface to his translation of Eusebius's *Chronicle*, in *Eusibii Pamphili Chronici canones latini*, ed. John K. Fotheringham (London: Milford, 1923), p. 1.

The controversy about translation and textual circulation is, of course, an arena in which the battle over political and economic privilege is played out. But the commonplaces about translation—word for word, sense for sense, style, *sentence,* truth, and all their attendant values—are never politically innocent. A genealogy of their reconfiguration reveals how they can stand in for and mark out the terrain of those social pressures which constitute the textual invisible, and how in turn, in their conceptual complexity and slipperiness, they reshape the form that discourses of communality take.

Written French and Latin at the Court of France at the End of the Middle Ages[1]

Serge Lusignan

Medieval France was fundamentally bilingual, but this medieval bilingualism, in which a scholarly, learned language coexisted with a vernacular mother tongue, was very different from bilingualism as it is understood today. The following pages treat the relations between French and Latin by analyzing, first, several instances of translation from learned Latin into French and, second, the use of both languages by royal notaries in the royal court of the fourteenth and fifteenth centuries. During that period many French translations were done at the request of the French kings or of members of their family. Translation was particularly encouraged by Charles V (1338 to 1380), resulting in, for example, Augustine's *City of God* by Raoul de Presles, Aristotle's *Nicomachean Ethics* and *Politics* by Nicole Oresme, and John of Salisbury's *Policraticus* by Denis Foulechat. During the same period, the French language was being used as an administrative tool within the chancellery—indeed, some of the king's translators (Raoul de Presles or Laurent de Premierfait) came from the legal milieu. But two different ideologies still characterized the use of the learned and the vernacular languages.[2]

---

[1]This paper results from research generously subsidized by the Social Sciences and Humanities Research Council of Canada and by the FCAR of the Government of Québec. I would like to thank Claire Boudreau and Nadine Tremblay, who acted as my principal research assistants, and George Ferzoco and Jeanette Beer, who revised my English.

[2]The following ideas are explored in the first two chapters of Serge Lusignan, *Parler vulgairement: Les intellectuels et la langue française aux XIIIe et XIVe siècles* (Paris: Vrin and Montréal: Presses de l'Université de Montréal, 1986).

Latin was described as a language ruled by grammar, whereas French, like other vernacular tongues, was considered to be without rules. The former was learned at school with the help of books; the latter was acquired through the imitation of one's mother or wet nurse. Philosophers considered that Latin was the only appropriate language for the transmission of knowledge, while French was unfit for that purpose. College and university statutes reflected the same idea by forbidding the use of the vernacular within school limits.[3]

In the context of religion, the sacred rites were conducted exclusively in Latin, even if preaching to laymen could largely be done in the vernacular, and the Bible and prayer books were read in French by the nobility.[4] Glossing the biblical episode of Babel, and John 19:20 or Luke 23:38 in which "Jesus of Nazareth, king of the Jews" was written in Hebrew, Greek, and Latin on the Holy Cross, commentators explained that Hebrew was the original human language, which was kept as such, notwithstanding the confusion of Babel, so that Jesus could speak a language not corrupted by sin. Greek descended from Hebrew, and Latin from Greek, which explained the singular and sacred nature of the three languages. Discussions by theologians concerning language to be used for sacramental formulas revealed the same attitude: Latin appeared to be the only language for the sacred.[5]

This opposition between Latin and vernacular was visible also in the organization of medieval society and contributed to the distinction between clerics and laymen. During the fourteenth century, it was impossible to be recognized by any judge as a clerk without some ability to read, which ultimately presupposed a minimal knowledge of Latin. Thus, clerks formed a separate social group; they were exempted from certain social

---

[3]Serge Lusignan, "Le français et le latin dans le milieu de l'École à la fin du moyen Âge," *Parlure* 6 (1990): 3–23.

[4]Michel Zink, *La Prédication en langue romane avant 1300* (Paris: Champion, 1982), and the entry "Bible en français" in the *Dictionnaire des lettres françaises*, vol. 1, *Le Moyen Âge*, ed. Genevieve Hasenohr and Michel Zink (Paris: Fayard, 1992).

[5]Irène Rosier, "Signes et sacrements. Thomas d'Aquin et la grammaire spéculative," *Revue des sciences philosophiques et théologiques* 74 (1990): 392–436.

responsibilities and they were tried in canon law tribunals. Their criminal offenses were outside the jurisdiction of lay justice, which was harsher than that of the Church.[6]

Such was the socio-linguistic system that defined relations between Latin and French during the fourteenth century. A further set of differences confronted the medieval translator. The French language appeared inadequate to render the proper level of rhetoric for *auctoritas*.[7] Translators often discussed this question in their prologues. Concerning their competence in Latin, it seems clear that fourteenth-century translators felt more at ease with medieval Latin, some frankly admitting their difficulties in understanding classical Latin. But whether classical or medieval, it seemed to them impossible to render Latin into French appropriately. They saw serious stylistic problems also. To move a work from the Latin language to

---

[6]Robert Génestal, "Le procès sur l'état de clerc aux XIIIᵉ et XIVᵉ siècles," *École pratique des Hautes Études, Section des sciences religieuses* (1909–10): 1–39; and Robert Génestal, *Le privilegium fori en France du Décret de Gratien à la fin du XIVᵉ siècle*, 2 vols. (Paris: Leroux, 1921–24).

[7]Among recent publications about translation in the Middle Ages are: *The Medieval Translator: The Theory and Practice of Translation in the Middle Ages,* ed. Roger Ellis (Cambridge: Brewer, 1989); *Medieval Translators and Their Craft,* ed. Jeanette Beer (Kalamazoo: Medieval Institute Publications, 1989); *Traduction et traducteurs au Moyen Âge,* ed. Genevieve Contamine (Paris: Éditions du CNRS, 1989); Rita Copeland, *Rhetoric, Hermeneutics, and Translation in the Middle Ages: Academic Traditions and Vernacular Texts* (Cambridge: Cambridge University Press, 1991); and *Rencontres de cultures dans la philosophie médiévale: Traductions et Traducteurs de l'Antiquité tardive au XIVᵉ siècle,* ed. Jacqueline Hamesse and Marta Fattori (Turnhout, 1990). On translation from Latin to French see Jacques Monfrin, "Humanisme et traduction au Moyen Âge," *Journal des savants* (1963): 161–90; Jacques Monfrin, "Les traducteurs et leur public en France au Moyen Âge," *Journal des savants* (1964): 5–20; Jacques Monfrin, "La connaissance de l'antiquité et le problème de l'humanisme en langue vulgaire dans la France du XVᵉ siècle," in *The Late Middle Ages and the Dawn of Humanism Outside Italy* (Louvain: University Press, 1972), pp. 131–70; Claude Buridant, "*Translatio medievalis.* Théorie et pratique de la traduction médiévale," *Travaux de linguistique et de littérature* 21 (1983): 81–136; Lusignan, *Parler vulgairement*; and François Bérier, "La traduction en français," *Grundriss der romanischen Literaturen des Mittelalters* 8/1 (1988): 219–65 and 400–01. The *Dictionnaire des lettres françaises*, vol. 1, contains updated notices and bibliographies on all French translators.

French meant not only a linguistic transfer but also a rhetorical lowering of the original. Many translators argued that what sounded superb in Latin appeared dull when translated in French. Beneath the argument was the rhetorical theory of three styles (*Rethorica ad Herennium* IV, 8, 11). Medieval translators believed that what a Latin work expressed in "oratio gravis" was lowered to "oratio attenuata" when translated in French. As Jean Daudin formulated the problem in the prologue to his translation of Petrarch's *De Remediis utriusque Fortunae* dedicated to Charles V:

> Car, combien que en moult de choses le langage françois ne soit pas grandement differant du latin, nientmoins y a il très grant foison de mos latin qui à peine pevent estre dis ou ne pevent estre dis en françois qu'ilz ne perdent l'eloquence et aornement du latin.[8]

The rhetorical gap between the original work and its French translation was perceived both in the construction of sentences and in the choice of words. As to the first, most translators agreed that word-to-word translation was impossible. In his prologue to the translation of Thomas of Cantimpré's *Bonum universale de apibus,* in 1372, Henri du Trévou stated the problem thus:

> Aucune foiz ou l'aucteur du livre et les docteurs et philosophes ont pour le plus bel et rectorique latin querir transporté les dictions pour quoy françois ainsi ordoné seroit pesant et moins cler a entendre, i'ai la sentence mise rez a rez comme i'ay pensé que il l'eussent dit eulz meismes se il parlassent françois.[9]

The same rhetorical distance was felt with vocabulary, as Laurent de Premierfait noted a few decades later: "La magesté et la gravité des paroles et sentences sont moult humiliees et amoindries par mon langaige vulgar qui par necessité (use) de motz petits et legiers."[10]

---

[8]Lusignan, *Parler vulgairement*, p. 168.

[9]Quoted from the only existing manuscript, Brussel/Bruxelles, Koninklijke Bibliotheek Albert I/Bibliothèque royale Albert I, 9507.

[10]Quoted from Laurent de Premierfait, Prologue to the translation of Cicero's *De amicitia* (Paris: Bibliothèque nationale, Fr. 1020, fols. 44–54).

Translators did not remain passive toward this perceived weakness of the vernacular, and during the fourteenth century literary French underwent a re-Latinization of its structures and vocabulary resulting, at least in part, from the dissatisfaction of French translators with their native language. This re-Latinization was examined many years ago by Ferdinand Brunot, and Rychner, Löfstedt, Buridant, and Ouy and Catach, among others, have more recently substantiated his conclusions.[11] For example, Buridaïnt has shown, by a comparison of Jean de Meun's and Jean de Vignay's translation of Vegetius, that Jean de Vignay preferred to create neologisms to translate some Latin technical words, even if French had an equivalent, attested by Jean de Meun's translation. For instance, to translate *cohors* Jean de Vignay introduced in French the neologism *cohorte* instead of using Jean de Meun's more familiar word *compeignie*. Many of these neologisms have not survived, but many are still in use, especially in technical and abstract contexts. Ouy and Catach showed the importance of this re-Latinization also for the history of French orthography. Jean Rychner even concluded: "Au demeurant, la langue des traducteurs n'a peut-être pas l'importance que certains lui ont prêtée, parce qu'elle est sans doute dans une large mesure langue de traduction, et parfois même langue de mauvaise version latine."[12] In the process of translation, the French language developed a mimetic

---

[11]Ferdinand Brunot, *Histoire de la langue française des origines à nos jours*, vol. 1, *De l'époque latine à la Renaissance,* new ed. (Paris: Colin, 1966); Jean Rychner, "Observations sur la traduction de Tite-Live par Pierre Bersuire (1354–1356)," *Journal des savants* (1963): 242–67; Nina Catach and Gilbert Ouy, "De Pierre d'Ailly à Jean Antoine de Baïf: une exemple de double orthographe à la fin du XIVᵉ siècle," *Romania* 97 (1976): 218–48; *Li abregemenz noble honme Vegesce Flave René des establissemenz apartenanz a chevalerie, traduction par Jean de Meun de Flavii Vegeti Renati viri illustris Epitoma institutorum rei militaris,* ed. Leena Löfstedt (Helsinki: Suomalainen Tiedeakatemia, 1977); Claude Buridant, "Jean de Meun et Jean de Vignay, traducteurs de l'*Epitoma rei militaris* de Végèce. Contribution à l'histoire de la traduction au Moyen Âge," in *Études de langue et de littérature française offertes à André Lanly* (Nancy: University of Nancy II, 1980), pp. 51–69; and Flavius Vegetius Renatus, *Li livres Flave Vegece de la chose de chevalerie,* ed. Leena Löfstedt (Helsinki: Suomalainen Tiedeakatemia, 1982).

[12]Jean Rychner, "Observations sur la traduction de Tite-Live par Pierre Bersuire (1354–1356)," *Journal des savants* (1963): 265.

relation with Latin, which ultimately contributed to the diversification of
French linguistic skills.

As for the language encounter experienced in the royal chancellery,
kings of France had always had religious clerks to write their diplomas in
Latin,[13] although the royal chancellery as an organized body with professional notaries emerged only in the thirteenth century. During the reign
of Louis IX (d. 1270) the French language was used on some occasions,
and in the first decades of the fourteenth century the vernacular was as
widely used as Latin in official documents of the royal administration. Latin
remained the exclusive language for diplomacy and for certain kinds of
documents such as letters of nobility or of enfranchisement. But in other
areas of administration either Latin or French was used, depending on
whether the king was writing to church institutions and clerics or to
laymen, to the central region of France or Languedoc or the northern part
of the realm.[14] Thus, for many purposes either French or Latin was
employed, and the royal chancellery had to be truly bilingual. As early as
1342, royal ordinances concerning royal notaries made it clear that they
should be competent in both languages: "souffisans pour faire lettres tant
en latin comme en françois selon que l'office requiert."[15] The French
language acquired status as an administrative language, long after it
acquired status as a literary language.

---

[13]For the early functioning of royal chanceries see Jeanette M. A. Beer, *Early Prose in France:
Contexts of Bilingualism and Authority* (Kalamazoo: Medieval Institute Publications, 1992).

[14]This question is far from having received a full historical treatment. However, one can
consult: "La langue vulgaire dans les documents diplomatiques" in Arthur Giry, *Manuel de
diplomatique* (Paris: Hachette, 1894), pp. 464–76; Georges Tessier, *Diplomatique royale
française* (Paris: Picard, 1962), pp. 239–40; Kurt Baldinger, "L'importance de la langue des
documents pour l'histoire du vocabulaire gallo-roman," *Revue de linguistique de langue
romane* 26 (1962): 309–30; L. Carolus Barré, "L'apparition de la langue française dans les
actes de l'administration royale," *Académie des Inscriptions et Belles Lettres. Comptes rendus*
(1976): 148–55; and Jacques Monfrin, "L'emploi de la langue vulgaire dans les actes
diplomatiques du temps de Philippe Auguste," in *La France de Philippe Auguste: Le temps
des mutations,* ed. Robert-Henri Bautier (Paris: Éditions du CNRS, 1982), pp. 785–92.

[15]Octave Morel, *La Grande Chancellerie royale et l'expédition des lettres royaux de l'avènement
de Philippe de Valois à la fin du XIVᵉ siècle (1328–1400)* (Paris: A. Picard, 1900), p. 76.

A unique piece of evidence exists on the subject: the *Art notarié de la chancellerie royale* compiled by Odart Morchesne in 1427. This work is in the long medieval tradition of *artes dictaminis*. Compilations of models of letters first appeared during the Merovingian period, enabling political administrations to continue to write letters in contexts where Latin literacy was fading. The tradition of *artes dictaminis* survived throughout the medieval period as a mean of teaching the arts of writing in Latin, but Morchesne's work was an innovation, in using the *ars dictaminis* to teach the art of writing in French. Compilations of models of letters in French had already appeared in England during the fourteenth century but appear not to have circulated in France.[16]

Morchesne compiled his *Art notarié* by using actual letters of chancellery[17] stripped of all *ad hoc* references. Names of persons were replaced by such phrases as "a un tel," names of places by "a tel lieu," and dates by "a telle date," or, alternatively, blanks were left for specifics. Fortunately, Morchesne was not totally systematic in this: some names of persons, places, and dates remain, giving important clues to understanding the history of the treatise. Also, letters were accompanied by "notae" that offered further explanation concerning the circumstances in which particular

---

[16]For the history of the Latin *artes dictaminis* during the medieval period, one can consult: James Jerome Murphy, *Rhetoric in the Middle Ages: A History of Rhetorical Theory from St. Augustine to the Renaissance* (Berkeley: University of California Press, 1974), esp. chap. 5, "*Ars dictaminis*: The Art of Letter-Writing"; and Martin Camargo, *Ars dictaminis, ars dictandi* (Turnhout: Brepols, 1991). For vernacular *artes dictaminis* in England and their diffusion see M. Dominica Legge, *Anglo-Norman Letters and Petitions from All Souls MS. 182* (Oxford: Blackwell, 1941); and Lusignan, *Parler vulgairement*, pp. 94–97 and 194.

[17]On the arts of notaries of French chancellery and on Odart Morchesne see C.-V. Langlois, "Les plus anciens formulaires de la chancellerie de France," *Notices et extraits des manuscrits de la Bibliothèque Nationale et des autres bibliothèques* 35, 2nd partie (1897): 793–830; Morel, *La Grande Chancellerie royale*; S. Vitte, "Formulaires de la chancellerie royale conservés dans le fonds Ottoboni," *Mélanges d'archéologie et d'histoire. École française de Rome* 48 (1931): 185–214; Georges Tessier, "L'activité de la chancellerie française au temps de Charles V," *Le Moyen Âge* 51 (1938): 14–52 and 81–113; and Georges Tessier, "Le formulaire d'Odart Morchesne (1427)," in *Mélanges dédiés à la mémoire de Félix Grat*, vol. 2, *Diplomes et chartes* (Paris: Pecqueur-Grat, 1949), pp. 75–102.

letters were to be used or special wording to which notaries should pay special attention. Letters are grouped in seventeen chapters, which correspond to seventeen areas of chancellery competence. Letters of privilege to plead by attorney are followed by letters of safeguard, delay of payment of a debt, and feudal homage. Other chapters are devoted to nominations to offices or ecclesiastical benefices, and to financial administration. The treatise concludes with charters.[18]

Odart Morchesne was a notary and secretary of Charles VII. He compiled his treatise when the king was reorganizing his administration at the time of the Bourges monarchy and the Anglo-Burgundian occupation of Paris. Some letters are thus dated from Poitiers, Bourges, Chinon, or Loches. Morchesne's compilation possibly originated in the need to reconstruct a new chancellery able to train new notaries, without access to the archives of the realm that had been left in Paris. This would explain why his art of letter writing was among the first to be composed for the French chancellery, which, however, had formally existed for more than two centuries. Whatever the reason, Morchesne created a new genre for his milieu. There are twelve manuscripts extant of the *Art notarié de la chancellerie royale,* some being exact copies of the original, others being versions augmented by new letters. For the present study, I am using the copy contained in Paris, Bibliothèque nationale, Fr. 5024, which seems to be the author's own manuscript.[19]

Morchesne compiled 274 model letters, 93 of which are in Latin and 181 in French. Latin appears to be the exclusive language for church matters, diplomacy, and for addresses of a certain social status. Otherwise the language was a matter of choice. The following example provides the Latin and French versions of an almost identical text. The use of French

---

[18]On the nature of these categories of letters, see Giry, *Manuel de diplomatique,* and Tessier, *Diplomatique royale française.*

[19]These are the results of my own study of the manuscript tradition, which has been published under the title "La transmission parascolaire de savoirs juridiques: les arts épistolaires de la chancellerie royale française" in the proceedings of the colloquium *Éducation, Apprentissages, Initiation au Moyen Âge* (Montpellier: Centre de recherche interdisciplinaire sur la société et l'imaginaire au Moyen Âge, 1993), pp. 249–62.

was obviously suggested when the letter was addressed to lay persons (*a tel et a sa femme*), whereas Latin must be preferred for the clergy (*decano et capitulo ecclesie Aurelianensis*):

Grace a plaidier par procureur

Charles par la grace de Dieu roy de France, a tous ceuls qui ces presentes
Karolus   Dei gracia   Francorum rex, universis   presentes
[Charles, by the grace of God king of Frenchmen, to all who will see]

lettres verront   salut.   Savoir faisons nous de grace especial avoir octroyé
litteras inspecturis salutem. Notum facimus nos   de gracia speciali concessisse
[these letters, hail. Let us make known that by our special grace we have conceded]

a tel et a sa femme

dilectis nostris decano et capitulo ecclesie Aurelianensis
[to our beloved dean and chapter of the church of Orléans]

que eulz tant conionctement comme diviseement en toutes   leurs causes et
ut ipsi tam coniunctim   quam divisim   in omnibus suis causis et
[that together or separately in all their suits and]

quereles meues et a mouveroir contre tous   leurs adversaires
querelis motis et movendis contra quoscumque suos adversarios
[disputes moved or to be moved against any of their opponents]

par devant tous   juges   seculiers de nostre royaume,
 coram   quibuscumque judicibus   regni nostri   secularibus,
[before all secular judges of our realm,]

en demandant, en defendant, soient receuz par procureur en parlement et dehors
agendo   et defendendo,   in parlamento et extra per procuratorem
[as plaintiff or defendant, can be represented by an attorney in parliament as elsewhere]

iusques a un an.
usque ad annum admictantur.
[for one year.]

(Odart Morchesne, *Art notarié de la chancellerie royale*, Paris, B.N. Fr. 5024, fol. 1r)

The high degree of parallelism between the two versions of this—and other—letters is immediately striking. The only important difference in the sequence of words is that quite often verbs are at the end of propositions in Latin, for example, the final *admictantur*. Otherwise, syntagmatic constituents of sentences follow the same order and strictly correspond one to the other. Within syntagms, small inversions are justified by the different position, relative to nouns, of adjectives and determinants in French and Latin. A good example of this phenomenon is seen in the French syntagm "juges seculiers de nostre royaume" and its Latin counterpart "judicibus regni nostri secularibus." In general, the morphological nature of words exactly corresponds in the two languages. Of course, French must compensate with prepositions for its lack of case system. The uses of *inspecturis* and *notum* also illustrate the greater flexibility offered by participial constructions in Latin.

Semantically, many of the significant nouns, adjectives, adverbs, and verbs share a common root. This is particularly the case with juridical and technical terms: *lettres - litteras, grace especial - gracia speciali, causes et quereles - causis et querelis, procureur - procuratorem*, and so on. In fact, when reading Morchesne's *Art notarié* as well as other administrative sources of that period, we are left with the impression that there exists in the juridical language a clear tendency to tune French and Latin to the same semantic roots. Of course, French is a Romance language and these roots normally are borrowed from Latin. However, in rare cases the roots have a vernacular source: *saisina* in Latin, *saisine* in French (a key term in medieval customary law, which is of Germanic origin); *namptum* (a pledge), *namp* (of Saxon origin); or *atornatus* and *attourné* (an Anglo-Norman term).

Unfortunately, not one of our sources gives us any clue about the relative ease experienced by notaries when writing in one language or in the other. But in reading parallel letters, one has the impression that words came as easily in both languages. Notaries do not seem to have encountered the same problems of vocabulary as medieval translators. Things move so fluently from one language to the other that, when I look at letters such as the one I have edited above, it is almost impossible to determine which language is the source language. At the same time, one cannot fail to recognize that the Latin of the chancellery remained distant from both classical Latin and even medieval literary Latin. Most translators of learned Latin texts affirmed that a word-to-word translation was absolutely impossible, whereas in letters of chancellery word order showed a high degree of parallelism in both languages. Morchesne attests to a linguistic situation where the Latin language developed a mimetic relation with French. This last conclusion can be supported by the following advice, written in 1336 by a member of the French Parliament, concerning the style to be used in Latin to transcribe oral testimonies given in French for the purpose of a trial:

> Et si inveniat verba in gallico extranea vel dubia, ita quod nesciat proprie facere latinum, ponat ad placitum juxta gallicum et etiam gallicum post latinum, servando verba assueta poni in arrestis curie, et planum latinum et grossum, pro laicis, amicum et propinquum vocabulis in gallico in articulis positis et sentenciis predictis. (P. Guilhiermoz, *Enquête et procès. Étude sur la procédure et le fonctionnement du Parlement au XIVe siècle* [Paris, 1892], pp. 223–24)
> [And if you find strange or dubious French words, for which you do not know the Latin translation, do your best to imitate such words in Latin and even give the French word after the Latin word, and use the usual vocabulary for court sentences, and a plain and rough Latin, congenial and close to the French vocabulary used in (lower) court arguments and judgments, for the sake of laymen.]

The same text then advises people to avoid constructions such as the ablative absolute and gerundive, and to prefer constructions in the third person, which are termed "via plana," suggesting that relations between French and Latin were not always transparent for notaries of the chancellery. As late as the beginning of the fifteenth century, the French language remained inadequate for ornate style, even under the pen of royal notaries. Their parallel texts echo the complaint of royal translators concerning the inadequacy of French to render the style of great Latin authors. They also remind us that some royal secretaries were remarkable Latin stylists, as was Jean de Montreuil (1354–1418). After all, the royal chancellery of Charles VI was one of the birthplaces of French humanism.[20]

---

[20]Ezio Ornato, *Jean Muret et ses amis: Nicolas de Clamanges et Jean de Montreuil. Contribution à l'étude des rapports entre les humanistes de Paris et ceux d'Avignon (1394–1420)*

Should we conclude then, that notaries were more at ease with Latin than with French regarding written expression? The *Art notarié* is again useful to answer this question. Morchesne's purpose obviously was didactic. Each letter was given a title and these titles, with sequence numbers of the letters within the seventeen chapters of the treatise, were listed in a table of contents at the beginning of the manuscript. Users were provided with these tools to facilitate information retrieval, a process familiar to someone trained in the schools. Futhermore, as was formerly noticed, each letter or group of similar letters was accompanied by explanatory notes. These *notae,* to use Morchesne's own term, were made of one to several short paragraphs that explain how to make good use of each model letter. All titles, with the exception of two or three, and absolutely all *notae* were in French, even when they concerned letters exclusively in Latin. In Morchesne's manual, French was the didactic language to teach letter writing in French as well as in Latin. The following are two *notae* about letters in Latin nominating someone to an ecclesiastical benefice:

> Nota que toutes et quantesfoiz qu'on parle d'une eglise cathedrale ou metropolitaine, on ne doit point nommer le saint ou la sainte dont elle est fondee, ne dire ne "metropolitaine" ne "cathedrale," mais seulement "l'eglise de tel lieu." Et quant c'est pour autres eglises collegiales ou parrachiales, on le y doit mectre, a la difference de l'eglise cathedrale, comme en disant ainsi: "ecclesie collegiate Beate Marie," vel "Beati Aniani" in Bicturia," vel "N."

> Item, nota que ce mot "solennitatibus" se doit escrire par deux "n," et par une "l," et non pas par "m" et par "p" comme souventeffoiz on l'escript et ainsi "le." (Paris, B.N., Fr. 5024, fol. 66v)

> [Note that each and every time that one designates a cathedral or a metropolitan church, he should not specify the name of the Saint to which it is dedicated, nor mention "metropolitan" nor "cathedral," but simply write "the church of such place." But when one writes for the profit of a collegiate or a parish church, he

---

(Paris: Droz, 1969). A recent colloquium was devoted to the general question of the role of chanceries in the development of medieval culture: Germano Gualdo, ed., *Cancelleria e cultura nel Medio Evo* (Vatican City: Archivio Segreto Vaticano, 1990).

should specifically state, to the difference of a cathedral church, "collegiate church Saint-Mary," or "Saint-Agnan in Bourges," or "N."

Item, note that this word "solennitatibus" should be written with two "n"s and one "l," and not with an "m" and a "p" as too often seen, and thus "le."]

These *notae* exemplify that French could be used as a metalanguage to discuss linguistic questions about Latin. They also suggest that Latin remained a secondary language for royal notaries.

What conclusions are to be drawn about the linguistic situation from which royal translations of learned Latin texts as well as chancellery letters emerged? What was the linguistic nature of the encounter between Latin and French as literary languages in the milieu of the royal court of France in the fourteenth and early fifteenth centuries? Clearly there existed a situation of bilingualism: even if translations of learned works were difficult to their authors, the fact remains that they were executed and conveyed a message that kept something of the Latin original. Christine de Pizan, for instance, relied heavily on these translations for her knowledge of Latin culture.[21] Furthermore, in this situation of bilingualism, it appears that Latin was a secondary language.

At the same time, the relation between French and Latin can be characterized as a situation of diglossia. Each language had its own area of specialization where one could not easily follow the other. French did not master the high style of rhetoric, but Latin also lacked words to render some information expressed orally in French legal testimonies. In either situation, the less fit language developed a mimetic relation with the other.

The necessity for certain people to use both languages for certain purposes, and the mimetic aptitude that each language developed toward the other, makes it difficult to determine which of the two languages translated the other, as is the case with bilingual letters. I would suggest, then, that this linguistic situation is best explained by two complementary

---

[21]See, for example, the study of the sources of Christine de Pisan's *Le Livre des fais et bonnes meurs du sage roy Charles V*, ed. Suzanne Solente, preface to vol. 1 (Paris: Champion, 1936), pp. xxxii–lxviii.

hypotheses. On the one hand we may postulate that Latin and French performed as a unique linguistic system; on the other hand we should remember that Latin and French were two Romance languages. Du Cange had the right intuition, when he chose to illustrate the meaning of many Latin words not only with Latin but also with French quotations, in his *Glossarium Mediae et Infimae Latinitatis.*

Thus "bilingualism," "first and secondary languages," "diglossia," and "language interbreeding" are all notions that applied to the language encounter of French and Latin in the court of France at the end of the Middle Ages. But the scarcity of our sources prevents us from doing more than tagging the problems. A clear picture and a coherent description of the relation between the two languages are at the moment beyond our grasp.

Translation and Definition
in the Medieval Bilingual Dictionary

Brian Merrilees

Bilingual dictionaries are major tools for translation, but they are seldom compiled simply for the user seeking equivalents for the source language in the target language. If the provision of equivalents remains a prime purpose of the bilingual dictionary, it is clear that the compilation process expects of the user at least some proficiency in the source language. The degree of bilingualism required for the profitable understanding of medieval Latin-French dictionaries is the subject of this chapter, and, as we shall see, the nature of implied bilingual competence appears to change with the structural complexity of the dictionary concerned. We shall examine the nature and use of Latin and French as definitional and metalinguistic languages in some known medieval Latin-French dictionaries and attempt to relate that use to the dictionary structure. We shall also look at assumptions about directionality and language priority in bilingual dictionaries.

The *Abavus* and the *Aalma*

The two earliest Latin-French alphabetical dictionaries were the *Abavus* and the *Aalma*, both dating from the fourteenth century and both having a simple structure with simple definitional material.[1] The *Abavus*, a much reduced form of Papias's *Elementarium doctrinae*, and the *Aalma*, an epitome of part five of Johannes Balbus's *Catholicon*, have large numbers of entries that consist of a Latin headword glossed by a single French equivalent:

---

[1] *Recueil général des lexiques français au moyen âge (XIIᵉ–XVᵉ siècle)*, ed. Mario Roques, 2 vols. (Paris: Champion, 1936–38), vol. 1, *Abavus*; vol. 2, *Aalma*.

Abbas - *abé*	Ablativus.. - *ablatif*
Abbatissa - *abeesce*	Abluo.. - *laver*
Abbassia - *abaie*	Ablucio.. - *lavemens*
Abreviare - *abreger*	Abnegacio.. - *denoiemens*
Abreviatio - *abregance*	Abnego.. - *denoier*
(*Abavus*, BN lat. 7692)	(*Aalma*, BN lat. 13032).

The *Abavus* has three main versions (in five MSS), according to its editor Mario Roques, and if most of its French definitions are indeed limited to single equivalents of the Latin headwords, there are some multiple equivalents and occasionally a definitional phrase, especially in the later manuscripts:

Abdere - *mucer ou respondre*;
Abigere - *embler vel fortraire vel chacer en sus*;
Actuaria - *nef qui est menee de cordes*;
Aloe - *espece de oignement*; and
Agere - *faire vel demener vel trespasser*.

The *Aalma* is found in fifteen MSS, and despite its rather spare look both in manuscript and edited printed form, it turns out, as Hélène Naïs noted in her 1986 study, to be a rich inventory.[2] Again most of its Latin headwords are glossed or defined by single French words, but a much superior number than in the *Abavus* have multiple equivalents, as in the following examples:

Accedo .dis - *aprochier ou avenir*;
Accipiter - *esprivier ou faucon ou oitour*; and
Afficio .cis - *tourmenter, convoitier ou enfourmer*.

It even has what we can term definitions, with distinctions and subtleties, as in the examples:

---

[2]"Présentation d'une future concordance de l'*Aalma*," in *La Lexicographie au Moyen Âge*, ed. Claude Buridant (Lille: Presses Universitaires de Lille, 1986), pp. 185–96. Jean F. Shaw, *Contributions to a Study of the Printed Dictionary in France before 1539*, Ph.D. thesis, University of Toronto, 1997, has added three manuscripts to the list given by M. Roques.

Accingo..gis.. - *saindre ou lui aprester pour aler en bataille*; and
Carus .a .um - *chiers en .ii. significacions c'est qui est bien amé ou qui couste moult*

or examples such as:

Acus .acus - *aguille ou espingle ou ce a quoy on desmelle les cheveux*;
Adopto. tas.. - *adopter, c'est recevoir en lieu de filz*; or
Adulter .teri - *ribaut ou houllier qui va a la femme d'autruy*

where the definition in French is valid not just for the Latin lemma but also for the single French gloss. One can argue that in such a combination of single gloss and internal definition a French dictionary entry is nascent, at least in semantic form if not yet in linguistic attributes. The *Aalma* also retains and converts to French some encyclopedic definitions.[3]

Another important feature of the *Aalma* is the use of French as metalanguage, which for this paper will be interpreted as grammatical terminology, as well as all attributional and relational information other than the definitional.[4] The most obvious examples are the prepositions, which are frequently explained by French metalanguage:

Ab - *preposicion qui sert a l'ablatis*; or
Ad - *preposicion servent a l'acusatif. a ou au.*

Hélène Naïs also points to other linguistic terms that are present, as in:

Afatim - *(la moienne brieve) abundaument ou largement*; and
Afatim - *(la moienne longue) facundement - adverbes.*[5]

In these last, the French translates very common Latin terms, *media correpta* and *media producta*, which are also found in their original form elsewhere

---

[3]For example: Carolus.. li - *propre nom d'aucuns des rois de France ou d'autre. Charles*; cited by Naïs in "Présentation d'une future concordance," p. 188.

[4]See Brian Merrilees, "Métalexicographie médiévale: la fonction de la métalangue dans un dictionnaire bilingue du moyen âge," *Bulletin Du Cange: Archivum latinitatis medii aevi* 50 (1991): 33–70.

[5]Naïs, "Présentation d'une future concordance," p. 194.

in the text. We must note, at this point, however, that Roques's edition of
the *Aalma* intentionally omits most of the Latin metalanguage that occurs
in many of his twelve manuscripts, including the base text edited, Paris, BN
lat. 13032. In the letter M of that manuscript we found the following
examples of metalinguistic and definitional material not included by Roques
(the material omitted is underlined):

Macrobius .bii - *propre nom d'omme*, <u>interpretatur longa via</u>;
Magnopere - <u>adverbium, secundum magnum opus</u> *soingneusement*;
Maius .maii - *may, nom de mois* <u>et habet .i. vocalem</u>   m; and
Mane - *matin* <u>adverbium vel nomen indeclinabile</u>   n
    <u>Item mane interpretatur: numeravit deus regnum suum et complevit illud.</u>[6]

The major omissions in Roques's edition are the marginal indication of
gender for nouns and voice for verbs and, within the text, declensional and
conjugational forms, no doubt excluded for reasons of space and layout. It
would be wrong to overemphasize these lacunae, but their inclusion would
have made clear that some knowledge of Latin was expected of the
user/reader. In addition, the omissions also hide some of the structural
elements of the *Aalma* that our studies of medieval lexicography show to be
important. It must be remembered, of course, that if the language of
linguistic description in the examples quoted is French, the language being
described is still Latin.

Finally, there are a few examples of definitions in Latin used to gloss
Latin headwords, either in conjunction with French or, more rarely, alone:

Agazo.. - *gardeur d'asnes, de jumens* vel domesticus minister officiorum;
Melancolia.. - *une des quatre qualitez humainez* que sunt sanguis, colera, melencolia
    et fleuma; or
Melo eciam olim deus est Nilus.

The *Glossarium gallico-latinum*—A French-Latin Dictionary

One of the first attempts to create a French-Latin dictionary was not
really a success as an alphabetical lexicon. Its ordering depends on the order

---

[6]Folios 85v–87r.

of the Latin glosses, formerly definitions, and not the French headwords. The dictionary stands alone in a fifteenth-century manuscript, BN lat. 7684, and if at first sight it might appear to be alphabetical, an eighteenth-century hand warns us that it is "non accurato litterarum ordine scriptum." Closer examination reveals what has happened. The compiler has clearly intended to set all French words beginning with the same letter together, but to achieve this he ran through his Latin-French source as follows: from the Latin A he took all French words beginning in A in the order of their occurrence in the source text; then he went through the Latin B and again took all the French words in A and added them to his first group; then through C, through D, and so on. French words in B were next again beginning with Latin A, following the same method. The result is a sort of French-Latin dictionary but the determination of the order is only in part the first letter of the French word and very much that of the Latin glosses. To find any particular French word one needs to run through an entire letter.[7]

But if this is rather like a first draft on the way to a recognizable French-Latin lexicon, we should not underestimate its importance methodologically nor as an indication that French is a semantic if not fully linguistic object in late medieval France. Because of the simplicity of its structure, the *Glossarium gallico-latinum* is probably to be classed with the *Abavus* and the *Aalma,* as most French headwords, though not all, are translated by single Latin glosses. The following entries seem unexceptional in their style:

Abbé	abbas .tis	m
Abbasse	abatissa .sse	
Abbeye	abbatio .cis	f
Ayole	abamitta .tte	f
Arriere chacer	abigo .gis, abegi, abigere, abactum a	
Abominer	abominor .aris .atus sum vel fui .ari a	
Abominacion	abominacio	f
Abominable	abominabilis .le	o
Abominablement	abominabiliter	

---

[7]The source is related to the *Dictionarius* of Firmin Le Ver (1440; ed. Brian Merrilees and William Edwards, Turnhout: Brepols, 1994), but not exactly in the form found in Paris, BN n.acq.fr. 1120.

but these next reflect traces of the underlying structure of the source text:

Acuser	accuso .sas .satum *encuser*	a
Accusé	accusatus .ta .tum *encusé*	d
Accusement	accusatio .onis *encusement*	f
Aigrir	aceo .ces	n
Accesco .scis	*commencer a devenir aigre.*	

In these last entries the French repeated as a gloss is a reminder that the French was originally definitional but that only one word has been chosen as a new lemma. In the last example, "Accesco," the compiler has forgotten his objective of setting French in the lemmatic position. Occasionally one French lemma will serve for more than a single Latin gloss, but in this case each gloss had earlier been an independent lemma:

Adjoustement	addicio .onis	f
	addimentum, idem	n
	additamentum .ti, idem	n.

Metalanguage in French is not frequent in the *Glossarium gallico-latinum* and only a few rare examples are found.[8] Generally, the simple definitional structure parallels the simple organizational structure.

The Latin-French Lexicon in Montpellier H110 and Stockholm N78

The Latin-French lexicon found in Montpellier H110 and Stockholm N78 is one of the two larger and more complex of the bilingual dictionaries compiled in medieval France, the other being the *Dictionarius* of Firmin Le Ver. The first manuscript dates from the late fourteenth, the second from the mid-fifteenth century; the Le Ver was completed in 1440.[9]

---

[8]There are some examples: *Dedessus* - desuper - adverbium vel *preposition servant a accusatif, Espicial* - come l'en dit: mon amy espicial.

[9]The datings for the Montpellier and Stockholm manuscripts are as yet approximate, but in the explicit to the *Dictionarius* Le Ver tells us that "per viginti annorum curricula et amplius cum maxima pena et labore insimul congregavi, compilavi et conscripsi" and that

In contrast to the *Abavus, Aalma,* and the *Glossarium gallico-latinum,* the *Montpellier-Stockholm* contains much Latin in its composition, but there is a fairly clear pattern to the distribution of Latin and French usage. Most of the definitional material is in French with, as Pierre Nobel has shown, extensive variety of kind. There are some entries with single equivalents, many with multiple equivalents, others still with explicative definitions:

Abusive - adverbium qualitatis - *quant on fait contre l'usage*

Acaris .dis - componitur ex ab et caris quod est gratia - *non gracieux, oublians les benefices receuz*

Acanto .as .avi .are - ex ad et canto .tas et mutatur 'd' in 'c' - *rechanter ou environ chanter*

Accedo .dis .cessi .cedere - ex ad et cedo .dis, cessi mutatur 'd' in 'c' - *aprochier*

Accelero .ras .avi .re - ex ad et celero .ras et mutatur 'd' in 'c' - *haster*

Accendo .dis .di .dere - ex ad et candeo .des et mutatur 'd' in 'c' - *alumer ou embraser*

Accentuo .as - verbum frequentativum - *souvent chanter, accentuer ou pronuncier.*

Almost all entries, however, contain attributional material in Latin relating to the Latin headword, that is grammatical, phonetic, or orthographical data, etymological information, including derivation and composition. Several entries contain definitional connectors such as *id est, dicitur, interpretatur,* etc. Generally one can say that most definitional material is in French and almost all metalinguistic material in Latin. There is, nonetheless, a substantial amount of Latin definitional material, which is preferred in certain circumstances:

a) There are a large number of transposed Greek and other foreign words which are usually glossed in Latin, sometimes with a French gloss added, giving a trilingual parallel:

"Qui dictus dictionarius anno domini millesimo quadringentesimo quadragesimo mensis Aprilis die ultimo completus fuit et finitus" (April 30, 1440). For Montpellier H110 see the preliminary study by Pierre Nobel, "La traduction du *Catholicon* contenue dans le manuscrit H110 de la Bibliothèque Universitaire de Montpellier," in Buridant, ed., *La Lexicographie,* pp. 157–83.

> Acha - grece, amenitas latine *doulceté*,
> Achas - grece, tristis latine, or
> Achobor - grece, mus latine *soris*;

b) Some relatively simple words are accompanied by an explanation of their sense and use in Latin:

> Abs - in quibusdam pro ab cum dictionibus insipientibus a 'c' componitur ut abscondo, abscindo et hunc a, ab, abs fere eandem significationem, galice *de*, or
>
> Accio .cis - ex cieo componitur cum ad et dicitur accieo .es, accivi, accitum et accio, actis .ivi .itum - *appeller ou huchier* et dicebatur accio, actis in eodem sensu secundum antiquos et ab utroque istorum descendit verbum desiderativum in 'so'; ab arcio antiquo debet dici accesso .sis sed quia arcesso descendit ab arceo .es et ideo causa differentie mutatum est primum 's' in 'r' in eo quod descendit ab arcio antiquo et dicitur arcerso .sis - Item ab accio moderno descendit acccesso .sis sed quia ab accedo .dis similiter descendit accesso .sis ideo causa differentie in eo quod venit ab accio mutatum est primum 's' in 'r': accerso .sis - invenitur ergo arcerso ars, arcio(?), arcesso ab arceo, accerso ab accio, accesso ab accedo - invenitur aliud verbum quarte coniugationis derivativum ab accerso in eadem significatione cum eo, scilicet accersio .sis;

c) There are some Latin headwords glossed in Latin only:

> Accidere - malum contingere facto, obtingere sorte, evenire,
> Acciare - facere ferrum durissimum, or
> Accessio - est emolumentum, lucrum; and

d) A few Latin headwords are glossed in Latin and French:

> Adnutum - .i. facile *legier*,
> Affore - .i. advenire *advenir*,
> Avocare - .i. separare *decevrer*, or
> Avello .lis .li .lere - aufferre, extirpare *c'est esrachier*.

The *Montpellier-Stockholm* lexicon has some bilingual features that are also found in the *Aalma*, all of which are evident in the other large bilingual dictionary of the pre-printing period, the *Dictionarius* of Firmin Le Ver.

These are:

1) the use of French in internal definitions;
2) the generalization of definitions;
3) the use of French as metalanguage; and
4) the fusion of Latin and French in some definitions.

Although the Le Ver *Dictionarius* and the *Montpellier-Stockholm* differ somewhat in presentation and structure, the two can be examined together in terms of the relationship of French and Latin within each text.

The *Dictionarius* of Firmin Le Ver

With the *Dictionarius* of Le Ver (*DLV*) we move to a different kind of bilingual dictionary. Here French is not the principal language of definition, although it is massively present. Both Latin and French serve as definitional languages in all possible combinations as we outlined in an earlier study: Latin only; French and Latin in equal and unequal proportions; and French only.[10] As in the *Montpellier-Stockholm* (*M-S*), there are extended definitions in both Latin and French, but the distribution of the two languages in the *DLV* does not parallel the other work.

"Internal" Definitions

There are at least two kinds of internal definitions that are apparent in the *DLV* and also found elsewhere. The first is especially a feature of the *DLV*'s particular bilingual character, which leads to a kind of internal matching of Latin glosses by French glosses:

Abiectarius .rii - .i. carpentarius, qui operatur de abiete *qui oeuvre de sapin*;
Abnormis et hoc .me - .i. sine regula, turpis, deformis *sans rieule, lais, deformés* -
  comparatur;
Absentaneus .ea .eum - qui se semper absentat *qui se absente tousjours*;
Absisto .stis, abstiti, caret supino - .i. longe stare vel cessare vel discedere *estre loings
  ou cesser ou aler s'ent*;

---

[10]Brian Merrilees and William Edwards, "Le statut du français dans le *dictionarius* de Firmin Le Ver," in *Du Manuscrit à l'imprimé* (Montréal: CERES, 1989), pp. 37–51.

Acceptus .pta .ptum - .i. carus, placitus, gratus, iocundus, acceptabilis .i. *chier,*
plaisans, agreables, joieux, acceptables; or
Ambio .bis .bivi .bire, ambitum - .i. circumdare *avironner* vel cupere *convoitier* et
proprie honorem *convoitier honneur.*

Sometimes the Latin seems to match the French that precedes:

Barbitonstrix .stricis - *barbiere, femme qui reit barbe* mulier que tondet barbam; or
Diptongus .gi .go - .i. *diptongue* scilicet *quant ii voieulx font une sillabe* .i.
conglutinatio duarum vocalium in eadem sillaba.

There are few of this type in the *M-S*, and most are in entries that are in
essence trilingual:

Accida - grece, genus pigmenti colati *une maniere de pigment*;
Acclus - Tuscorum lingua - .i. iunius mensis *ou mois de l'an, juing*;
Acha - grece, amenitas latine *doulceté*; or
Machinula .le - parva machina *petit engin ou composicion.*

A second kind of internal definition is where a French gloss is followed by
a French definition, which applies in the first instance of course to the
Latin lemma but which is equally applicable to the French:

DLV:
Acinacium .cii - .i. *gosse* vel cortices uvarum que post expressionem proiciuntur .i.
lenne, le marc qui demeure aprés le pressurage;
Legumen .minis - .i. *leguns* .i. *tramois, potages, si come feves, pois, esche*; or
Loramentum .menti - .i. *pilotemens, pilotis de bois fichiés en terre sus quoi on fait*
edefiche .i. concathenatio lignorum que solet fieri in fundamentis edificiorum
ubi non potest inveniri terra solida ad fundandum edificium.

M-S:
Adolescencia .cie - *jeunesce, fleur de aage qui dure de puis xv ans jusques a xxviii.*

In some cases the provision of a French example adds to the sense of a fully
developed internal entry:

Agnomino .nas .natum - *sournommer* .i. *appeller par son sournon, sicome Jehan du*
Bois .i. agnomine vocare vel agnomen imponere (*DLV*).

and in general the use of exemplary explanation adds an enlivening dimension to the French:

> Ablacto .ctas .ctatum - *ensevrer, sicome enfant on oste de la mamelle* .i. a lacte removere, extrahere et separare; or
> Balbutio .tis .tivi .tire - .i. male et incongrue loqui .i. *besguier, baubeter, sicome parlers de petis enfans qui ne scevent parler.*

Generalization of the Definition

There was a strong element of the encyclopedic in earlier monolingual Latin dictionaries such as the *Catholicon* with provision of specific information on some proper names or for important concepts, especially the theological. Both the *M-S* and the *DLV* are prone to generalize or simplify this information into generic terms. In the 1483 Venice edition of the *Catholicon*, the entry "Anima" is followed by almost one and one-half columns of text. In the *DLV*, the same entry is simply:

> Anima, anime - *ame* - ab alo, alis dicitur, eo quod nos alat - *ame* .i. vita corporis.

The *DLV* in many cases prefers a generic translation in Latin and a specific equivalent in French:

> Abrotanum .tani - herba est .i. *auroine*;
> Allauda .de - *alouette* avis quedam;
> Macedo .donis fuit quidam rex, unde; or
> Macedonia .donie - terra eius *Macedoine.*

The *M-S* can vary, with either Latin or French being generic:

> Achala .le - provincia terre *la province de Troye*;
> Athenis - flumen Gallie *un fleuve*; or
> Athesis - flumen Verone *un autre fleuve.*

Metalanguage

The metalanguage in all medieval Latin-French bilingual dictionaries is almost exclusively Latin, but all show some cases of the use of French for metalinguistic purposes. In some cases this is a translated equivalent of the appropriate Latin term or expression. . . . Often these translations seem like an unconscious reflex as though the compiler or scribe may not have been aware of the change. The following examples are taken from Le Ver's *Dictionarius*, though we are aware that French metalanguage appears earlier in the *Aalma* and that French grammatical terminology can be traced to the twelfth century:[11]

> A - *est une preposition qui sert a l'ablatis*;
> A - *est ossi interjection de douleur*;
> Affore - *estre presens - infinitis de* assum, ades;
> Botrio .trionis - *ossi le dit on pour vergus*; and
> De - *preposition qui sert a l'ablatis case,* ut: de deo, de pane, etc.

The *Montpellier-Stockholm* also has a number of examples of a similar nature, as well as some that are fuller:

> Achas - *propre nom* - interpretatur apprehendens.. (Stockh.);
> Ancillor .aris - vide in Ancillo et nota quod ancillo est verbum deponens...quod sub voce passivi habet sensum activi - *c'est celuy qui a la lettre du passif, c'est a dire qui se decline comme verbe passif et a la significacion active si come* ancillor *je amenistre* - .laris et .lare *du amenistre*;
> Adortor .aris - *anciennement estoit verbe commun*[12] et dicitur ex ad et quero [*sic*] - *acquerir ou prendre*; and
> Age - *adverbe - c'est dire, faire ou commencier*.

Most of the terminology we have found is, in form, a simple adaptation of the Latin, and we remain aware that its reference point remains Latin. However, small as the amount of French metalanguage is in texts such as the *DLV* and the *M-S*, its use reflects the increased complexity of those two dictionaries compared to the others we have discussed, a more direct heritage of the large unilingual Latin lexicons of Papias, Hugutio, and Johannes Balbus.

---

[11]See, in particular, Thomas Städtler, *Zu den Anfängen der französischen Grammatiksprache: Textausgaben und Wortschatzstudien* (Tübingen: Niemeyer, 1988).

[12]Cf. "commune antiquitus fuit," in Papias, *Elementarium doctrinae*, ed. Violetta de Angelis (repr. Turin: Bottega d'Erasmo, 1966).

Language Mixing

If it may seem speculative, as we noted in the previous section, to reflect on the intentions of compiler or scribe, we can turn to another feature of the *DLV* and the *M-S* that indicates how closely Latin and French were integrated in these manuscripts. Both texts show definitional and metalinguistic material that combines the two in some fashion even to the point where expressions begin in one language and end in the second:

DLV:

Agnatus .ti vel Agnata .te possunt substantive declinari et nota quod agnati sunt
    cousin du costé du pere, cognati sunt *cousin de par la mere;*

Laberintus .ti - .i. perplexum edificium, sic erat domus Dedali *ou nulz qui y entre*
    n'en scet issir; or

Ultra eciam est prepositio *servans a l'accusatis* quando regit casum - .i. *oultre,* ut:
    ultra Renum *oultre le Rin.*

M-S:

Achivi - *Grieux descendans* de filio Iovis;

Munus .eris - a munio .nis - *don deservy* sed donum est ex gratia; or

Musica .sce - a mus pro terra vel pro *souris* dicitur - *mouche.*

A further proof that a measure of bilingualism was expected is to be found in the use of *etc.* following a French definition. In many cases the *etc.* indicates that the reader will be capable of providing his own translation:

Abominarium .rii - .i. liber ubi abominationes scribebantur *le livre etc.;*

Accinctus .a .um - .i. preparatus, ornatus *chaint, etc.;* and

Adiectivo .vas .vatum - adiectivum facere vel adiective ponere *faire adjectis ou etc.*

One could argue that these examples are of incidental importance for an analysis of bilingual dictionaries, but I rather think they signify an inherently bilingual state of mind of the lexicographer and of his expectations for his audience. A clean dichotomous or diglossic functioning of each language in a separate sphere is not what the data show. If the overriding purpose is the explanation of one language by the other, none of these dictionary texts functions in a unidirectional manner. The interplay of language is apparent at every step. Indeed, the preface to one of the copies of the *Aalma* indicates that bidirectionality is part of the compiler/scribe's intention, as is suggested in this prologue to a copy of the *Aalma* in BN lat. 14748:

> Afin que plus tost et plus prestement les escoliers et autres puissent mettre le latin en françois et le françois en latin des moz de gramaire et par especial du livre nommé *Catholicon*, En ce livret nommé le *Mirouer des nouveaux escoliers* est mis le latin et après le françois des moz plus necessaires et acoustumez contenus ou dit *Catholicon* et d'aucuns autres moz.

It is clear then that the user of bilingual dictionaries was expected to function in both languages even to the extent of knowing how to locate words in the first language through the second. This confirms evidence that we have already provided, which implies that the compiler was comfortably bilingual and sought more than just minimal bilingual competence from his intended audience.

Translation and Neologisms

There are many other aspects of dictionary translation that we have not touched in this chapter. One in particular is the use of neologisms. Firmin Le Ver was an unusual creator of neologisms in that most of the new words he chose to render Latin headwords failed to survive in French and are to be found only in his *Dictionarius* and two related texts, the *Glossarium gallico-latinum* of BN lat. 7684 that we have already examined and an incunable, the *Vocabularius familiaris*, published by Guillaume Le Talleur around 1490 and again by Martin Morin in 1500. Le Ver creates a number of new forms that can be divided into two kinds. The first is comprised of those which closely correspond to the Latin lemma and gallicize the resulting form:

amabilitas	*amabletés*
expedibilitas	*expediabletés*
favorabilitas	*favorabletés*
finibilitas	*finabletés*

habitabilitas	*habitabletés*
hospitabilitas	*hospitabletés.*

The second type deconstructs the Latin and uses an established base in French:

acceptabilitas	*agreabletés*
accessibilitas	*approchabletés*
agibilitas	*faisabletés*
appetabilitas	*desirabletés*
binitas	*deusimetés*
brevitas	*courtetés*
ledibilitas	*blechabletés.*

We have argued in a recent paper that many of Le Ver's French neologisms appear to be created to match derived Latin subheadwords generated in his macro-entry presentation. They remain hapaxes, confined to their dictionary context, neither attested in other texts nor even recorded by the *Französisches Etymologisches Wörterbuch*. For a consideration of neologisms in the Montpellier lexicon, we again refer to the preliminary study published by Pierre Nobel in 1986.[13]

The Integration of French in the Dictionary Structure

Dictionary entries are at their simplest level composed of headword and definition (lemma and gloss), but few dictionaries are limited to just that form. In recent research we have been analyzing the development of attributional and other metalinguistic information in medieval lexicography from Papias through to Le Ver, and we have paid particular attention to three positions where such ancillary information is to be found. These are the post-lemmatic, the post-definitional, and the marginal. Although all three might be used by simple dictionaries such as the *Abavus* or the *Aalma*, their regular and frequent use is the mark of more complex compilations such as the *Montpellier-Stockholm* and, especially, Le Ver's *Dictionarius*. In

---

[13]Nobel, "La traduction du *Catholicon*," pp. 165–66.

most cases the language used in these three positions is Latin. French does occur in the post-lemmatic and the post-definitional, but never in the marginal position, which is reserved for abbreviations indicating gender for nouns and voice for verbs. In a dictionary as highly organized as the *DLV* the range of definitional positions also increases the structural complexity and, because both Latin and French serve as definitional languages, questions of language priority are introduced.[14] These are elements that are also related to the bilingual character of the *DLV* and that we have only begun to explore.

Medieval Latin-French dictionaries represent an important stage in the development of the dictionary in France and in the increasing importance of the French language. The full integration of French into a unilingual dictionary will take a further century, but by then we are no longer in the realm of bilingual translation.

---

[14]So far our sample analyses show that French occurs as the first definition in about 35 percent of entries, but this has to be weighed with other considerations inherent in Le Ver's macro-entry structure, which allows a certain flexibility in the matching of subheadwords and implied definitions.

Troy Book:
How Lydgate Translates Chaucer into Latin

Christopher Baswell

This essay explores some dynamics of linguistic prestige, political power, and national myth in the second decade of the fifteenth century, when England was still militantly pursuing its dreams of continental empire under the leadership of Henry V, even as its linguistic, judicial, and administrative habits divided it ever more deeply from the Continent. England in the later fourteenth and fifteenth centuries was a nation actively involved in cultural and political self-translation. It still cherished imperial ambitions to replicate King Arthur's conquests and reverse the *translatio imperii* that had brought Brutus to England, and thereby to re-establish the Angevin empire that had earlier exploited this same set of myths. And yet England was a nation increasingly functioning in a native language with a resurgent cultural and political authority. In these decades, Middle English was beginning to dominate in the insular worlds of the court, education, law, and to some extent even religion.[1] By examining John Lydgate's *Troy Book,* written at the express commission of Henry, I will try to articulate the shifting claims and intentions of the English language as a bearer of imperial myth. In particular, I explore the paradox of renewing a myth of continental empire by translating a Latin text into an insular tongue that excludes the very continental objects of its imperial message.

The *Troy Book* announces itself as a translation of the *Historia destructionis Troiae* of Guido delle Colonne, but inserts alternate narrative

---

[1]For a review of these developments see John H. Fisher, "A Language Policy for Lancastrian England," *Proceedings of the Modern Language Association* 107 (1992): 1168–71.

and linguistic sources, particularly in the form of Geoffrey Chaucer's *Troilus and Criseyde*. Lydgate thus imports Chaucer and Chaucer's English as competitors, even successors, to Guido and the authority of his Latin. I will claim that the *Troy Book* aims, by these means, to create an English language of imperial exclusivity and stature. Lydgate does this largely by a series of strategies raising the hierarchical register of English to that of Latin; and in particular he does so by repeatedly inserting Chaucerian narratives and language into his translation of Guido's Latin. That is, Lydgate carries Chaucer over—translates him—into a "Latin" author.

Commissioned just before his accession to the throne and written right across the reign of King Henry V, Lydgate's *Troy Book* is elaborately and explicitly sited in the historical circumstances of its author and patron. Further, it shows an extremely articulate engagement with forms of linguistic authority and a very self-conscious sense of the imperial work of *translatio*.[2] The book announces itself as a faithful translation of Guido delle Colonne's enormously popular *History of the Destruction of Troy*, but it takes on more of Lydgate's own voice and perspective as it goes on.[3] In particular, at

---

[2] *Lydgate's Troy Book. A.D. 1412–20*, ed. Henry Bergen, 4 vols. in 3, EETS, e.s., 97, 103, 106, 126 (London: K. Paul, Trench, Trubner & Co. Ltd., 1906–35; repr. 1975). In an important and richly learned new article, Lee Patterson explores the historical setting of Lydgate's poetry and Henry V's kingship, especially his campaigns in France, as well as the historiographical construction in the same period (partly by Lydgate) of a unified English identity, with Henry as its defining monarch. See "Making Identities in Fifteenth-Century England: Henry V and John Lydgate," in *New Historical Literary Study: Essays on Reproducing Texts, Representing History*, ed. Jeffrey N. Cox and Larry J. Reynolds (Princeton: Princeton University Press, 1993), pp. 69–107.

[3] For a systematic comparison of the two texts see Bergen, ed., *Lydgate's Troy Book*, 4: 93–210. Guido delle Colonne, *Historia destructionis Troiae*, ed. Nathaniel Edward Griffin (Cambridge, Mass.: Mediaeval Academy of America, 1936); trans. Mary E. Meek (Bloomington: Indiana University Press, 1974). Lois Ebin offers a useful analysis of Lydgate's strategies in handling Guido, as he moves from Guido's thirty-five brief books "into five distinct units designed structurally to emphasize the theme of the loss which results from war"; see her *John Lydgate* (Boston: Twayne, 1985), pp. 42–52. For Lydgate's general fidelity to the substance of Guido see C. David Benson, *The History of Troy in Middle English Literature: Guido della Colonne's Historia Destructionibus Troiae in Medieval England* (Woodbridge: Brewer, 1980), pp. 113–15.

several crucial points, Lydgate inserts Geoffrey Chaucer's Troy into the framework of Guido's narrative. By this and other means, he replaces an initial rhetoric of the inimitability of the Latin Guido with a rhetoric of the inimitable English Chaucer. Chaucer's laureate status and Chaucer's English thus become the sources of an accessible but elevated national poetic language. And that language, readable by many but imitable by almost none, bodies forth a poem of England's imperial and genealogical origin— Troy—in which is implicit an argument for England's current imperial claims on the Continent.[4] There is thus a double imperial project in the *Troy Book*. Lydgate not only tells the history of Troy and suggests its revival among its British descendants but also repeatedly pulls the poem's focus to the verbal medium of its narrative, to Chaucer as its source, and by implication to himself as the surviving if inadequate channel of that source.

Lydgate brackets the *Troy Book* with an elaborate Prologue and even longer closing verses, by which he inserts the Trojan narrative within this double dynamic. First, in the Prologue and final section, he raises themes of writing, its crucial contribution to (a highly ideological) truth and the survival of truth, and the mobility of truth across times and languages. I will return to these points below. Second and just as important, though, Lydgate uses his opening and closing verses to generate a second story of *translatio* in addition to that of Troy. That is, he carefully narrates the historical moments at which he began and completed his translation of Guido; and he includes thereby a more inferential narrative of the imperial projects his patron was engaged in during that same period: accession to the English throne by patrilineage, continental conquest, marriage to Catherine Valois, daughter of the king of France, and the diplomatic activities that made him heir to the throne of France.

---

[4]For a discussion of Lydgate and Chaucer in the *Troy Book* see C. David Benson, "Critic and Poet: What Lydgate and Henryson Did to Chaucer's *Troilus and Criseyde*," *Modern Language Quarterly* 53/1 (1992): 23–33. Lydgate's later work as an imperial and genealogical propagandist under Henry VI is discussed by J. W. McKenna, "Henry VI and the Dual Monarchy: Aspects of Royal Political Propaganda, 1422–1432," *Journal of the Warburg and Courtauld Institutes* 28 (1965): 153–55. For a broader survey of national propaganda see P. S. Lewis, "War Propaganda and Historiography in Fifteenth-Century France and England," *Transactions of the Royal Historical Society*, 5th series, 15 (1965): 1–21.

Together, these strategies make Lydgate and Henry V into intriguing mirror figures, using words and acts respectively to translate Troy and revive its empire for its British heirs. In a recent essay on Lydgate and Henry V, Lee Patterson presents telling arguments for an overt and uninterrupted English rhetoric of unity and identity, as much for English empire as for its new emperor, Henry V; and he finds that rhetoric both in Lydgate's poems (particularly the *Siege of Thebes*) and in contemporary English history writing. But this rhetoric of unity, Patterson suggests, has a double and ultimately incompatible focus:

> On the one hand, it had insisted on English integrity versus French duplicity, presenting England as politically unified and ethically coherent while France was riven by internal divisions and corrupted by duplicity. Yet on the other hand, it had also claimed that the war was undertaken to heal the rift between the fraternal nations England and France.[5]

Patterson suggests the anxiety around this rift reveals itself, in part, in Lydgate's "discourse of identity and difference . . . deployed with an insistence, even an obsessiveness that pushes it to the breaking point."[6]

Patterson's demonstration of comparable stresses in Lydgate's poems and history writing and public rhetoric is compelling.[7] In what follows, however, I will be looking at what I consider to be more self-consciously contested moments in the *Troy Book*—delays, ruptures, *mises en abyme*. These, I show, suggest a rather different though equally stressful contest to generate and then lay claim to an English verbal eloquence worthy of an English imperial poet.[8] This is enacted in a poem whose creation is explicitly coterminous with the monarch's efforts to claim imperial power

---

[5]Patterson, "Making Identities," p. 89.

[6]Patterson, "Making Identities," p. 92.

[7]Patterson, "Making Identities," pp. 92–95.

[8]Patterson includes the *Troy Book* in his discussion, but somewhat as a straw man, an instance of controlled imperial mythmaking against which he situates what he sees as the greater strains and complexities of the *Siege of Thebes* and the "Title and Pedigree of Henry VI." See "Making Identities," pp. 74, 80, 82, and 97.

in France, a power elaborately linked to the story of Troy. Yet the two claims to power, linguistic and imperial, finally are enacted in quite contrary ways, through the absence or presence of a legitimating beloved: Lydgate's mourning of his beloved master Chaucer (encoded, we will see, as the abandoning Criseyde), and Henry's importation of a unifying imperial bride (who will reverse the sliding of Criseyde and the results of the rape of Helen).

In the Prologue, Lydgate carefully situates how he began his translation, "For to obeie with-oute variaunce / My lordes byddyng fully and plesaunce" (Prologue, lines 73–74).[9] This commission comes while "Henri the firthe" (Pro., line 96) is yet on the throne and Lydgate's patron is still

> the worthy prynce of Walys,
> To whom schal longe by successioun
> For to gouerne Brutys Albyoun. (Pro., lines 102–04)

Lydgate goes on to date the exact moment of taking up Henry's commission, in October of the fourteenth year "of his fadris regne" (Pro., line 124), adding an elaborate astrological periphrasis.[10] Within six months, the worthy Prince of Wales had become King Henry V, in a "successioun" quite different from that of his father, though not without its own initial strains.[11]

Roughly eight years later (the dating is tricky), Lydgate completes his redaction of Guido and turns again to his patron, dedicating the work now to King Henry the Fifth—"Herry the Fyfthe, the noble worthi kyng" (5.3376)—in the eighth year of his reign and after his conquests in France. So Henry has been engaged in an eastward *translatio imperii* even as Lydgate has translated the great story behind the Trojans' westward *translatio imperii*. Harry the Fifth thus replicates but inverts the Trojan disaster, echoing his nation's and his ancestors' imperial prehistory but at

---

[9]All quotations are from the Bergen edition.

[10]For this and other such astrological passages see Derek Pearsall, *John Lydgate* (Charlottesville: University Press of Virginia, 1970), p. 126.

[11]See Patterson, "Making Identities," pp. 77–79.

the same time redeeming it in these altered circumstances. Such related acts of militancy fulfill Henry's aim of chivalric imitation, articulated in the Prologue; he wanted Lydgate's translation to help remember "the prowesse of olde chiualrie" and

> To fyn only, vertu for to swe,
> Be example of hem, and also for to eschewe
> The cursyd vice of slouthe and ydelnesse. (Pro., lines 78, 81–83)[12]

Henry V, as much as Lydgate, translates Troy into English.

In the eight or so years that Lydgate worked at his translation, Henry V was pursuing a war of imperial reclamation in Normandy and France, which culminated in his marriage with Catherine, daughter of Charles VI of France, and the Treaty of Troyes.[13] The closing section of *Troy Book* leads the reader through these events. It calls Henry "Of Normaundie the myghti conquerour," who has "conquered his herytage ageyn" and will "regne in Fraunce by lyneal discent" (5.3381–91). Henry's succession is guaranteed not just by lineage, though. The Treaty of Troyes, sealed 21 May 1420, made him heir to Charles VI, and his marriage with Catherine took place June the second.[14] The closing section of *Troy Book* refers explicitly to both triumphs, beginning with the treaty:

> He to reioisshe, with-oute more delay,
> Septer & crowne after the kynges day,
> As it is clerly, in conclusioun,
> Enrolled vp in the conuencioun. (5.3395–98)[15]

The long process of Henry's spectacular continental victories (such as Agincourt), followed by inconclusive campaigns, protracted negotiations,

---

[12]"Only for the purpose of pursuing virtue / By their example, and also to avoid the vice of sloth and idleness."

[13]See Patterson, "Making Identities," pp. 79–83, 87–89, and further references there.

[14]Ernest F. Jacob, *The Fifteenth Century, 1399–1485* (Oxford: Clarendon, 1961), pp. 183–87.

[15]Patterson discusses similar references to the Treaty of Troyes found in the *Siege of Thebes*, "Making Identities," pp. 74–75.

and painful diplomacy, could have seemed strikingly analogous to Lydgate's narrative of ancient events in Troy.[16] Other aspects of Henry's reign, though, must equally have suggested an inversion and vindication of the fall and dispersal of his distant mythic ancestors. In the very months that Lydgate was finishing up his translation, Henry was moving in France and his conquered lands of Normandy with a retinue that included his new wife, Catherine, King James of Scotland, who was his long-time prisoner, the duke of Bedford, and several other English earls; he was acting jointly with Philip, duke of Burgundy; and he was the acknowledged heir to the throne of France. Taken together, this could be presented as a picture of spectacular imperial triumph, and the consolidation (however temporary it later proved to be) of lands long divided and contested: "To maken oon that longe hath be tweyne" (5.3410). It makes a telling moment in which to present Henry as a reverser of the Trojan disaster who replicates its greatest power while avoiding its weaknesses.[17] And it was an important moment for Lydgate to insert himself into the myth of restoration by presenting the Englishing of Troy to the Englishman who has replicated Troy's triumphs and redeemed its disasters.

The whole closing section of the *Troy Book* thus encodes England as a mirror of Troy, reviving its imperial glory but inverting those self-destructive sins that the book's readers have just encountered. As we have seen, Lydgate now emphasizes treaty, not military power, as the basis of

---

[16]For a survey of Henry's campaigns and negotiations in France see Jacob, *The Fifteenth Century*, pp. 149–89; and Ernest Jacob, *Henry V and the Invasion of France* (London: Hodder & Stoughton, 1947).

[17]Henry is represented, in fact, as an almost Christ-like redeemer. His peace will restore "the tyme . . . aureat" (5.3399–3400), Lydgate says, in a passage that echoes Virgil's Fourth Eclogue, often interpreted throughout the Middle Ages as a prophecy of Christ. And in a nicely ambiguous line, Henry is later called "The souereyn lord and the prince of pes" (5.3416). A contemporary sermon explicitly views Henry as a savior and celestial warrior; Roy M. Haines, "Church, Society and Politics in the Early Fifteenth Century as Viewed from an English Pulpit," *Studies in Church History* 12 (1975): 143–57, esp. pp. 150–51, 155. In an analogous move, the coinage of the still-infant Henry VI will present him as a savior; see McKenna, "Henry VI and the Dual Monarchy," p. 149. For the elaborate praise paid to Henry's own piety see Patterson, "Making Identities," p. 84.

Henry's imperial stature. He focuses, too, on the peace-making role of marriage by diplomatic arrangement, not rape:

> And alliaunce of the blod royal,
> That is knet vp by bonde of mariage,
> Of werre shal voide aweie the rage,
> To make pes with brighte bemys shyne. (5.3420–23)

Catherine replicates but inverts Helen of Troy, through an exogamous marriage that will bring peace and combine two nations, not set them at war; and she and Henry successfully enact the Trojans' failed plan of a peace-making marriage between Polyxena and Achilles.[18]

Lydgate's hopes for Catherine's role as peace-maker between England and France, a "mene a-twixe bothe two" (5.3426), are expressed in lines that, I would suggest, tie the completion of his linguistic translation to Catherine's geographical translation from France to England:

> And I hope hir gracious arryvaille
> In-to this lond shal so moche availle,
> That Ioie, honour, and prosperite,
> With-oute trouble of al aduersite,
> Repeire shal, & al hertly plesaunce . . .
> . . . .
> Sothly, al this I hope ye shal sen
> Come in-to lond with this noble quene,
> That we shal seyn of hert, & feyne nought:
> Blessed be she that al this hath vs brought! (5.3429–42)

These lines narrowly situate the date at which Lydgate is composing the valedictory section of the *Troy Book*. Lydgate has already said it is about 1420, the eighth year of Henry V, but this could extend as late as 20 March 1421 by modern reckoning, depending on when Lydgate calculates

---

[18]For the elaborate narration of Achilles' infatuation with "Pollycene," and the negotiations for their marriage and an ensuing peace, see *Troy Book* 4.551–956, 1524–66, 2178–223, 2345–86, 2498–545 (where Achilles' military pride overcomes his love for Pollycene), 2589–619, and 3098–233 (where Hecuba plots the assassination of Achilles by Paris).

the New Year.[19] The marriage, 2 June 1420, has already taken place (it "is knet up," see above), but its peace-making impact is emphatically left in the future tense.[20] Now, Henry and Catherine returned to England in the first days of February 1421, stopping at Dover and Canterbury; Henry went on to London without Catherine, who followed on 21 February and was crowned on 23 February.[21] This moment of Henry's triumphal return, and the hope of a move from militant glory to marital peace, correspond very closely to the tone and detail of Lydgate's closing section in the *Troy Book*. I would hypothesize that this section of *Troy Book* records a ritual presentation of the narrative of one empire, made by Lydgate, to the ruler of its modern analogue, Henry V, at the moment of his triumph, as both look toward the arrival of their peace-making queen.[22]

The most powerful expressions of English dominance in such a setting are, of course, Lydgate's very language and the native British models it so persistently promotes. The Prologue and closing sections of the *Troy Book*, I now want to suggest, are as attentive to issues of linguistic dominion as they are to military conquest; and the body of the narrative they bracket also is a site in which a newly prestigious British eloquence (in the person of Chaucer) comes to contest and conquer its Mediterranean, Latin forebear (Guido).[23]

---

[19]It is "a thousand & foure hundrid yere, / And twenti ner" (5.3368–76). For varying starting-points of the year of grace see C. R. Cheney, ed., *Handbook of Dates for Students of English History* (London: Royal Historical Society, 1970), pp. 3–6; for regnal years of Henry IV and V see p. 22.

[20]See the quotation just above, 5.3429–42.

[21]Jacob, *The Fifteenth Century*, pp. 192–95.

[22]In later lines, Lydgate asks God when Henry will have "al set in pes and reste, . . . / To sende hym home" (5.3452–55). This could suggest that the book is finished after the marriage but before Henry's return in February. But the return was known to be temporary; Henry still had war business to prosecute in France, to which indeed he had to return hurriedly in early June. I think these lines anticipate that necessity and look forward to Henry's second, final return "Long after, in Ioie and in quyete / For to regnen in his royal sete!" (5.3457–58).

[23]For a general discussion of Lydgate's linguistic ambitions in the *Troy Book* see Ebin, *John Lydgate*, pp. 47, 51–52.

As already mentioned above, Lydgate's Prologue thematizes a major linguistic project, along with its narrative setting of Lancastrian patronage and succession. The Prologue situates translation and writing—and the powers and interests inherent therein—more generally along three issues: nationhood, class, and history itself. Prince Henry commissions this translation, it is claimed, for reasons of broad accessibility to high and low estates alike, and for national pride:

> By-cause he wolde that to hyghe and lowe
> The noble story openly were knowe
> In oure tonge, aboute in euery age,
> And y-writen as wel in oure langage
> As in latyn and in frensche it is;
> That of the story the trouthe we nat mys
> No more than doth eche other nacioun:
> This was the fyn of his entencioun. (Pro., lines 111–18)

Such a connection of language and national identity aims to erase the polylingualism of the English past, even its present. Instead, it seeks to identify a nation with each language, and with a more or less overt political purpose. For the emphasis of the passage just quoted shifts language distinctions from the earlier paradigm of class (aristocratic French *vs.* mercantile and common English) to the paradigm of geographical nationhood; distinctions of class and genealogy are implicitly erased, and all Englishmen are invited to line up behind Henry's imperial claims. Lydgate's move is fully consonant with the notion of a Lancastrian language policy, reaching out toward the commons, as recently discussed by John Fisher.[24]

Within this context, Henry and Lydgate turn to the authoritative, antique source of the "Troye Boke, I-made be dayes olde" (Pro., line 148).

---

[24]"A Language Policy," pp. 1168–80, esp. pp. 1170–71. Fisher presents strong arguments that Lydgate may have been in the immediate circle of the future Henry V while Henry was studying at Oxford in the years between 1398 and 1403; see pp. 1172–73. Fisher discusses the passage quoted above, p. 1176. Pearsall cites the passage as well, and rightly calls the *Troy Book* a "status symbol, an attempt to define and consolidate the new status of English," *John Lydgate*, p. 125. See also Patterson, "Making Identities," p. 82.

Lydgate then breaks up this single "book," however, into its variant and sometimes *un*truthful ancient versions (Homer, Ovid, Virgil, Dares and Dictys, Cornelius Nepos) before citing its truest if more recent redactor, "but late in comparisoun" (Pro., line 353) with the preceding list:

> And of Columpna Guydo was his name,
> Whiche had in writyng passyng excellence.
> For he enlvmyneth by crafte & cadence
> This noble story with many fresche colour
> Of rhetorik, and many riche flour
> Of eloquence to make it sownde bet
> He in the story hath ymped in and set,
> That in good feythe I trowe he hath no pere
> To rekne alle that write of this matere,
> As in his boke ye may beholde and se. (Pro., lines 360–69)

Lydgate's admiring description beautifully performs and almost covers over the shifting valuation of ancientness and rhetorical skill that was typical of late medieval redactions of classical story. Guido transmits a book from "dayes olde," but authority in his case has shifted (in theory) from antiquity to accuracy, a value, however, which quickly shades (in practice) into "crafte & cadence."[25]

This slippage among rhetoric, oldness, and accuracy as sources of authority begins a process of "antiquating" and authorizing Guido. He too is thus placed in a hierarchy, in which Lydgate assumes—or initially claims to assume—a very lowly position. That textual humility may be as problematic, though, and ultimately as contested, as the social humility he assumes before Henry.

Lydgate does, repeatedly and explicitly, assert his incapacity and the incapacity of his very language, in the face of Guido's Latin eloquence. Lydgate protests:

---

[25]For the double appeal of Guido's "truthfulness and eloquent style" see also Ebin, *John Lydgate*, pp. 41–42. For discussion of this passage and Lydgate's attitude toward Guido's style see Benson, *History of Troy*, pp. 98–106.

> I am so dulle, certeyn, that I ne can
> Folwen Guydo, that clerke, that coryous man,
> Whiche in latyn hath be rethorik
> So set his wordis, that I can nat be lyke. (2.169–72; see also 159–202)

Later he again asserts, "I wante flouris also of rethorik, / To sue his florischyng or his gey peynture" (2.3680–81). One could multiply examples indefinitely.[26]

For all the authority of his Latin rhetoric, however, and the militant and chivalric examples in his narrative, Guido presents problems. Not only is he introduced as a stylist who cannot be imitated but further, whatever his accomplishment, Guido is foreign; he writes in Latin, and Latin is not what King Henry is after. In reaction to both of these problems, Lydgate increasingly inserts the voice, and the sentence, of his alternate, native master, Chaucer. Lydgate will increasingly replace a Latin model of rhetorical linguistic accomplishment—"O Guydo maister" (Pro., line 372)—with a native model of accomplished eloquence in the person of "My maister Chaucer" (5.3521; see also 3.4197 and 4215).[27] In the very process of the translation, then, Lydgate translates Chaucer's English into the social and political position that at the beginning was registered by Guido's Latin. This shifting voice produces another kind of national contest that is parallel with the militant national contests of Trojans and Greeks, British and French: a linguistic contest to succeed Guido's Latin with an English eloquence that is nonetheless as laureate as its predecessor.[28] The voice of

---

[26]Pearsall, *John Lydgate*, surveys these and other examples of Lydgate's persistent habit of amplification, especially in terms of Lydgate's debt to the tradition of rhetorical topics; see pp. 129–51.

[27]Lydgate's very word order may reflect the shift from Latin to English models. Further, this overt insertion of Chaucerian language within Guidonian narrative neatly complements Lee Patterson's point that Lydgate inserts the *Siege of Thebes* into the *Canterbury Tales*, as a story told on the return journey; see Patterson, "Making Identities," pp. 75–77. For further examples of Lydgate's imitation (often clumsy) and echoing of Chaucer, see Benson, *History of Troy*, pp. 99–104; and for Chaucer's influence on Lydgate's sense of classical history see Benson, *History of Troy*, pp. 107–13.

[28]Fisher discusses the setting of politics and patronage behind the production of deluxe Chaucer manuscripts about this same time; see his "A Language Policy," pp. 1173–75.

Chaucer begins calling as early as the Prologue, where occasional Chaucerian phrases emerge even as ancient texts and Guido's authority are being
praised. Lydgate honors those ancient writers who place the truth in books,
"And with the keye of remembraunce it schet" (Pro., line 224), yet the
writer he actually echoes in this praise is Chaucer and his famous image in
the Prologue to *The Legend of Good Women*: "And yf that olde bokes were
aweye, / Yloren were of remembraunce the keye."[29] At the close of the
Prologue, we have seen, Lydgate turns to the inimitable excellence of Guido
among narrators of Troye:

> To whom I seie, knelyng on my knee:
> Laude and honour & excellence of fame,
> O Guydo maister, be vn-to thi name,
> That excellest by souereinte of stile
> Alle that writen this mater to compile.
> Whom I schal folwe as nyghe as euer I may. . . . (Pro., lines 370–75)

This gesture of humble deference again has a noble progenitor in the
Chaucer of *The Legend*, who also takes to his knees in deference to
Alceste and then addresses Virgil in terms strikingly similar to Lydgate's
praise of Guido:

> Glorye and honour, Virgil Mantoan,
> Be to thy name! and I shal, as I can,
> Folwe thy lanterne, as thow gost byforn. . . . (The Legend of Dido, lines 924–26)[30]

This begins an important triangulation, in which Guido receives praises
once accorded to Virgil, but Lydgate is allowed thereby to speak in the
words and posture of Virgil's English follower and his own poetic
progenitor, Chaucer.[31]

---

[29] F Prologue, lines 25–26. *The Riverside Chaucer*, 3rd ed., Larry D. Benson, general ed.
(Boston: Houghton Mifflin, 1987); all further quotations are from this edition.

[30] For Chaucer on his knees see F Prologue, lines 115–17, 308–12, and 455.

[31] I argue elsewhere that exactly in the Prologue to *The Legend*, and in the The Legend of
Dido, Chaucer himself was laying claim to a literary canonicity in the company of Virgil
and Ovid. See Christopher Baswell, *Virgil in Medieval England: Figuring the* Aeneid *from*

Informed readers of Chaucer would have continued to hear reminiscences as the Troy narrative unfolded, though it is difficult to say whether they are conscious, or just the inevitable result of Lydgate's own profound reading in his English master.[32] Lydgate employs Chaucer to replace Guido's linguistic register more openly at moments of excitement or high emotion. So when Paris first sets eyes on Helen (2.3642–54), Lydgate echoes Chaucer's description of Troilus's first sight of Criseyde (*Troilus* 1.102, 206–08, 267–74).

Not surprisingly, the echoes and references to Chaucer become densest when Lydgate arrives at Guido's story of Troilus and Criseyde; this, as Pearsall says, "initiates a movement in the poem in which the imaginative response is enormously heightened and intensified."[33] Lydgate's initial description of Criseyde is a doubling of Chaucer's portrait. Compare only these lines by Lydgate:

---

the Twelfth Century to Chaucer (Cambridge: Cambridge University Press, 1995), chap. 6, "Writing Reading Virgil: Chaucerian Authorities in the *House of Fame* and the *Legend of Dido*," sections 5 and 6.

[32] Consider this sequence of echoes, within scarcely more than two hundred lines in *Troy Book*, 2: 2.84 "make yow a merour of this Lamedoun," cf. *Troilus and Criseyde* 1.365 "Thus gan he make a mirour of his mynde"; 2.138 "As olde bokes maken mencioun," cf. The Manciple's Tale, line 106 "As olde bookes maken mencioun"; 2.139 "And many worthi and many noble knyght," cf. the Knight in the General Prologue; 2.144–45 "I fele also / My penne quake & tremble in my hond," cf. *Troilus and Criseyde*, 4.13–14 "And now my penne, allas, with which I write / Quaketh for drede of that I moste endite"; and 2.288 "Hector the secounde" (often repeated), cf. *Troilus* 2.158 "Ector the secounde." For another Chaucerian echo around the imagery of the mirror (a trope so widespread that its status as a specific "echo" seems to me problematic), see Anna Torti, "From 'History' to 'Tragedy': The Story of Troilus and Criseyde in Lydgate's *Troy Book* and Henryson's *Testament of Cresseid*," in *The European Tragedy of Troilus*, ed. Piero Boitani (Oxford: Clarendon, 1989), pp. 174–75.

[33] Pearsall, *John Lydgate*, p. 141; part of this intensity, I would add, derives from Lydgate's awareness that he now enters the poetic terrain of his English master. For general discussion see Torti, "From 'History' to 'Tragedy'," pp. 171–84. In Lydgate's use of Chaucer in these passages, Torti also sees "the effort, uneven though it may be, to confer on English the status Latin enjoyed," p. 184.

of schap, of face, and of chere,
Ther myghte be no fairer creature. (2.4738–39)
. . . .
And Saue hir browes Ioyneden y-fere,
No man koude in hir a lake espien. (2.4748–49)

and those by Chaucer:

Therto of shap, of face, and ek of cheere,
Ther myghte ben no fairer creature. (*Troilus and Criseyde*, 5.807–08)
. . . .
And, save hire browes joyneden yfeere,
Ther nas no lak, in aught I kan espien. (*Troilus and Criseyde*, 5.813–14)

Here, as in the description of Troilus that follows, Lydgate virtually inserts Chaucer into Guido's narrative, allowing these widely read passages to efface the "eloquence" of Guido.[34] When Troilus himself falls in love in the *Troy Book,* "my maister Chaucer" again practically takes over the text:

Lo! here the fyn of false felicite,
Lo! here the ende of worldly brotilnes,
Of fleshy lust, lo! here thunstabilnes,
Lo! here the double variacioun
Of worldly blisse and transmvtacioun. . . . (3.4224–28)[35]

Indeed, the quotation above is part of a passage in which Lydgate interrupts Guido's entire narrative, already much expanded as Lydgate inserts an ever more Chaucerian redaction of Troilus and Criseyde. At this breach in the narrative, Lydgate explicitly turns to Chaucer as a writer in English who equals the accomplishment of Mediterranean eloquence. "For he owre englishe gilte with his sawes"; that British language had been "Rude and boistous" until Chaucer

---

[34]For Lydgate's description of Troilus see 2.4861–95 and compare *Troilus* 5.827–40; throughout it is much closer to Chaucer than to Guido, though Lydgate adds to both in emphasizing Troilus's steadfastness, 2.4875–95. See Torti, "From 'History' to 'Tragedy'," p. 173.

[35]Compare the famous lines in *Troilus* 5.1828–32 and 5.1849–54.

> Gan oure tonge firste to magnifie,
> And adourne it with his elloquence.
> . . . .
> So that the laurer of oure englishe tonge
> Be to hym yove for his excellence. . . .
> . . . .
> That the report neuere after faille,
> Nor the honour dirked of his name,
> To be registred in the hous of fame
> Amonge other in the higheste sete,
> My maister Galfride, as for chefe poete
> That euere was yit in oure langage. (3.4237–57)

By gestures such as these, Lydgate makes Chaucer a genuine competitor for the rhetorical authority involved in translating classical story for a Lancastrian culture. And he suggests that English can be eloquent on a level with the Latin tradition of Guido—so eloquent in fact that Chaucer can (as in several passages quoted above) usurp the Latin source altogether. It is in this context that Lydgate would have Chaucer "registred in the house of fame," echoing still another famous Chaucerian poem and the very place in that poem where Chaucer dreamed of his own authoritative sources.[36]

Lydgate is often explicit about his poetic dependence on "my maister Galfride," moreover, casting Chaucer as an impeccable but—significantly— absent master of English eloquence:

> And Chaucer now, allas! is nat alyue
> Me to reforme, or to be my rede,
> For lak of whom slougher is my spede—
> The noble Rethor that alle dide excelle;
> For in makyng he drank of the welle
> Vndir Pernaso, that the Musis kepe. (3.550–55)

This crux of authoritative eloquence and absence makes Lydgate at once a mourner and an heir to a specifically British eloquence. It makes

---

[36]For the authors of Troy and its aftermath see *The House of Fame*, lines 1464–85. Lydgate may be remembering that authorities are contested there, too, literally struggling with one another on the pillars where Chaucer's narrator sees them.

Chaucerian English a language of prestige that can replace Latin, but that prestige (and Lydgate's power) depend too on its near-inaccessibility and inimitability. Like Latin itself in late medieval England, Chaucerian authority is validated by inaccessibility, the very absence of its source, and by its narrow channel of passage to a later world: in this case, Lydgate himself.

Of course, other claims are being laid on Chaucer in this period, and his canonical prestige is enhanced by institutionalizing gestures connected to the Lancastrian throne and even (John Fisher suggests) connected to Lydgate's immediate circle. We witness this especially in the production of "authoritative," *grande luxe* copies such as the Ellesmere manuscript.

Even while he makes Chaucer a competitor with Guido and a wider tradition of Latin rhetoric, even while he suggests an institutionalized laureate status for Chaucer, Lydgate is laying a very private claim on his English "maister." Some of this claim has its own aims of self-institutionalization, as I have suggested above, since Lydgate implicitly casts himself as a new if inadequate Chaucer. Even as he deprecates his own skills, we have seen, Lydgate most openly assumes the physical posture and sometimes the exact words of the master. And, absent the very master, Lydgate makes himself the medium of imitating the accomplishment of Chaucerian eloquence. This is typical of what Derek Pearsall nicely calls Lydgate's "reverent self-consequence."[37] But Lydgate is also a smart and private reader of Chaucer, and seems to have recognized kinds of Chaucerian complication that resist such institutional practices.[38] I turn now to a pair of passages in which ambivalent, strangely skewed, and unresolved images explore some of this very uncertainty and suggest Lydgate's own deeper identification with Chaucer, Chaucerian texts and characters, and thematics of absence. Slips of memory, perhaps unintentional echoes, can destabilize Lydgate's authoritative language in the very gestures by which he would most register laureate eloquence—in the use of "colors" such as simile.

---

[37] Pearsall, *John Lydgate*, p. 126.

[38] For Lydgate's accomplishment as an intelligent reader of Chaucer see C. David Benson, "Critic and Poet," pp. 26–27.

Lydgate, I think, eager as he was to help institutionalize Chaucer as England's native *auctor* and source of a rhetorically respectable imperial history, was nonetheless too good a reader not to be nagged by a residual sense of Chaucer's refusals, Chaucer's slipperiness, and finally by a sense of Chaucer's real inimitability. I think that Lydgate registered his own readerly worries about the project of institutionalizing Chaucer in a couple of genuinely odd but echoing similes that occur just at the moment Chaucerian authority emerges most clearly in the *Troy Book*, when Criseyde is described in lines that, as shown above, virtually repeat Chaucer's. Before he delivers this near-quotation Lydgate brings his narration to a halt, and in this intrusive gap addresses the irresolvable paradox of Chaucerian authority. Lydgate's pen stumbles in approaching Criseyde, he says, because Chaucer has already described her with such mastery that "it were but highe foly" to add anything (2.4682). If he does not write about Criseyde, however, Lydgate will transgress the order of Guido's narrative, and abandon "the trouthe . . . Of Troye boke" (2.4687–88). Lydgate thus explicitly situates himself at an impasse between competing authorities, that is, Latin story and British tongue, Guido and Chaucer. In this narrative and linguistic double bind, Lydgate feels he is forced into some form of transgression or infidelity:

And thus I most don offencioun
Thorughe necligence or presumpcioun:
So am I sette euene amyddes tweyne!
Gret cause haue I & mater to compleyne
On Antropos & vp-on hir envie,
That brak the threde & made for to dye
Noble Galfride, poete of Breteyne,
Amonge oure englisch that made first to reyne
The gold dewe-dropis of rethorik so fyne,
Oure rude langage only tenlwmyne.
To God I pray, that he his soule haue,
After whos help of nede I moste crave,
And seke his boke that is left be-hynde
Som goodly worde ther-in for to fynde,
To sette amonge the crokid lynys rude
Which I do write; as, by similitude,

The ruby stant, so royal of renoun,
With-Inne a ryng of copur or latoun,
So stant the makyng of hym, douteles,
Among oure bokis of englische pereles.

. . . .

Yet for al that, now I wol not leue,
But ben as bolde as Baiard is, the blynde,
That cast no peril what weye that he fynde;
Right so wil I stumble forthe of hede
For vnkonnyng, & take no better hede,
  hir bewte to discriue. (2.4691–735)

These lines, interrupting the narrative of Criseyde, lead the reader through a series of echoes and images that cast Lydgate and Chaucer themselves, varyingly, as Criseyde and Troilus.

Lydgate finds himself at an impossible choice between service to the authority of Guido or of Chaucer and, "sette euene amyddes tweyne," he replicates Criseyde as she reviewed the impossible choice to which Pandarus had led her: "I am . . . At dulcarnoun, right at my wittes ende" (*Troilus and Criseyde*, 3.930–31).[39] If he is to write at all, though, Lydgate must set Chaucerian words, like gems, among his "crokid lynys rude"; and these will be like the royal ruby set in a ring of copper. This prominent "similitude" for Chaucerian diction itself echoes a famous sequence of similitudes in the *Troilus* that clusters around the affair of Troilus and Criseyde. Pandarus first compares Criseyde to a ruby set in a ring (2.584–85); Troilus weeps on "The ruby in his signet," then uses it to seal his letter to Criseyde (2.1086–88); Criseyde gives Troilus a brooch "In which a ruby set was lik an herte" (3.1371); and after she leaves Troy, Criseyde's empty palace is compared to a ring whose ruby has fallen out (5.549). Lydgate's skewed version casts the dead Chaucer as an absent Criseyde, desired but available only through textual recollection, and Lydgate himself as a sort of debased ("copur") version of Troilus, abandoned by his validating ideal and almost immobilized by the loss.

---

[39]Depending perhaps on how strongly this parallel invites the reader to dwell on Lydgate as "Criseyde," the reference to "Antropos" that follows may also summon up Criseyde's later oath by Atropos, *Troilus and Criseyde*, 4.1546–47.

In the final simile in the passage quoted above, Lydgate compares his own temerity to "Baiard . . . the blynde." Given the context of dense Chaucerian echo in the passage, the simile would seem doubly to recall Troilus at the moment he was first caught in love for Criseyde. Chaucer's narrator there begins with an apostrophe "O blynde world, O blynde entencioun!" and continues with the elaborate comparison of Troilus to "proude Bayard" (*Troilus and Criseyde*, 1.211, 218). Lydgate's blind Baiard—an image of foolish blundering—is not, indeed, exactly the same as Chaucer's well-fed horse, skipping in the traces, yet the echo rings to Chaucer, again summoning up Lydgate as a Troilus figure, aspiring to a verbal ideal that is always slipping away from him.[40]

This is an odd cluster of images, at once clearly echoing *Troilus and Criseyde* at moments of erotic desire and loss but not quite neatly parallel with the Chaucerian original. The echoes are at once rich, oddly indeterminate, and unresolved. Lydgate casts himself as Troilus, insofar as it is he who proposes the simile and whose text is the ring; and Chaucer, as ruby, is thus implicitly figured as Criseyde—uncertain, attractive, slippery, necessary, absent, inescapable. But Lydgate is also Criseyde, set at an impossible choice between authorities.[41] And, like Criseyde, Lydgate is the surviving figure of the two.

Lydgate draws the *Troy Book* to an end with the slow deliberation for which he is known, even notorious. He alerts his reader that "I haue no more of latyn to translate" (5.3360) but extends the final book by more than 250 lines, then adds over another hundred in the form of "Lenvoye" and "Verba translatoris ad librum suum." Despite *Troy Book*'s prodigious effort to promote and use the prestige of native, Chaucerian eloquence, merely the titles of these two closing elements should remind us that older hierarchies of language still obtain and that contests for dominance persist.[42]

---

[40]See *Middle English Dictionary* (Ann Arbor: University of Michigan Press, 1956) "baiard" (1c).

[41]We may even recall that soon after, Criseyde is unwillingly translated across the ethnic battle line of Trojans and Greeks.

[42]This is true even—perhaps especially—if the titles are purely scribal. Patterson discusses an interestingly analogous mix of English and Latin in a contemporary sermon, "Making Identities," pp. 94–95.

Further, the contests of authority are no more resolved within English than among its competitor languages. In these closing sections, Lydgate again evokes Chaucer through a series of echoes and direct references. Yet these too place Lydgate in a mixed and unresolved position in regard to that English master, and in regard to authority in general, both literary and political.

The final lines of the book proper offer a double expression of humility, in regard to Latin sources and English readers. Each is somewhat disingenuous. Lydgate says it would be "veyn, / Lik a maner of presumpcioun" (5.3364–65) to add anything to his Latin sources; yet any reader of Chaucer would long ago have recognized that the *Troy Book* is often expanded from Lydgate's British master, and readers who also have Guido in Latin (probably few) would know that Lydgate's own additions have been many.

After the encomium to Henry V discussed earlier, Lydgate widens his address to a more general and also a potentially critical audience. In another formulaic trope of humility, Lydgate—"boistous and rual" (5.3466), "Rude of konnynge" (5.3468)—begs their indulgence for his errors, "To correcte, rather than disdeyne" (5.3482). Yet he quickly shifts into a more aggressive tone, saying that no one is so critical as he "that can no skyl at al" (5.3501). He extends the point, employing a simile we have seen before:

> For to deme ther is noon so bolde,
> As he that is blent with vnkonnyng:
> For blind Baiard cast pereil of no thyng,
> Til he stumble myddes of the lake! (5.3504–07)

This echo of the *Troilus and Criseyde* at once transfers the accusation of heedless temerity on to Lydgate's potential critics and implicitly draws Lydgate's real model back to our attention.

Lydgate then directs his book to a different kind of reader, introduced abstractly, who quickly proves to be the readerly heir (as Lydgate has already figured himself the writerly heir) of the British master, Chaucer himself:

> For vn-to hem my boke is nat direct,
> But to swiche as hauen, in effect,
> On symple folke ful compassioun,

> That goodly can by correccioun
> Amende a thing, & hindre neuere-adel,
> Of custom ay redy to seie wel:
> For he that was gronde of wel-seyng,
> An al hys lyf hyndred no makyng,
> My maister Chaucer, that founde ful many spot—
> Hym liste nat pinche nor gruche at euery blot.
> . . . .
> Suffring goodly of his gentilnes
> Ful many thing enbracid with rudnes.
> And yif I shal shortly hym discryve,
> Was neuer noon to this day alyue,
> To rekne alle, bothe yonge & olde,
> That worthi was his ynkhorn for to holde. (5.3513–30)

Lydgate offers his work to critics whose "gentilnes" will qualify them as heirs to Chaucerian reading—of whom, it then proves, there are "neuer noon." Lydgate has thus set himself (as often throughout the *Troy Book*) as a humble supplicant, practically on bended knee. But we have seen that the poet on bended knee is itself a trope by which Lydgate can at once abase himself and replicate "My maister Chaucer." He submits himself now to correction, but only to correction of those who are worthy followers of Chaucer, and to be such a follower one must be as forgiving as was the master. And of course Chaucer by now almost belongs to Lydgate: "*My maister.*" Once again, the quality of Chaucer's excellence removes him from access to all but a few users. This makes possible a wide readership, but a narrow company of those who can use Chaucer to create new authority and ideology, or even criticize such users. Lydgate's own privileged access to Chaucerian rhetoric is asserted one final time, moreover, in the final couplet of the *Troy Book* proper, as he sends off "This litel boke" (5.3611), a phrase that loudly echoes the *Troilus and Criseyde* at its own close: "Go, litel bok . . ." (5.1786). Chaucer's phrase will be reproduced exactly in the opening line of the two-stanza "Verba translatoris ad librum suum" that closes the work: "Go, litel bok, & put the in the grace / Of hym that is most of excellence" (Verba, lines 1–2).

In "Lenvoye," addressed once again directly to Henry V, Lydgate praises Henry's accomplishments a final time. In doing so, he invokes, in quick succession, a series of phrases and images that link Henry with Chaucer and thus Lydgate himself. Lydgate first says he wishes Henry "To be registred worthi as of name / In the highest place of the hous of fame" (lines 13–14). This locates Henry in a Chaucerian space where, as we have seen, Lydgate has also placed Chaucer himself. In the House of Fame, Henry will wear "a crowne made of laurer grene / Vp-on thin hed" (lines 20–21); the only other individual linked with laurel in *Troy Book* is Chaucer, who gets "the laurer of oure englishe tonge" (3.4246). Even here, the prestige of conquest and the prestige of rhetorical authority remained linked, though their hierarchical relation remains unstable and unresolved. I would not, however, leave the *Troy Book* in some unresolved aporia, embodied in Lydgate's similitudes. Rather, I would promote Lydgate as a more self-aware and self-consciously pragmatic poet than is usually allowed. He experiences the complex identifications and the fracturing of boundaries—erotic, linguistic, imperial—implied in these metaphors; but he also carries on with his projects of unified imperial history.

Lydgate himself thus becomes a complexly fractured figure at crucial moments in his translation, when he suspends his narrative to refocus instead on the contest of Latin and British verbal authority. Further, he encodes in himself, in the weird *mise en abyme* of the Troilus-and-Criseyde similes, the unresolved crisis of generating a native rhetorical authority from a figure—Chaucer—whose very prestige stems from his absence and inimitability. Even as Chaucer is inserted within and finally (if temporarily) usurps the authority of the Latin original in the narrative of empire, the issue of his authority itself creates delays, gaps, and excess insertions in that same narration. The movement from a Latin to a British imperial tongue, like any such imperial translation, does not occur without occasional violence that creates rifts in the narrative (as in the social) texture. It is in queer and unresolved images such as these, I think, that the dialectic among translated classical authority, empire, and language does carry on, even in the context of fifteenth-century efforts to totalize English as a language of empire and to name Chaucer as the new voice of Lancastrian classicism.

Vernacular Valorizing:
Functions and Fashionings of Literary Theory in Middle English Translation of Authority[1]

Ian Johnson

This is a chapter about functions and reconfigurations of vernacularized literary theory, deriving from a learned tradition of commentary on the Bible and *auctores*, and found in the prologues and self-exegesis of translators of authoritative materials. But the concern here is not confined just to demonstrating the presence of such theory (prologue paradigms, scholastic literary roles, etc.).[2] Rather, the focus is on some turns taken by

---

[1] I am grateful to the Medieval Institute and to the Symposium Organizer, Jeanette Beer, for the generous hospitality which made it possible for this paper to be given. I am also grateful to Wendy Vacani and Julian Crowe for their help in translating one computer dialect into another.

[2] The highly important tradition of the scholastic prologue has attracted considerable modern scholarly attention. The conventional headings of the *accessus*, under which a text of an *auctor* was appraised—*utilitas* (the utility/value of a work), *intentio* (intentionality), *nomen libri* (title), *modus agendi* (procedure/style), *ordinatio/forma tractatus* (structure and order of materials), *nomen auctoris* (name, life [*vita auctoris*], and status of the author), *materia* (sources/subject matter)—were accorded a range of vernacular equivalents and significantly influenced the terminology and ideology of English translators' prologues. The fourteenth century saw this tradition being modified and sharpened up by an Aristotelian scheme founded on the universally applicable philosophical grid of the Four Causes. Thus, the efficient cause (*causa efficiens*) was the author; it could be *duplex*, e.g., God and Man, priest and Holy Ghost. The material cause (*causa materialis*) was the subject matter/sources of a work. The formal cause (*causa formalis*) was the form (structure, style, and literary procedures). The final cause (*causa finalis*) was the objective of text and author, thereby equating with *utilitas* and *intentio* from the earlier tradition. For more detailed discussion

theory as mediated in and by English culture, and in particular some attempted "clinching moments" of self-exegesis; in other words, some of the belaborings, preoccupations, trumpetings, and self-conceptions that stand out scenically, obtrusively, or insistently in the rhetorico-hermeneutic topography of paratextual discourse.

To express hesitancy as to one's fitness for the task was a hallmark of the decorous medieval translator. A particularly intriguing case of ostensibly genuine misgivings is to be found in the *prefacyon* to a fifteenth-century Carthusian meditative Life of Christ, the exegetical, moralizing, and prayerful *Speculum Devotorum.*[3] Its compiler tells us a valorizing tale, claiming that he was discouraged to the point of repeatedly considering abandonment of the whole project not only on account of his own spiritually slight *vita auctoris* but also because St. Bonaventure had written a Life of Christ:

---

and examples of the scholastic literary prologue and literary roles see A. J. Minnis, *Medieval Theory of Authorship: Scholastic Literary Attitudes in the Later Middle Ages* (London: Scolar Press, 1984), pp. 9–39, 73–117, 160–65; Richard W. Hunt, "The Introductions to the 'Artes' in the Twelfth Century," in *The History of Grammar in the Middle Ages: Collected Papers,* ed. G. L. Bursill-Hall (Amsterdam: John Benjamins, 1980), pp. 117–44; *Medieval Literary Theory and Criticism, c. 1100–c. 1375: The Commentary-Tradition,* ed. A. J. Minnis and A. Brian Scott with the assistance of David Wallace (Oxford: Clarendon, 1988), pp. 12–36; Ian Johnson, "Prologue and Practice: Middle English Lives of Christ," in *The Medieval Translator: The Theory and Practice of Translation in the Middle Ages,* ed. Roger Ellis (Cambridge: Brewer, 1989), pp. 69–85; and Ian Johnson, "The Late-Medieval Theory and Practice of Translation with Special Reference to Some Middle English Lives of Christ" (Ph.D. diss., University of Bristol, 1990), esp. pp. 49–159. For discussion of one of the most elaborate vernacularizations of the Aristotelian prologue in Middle English see Ian Johnson, "Tales of a True Translator: Medieval Literary Theory, Anecdote and Autobiography in Osbern Bokenham's *Legendys of Hooly Wummen,*" in *The Medieval Translator 4,* ed. Roger Ellis and Ruth Evans (Exeter: Exeter University Press, 1994), pp. 104–24.

[3] *The Speculum Devotorum of an Anonymous Carthusian of Sheen, Analecta Cartusiana* 12–13, ed. James Hogg (Salzburg: Universität Salzburg, 1973–74). I am very grateful to have had access to James Hogg's typescript introduction to his edition. Subsequent references are found in the text. For discussion of this work see Johnson, "Prologue and Practice," pp. 75–80; and Johnson, "Late-Medieval Theory and Practice of Translation," pp. 286–386.

> Also I haue be steryd ofte tymys to haue lefte thys bysynesse bothe for my
> vnworthynesse & also for Bonauenture a cardynal & a worthy clerke made a boke
> of the same matere the whyche ys callyd Vita Christi. (p. 2)

The *Speculum Devotorum* is in the tradition of the mighty *Meditationes Vitae
Christi,* an intimidating impediment to his Englishing and a precedent to be
matched.[4] The compiler's choice of the word *vnworthynesse* refers not only
to his literary deficiencies but also to his moral fallibility: he cannot hope to
match up to "a cardynal & a worthy clerke," who is not only scholastically
but also morally and spiritually superior, with a hagiographic *vita auctoris*
to buttress his works. Note the use of the term *matere* from the scholastic
prologue, here referring to the subject-matter of the *vita* and to the
meditative *matere* of the tradition of thinking on the Sacred Humanity, a
broader conception than that of the single textual source. Ironically, the oft-
pious word *steryd* denotes abandonment, not pursuit, of a devotional task.

Worse than having to compete with Bonaventure is having to reckon
with an English Carthusian predecessor, for the monk of Sheen was stirred
to give up "most of alle whenne I herde telle that a man of oure ordyr of
charturhowse had I turnyd the same boke into englyische" (p. 2), a
reference, presumably, to Nicholas Love's *Mirrour.*[5] It sounds as if the news

---

[4]The standard edition of this work is still to be found in *Opera Omnia Sancti
Bonaventurae,* vol. 12, ed. A. C. Peltier (Paris: Ludovicus Vives, 1868), pp. 509–630. For
a modern edition of the Passion-section see *Meditaciones de Passione Christi olim Sancto
Bonaventurae attributae,* ed. Sister M. Jordan Stallings (Washington D.C.: Catholic
University of America Press, 1965). For discussion of the huge influence of this work see
Johnson, "Late-Medieval Theory and Practice of Translation," pp. 160–65; Elizabeth Salter,
Nicholas Love's "Myrrour of the blessed lyf of Jesu Christ," Analecta Cartusiana 10 (Salzburg:
Universität Salzburg, 1974), pp. 39–46; *Smaointe Beatha Chriost .i. Innsint Ghaelge a chuir
Tomás Gruamdha Ó Bruacháin (fl. c. 1450) ar an Meditationes vitae Christi,* ed. Cainneach
Ó Maonaigh O.F.M. (Dublin: Institúid Árd-Léighinn Bhaile Átha Cliath [Dublin Institute
for Advanced Studies], 1944), English appendix pp. 325–26; and Michael G. Sargent,
"Bonaventura English: A Survey of the Middle English Prose Translations of Early
Franciscan Literature," in *Spätmittelalterliche Geistliche Literatur in der Nationalsprache,*
Analecta Cartusiana 106:2 (Salzburg: Universität Salzburg, 1984), pp. 145–76, esp. 148–54.

[5]Nicholas Love, *The Mirrour of the blessed lyf of Jesu Christ: A Translation of the Latin
Work Entitled Meditations vitae Christi,* ed. Lawrence F. Powell (Oxford: Clarendon, 1908).

came to him as a rather unpleasant surprise after he had started his work.
Whether or not after this he managed to see or read the *Mirrour* is not
certain. It would, though, be a little strange if this famous and much-
circulated Carthusian vernacular work, licensed and mandated against
Lollardy by Archbishop Arundel himself, and extant in more manuscripts
than any other English prose text of the fifteenth century, was completely
unseen by the monk of Sheen.

Had he actually looked at Love's *Mirrour,* he would have seen a
confident bid for vernacular canonicity buttressed by a comprehensive
repertoire of anglicized terminology drawn from Latin prologue paradigms,
and naturalized into idiomatic phraseology, whether Love is advertising his
own activity or, as here, assessing a tradition/source. The *matere,* with its
"pleyne [full and comprehensible] sentence" (p. 8), is "fructuouse." The
utilitas is the profit to be gained in stirring to the love of Jesus and the
edification of simple souls:

> The whiche scripture [i.e., biblical text] and writynge [i.e., parabiblical commen-
> tary, hagiography, devotional matter] / for the fructuouse mater ther of sterynge
> specially to the loue of Jesu / and also for the pleyne sentence to comune vnder-
> stondynge / semeth amonge othere souereynly edifienge to symple creatures. (p. 8)

"Fructuouse mater" indicates simultaneous consideration of *materia* and
utilitas. Love as a rule inter-relates and collocates paradigm categories *ad hoc*
as it suits his discussion. There is a similar fluency in combining prologue
categories in Love's discussion of his own activity, for example, the care he
takes to point out, concerning the *ordinatio/forma tractatus,* that the work
may be read according to the days of the week or the church year
(pp. 12–13).

One particularly arresting transformation of theory in this *proheme,*
however, is the rhetoricizing show that Love makes out of constructing the

---

The standard study of this work is Salter, *Nicholas Love's "Myrrour."* For an examination of
Love as translator in the light of academic literary theory see Johnson, "Late-Medieval
Theory and Practice of Translation," pp. 160–285. See also Michael G. Sargent's new
critical edition of the *Mirrour, Nicholas Love's Mirror of the Blessed Life of Jesus Christ* (New
York: Garland, 1992).

translatio (and I mean that in the senses of both *translation* and *metaphor/ transference*) that he enforces on the name of the book.[6] He makes a considerable display in bestowing the new title-metaphor of *The Mirrour of the Blessed Lyf of Jesu Christ* on the *Meditationes Vitae Christi,* a bestowal highlighted by the decorous marginal gloss "¶ Nomen libri," the appropriate category from the scholastic prologue. In his new title, Love seeks to embody the character and *sentence* of his work, as the "suspense-laden" *gradatio,* which constitutes the uncovering of the new name, aims to declare:

> ¶ And so for as moche as in this book ben conteyned dyuerse ymaginaciouns of cristes lyf⁚ the which lyf fro the bygynnyng in to the endyng euermore blessed and with outen synne / passynge alle lyues of alle othere seyntes / as for a synguler prerogatyf may worthely be cleped the blessed lyf of Jesu Crist. The whiche also be cause that it may not be fully discryued as the lifes of other seyntis / but in a maner of lickenes as the ymage of mannis face is schewed in the mirrour⁚ therfore as for a pertynent name to this book it may skilfully be cleped the mirrour of the blessed lyf of Jesu crist. (pp. 9–10)

Exposing and expounding his *titulus* bit by bit with unreluctant rhetorical delay, this exposition marks the climax of the materials original to Love which precede his Englishing of the pseudo-Bonaventurean *proheme.* The language of dialectic, i.e., "synguler prerogatyf" and "skilfully," helps to impose the new name. Argument and syntax are only satisfactorily resolved by the announcement of the full title, which is a distillation of, and micro-commentary on, the work that follows. At this point it may be recalled that the *Catholicon* defines (chapter) headings ("capitula") as capturing and containing in brief some of the worthwhile

---

[6]For further discussion of Love's *nomen libri,* medieval theory of imagination and mirror-titles, see Johnson, "Late-Medieval Theory and Practice of Translation," pp. 237–44. For an informative study of mirror-titles in medieval and Renaissance culture see Herbert Grabes, *The Mutable Glass: Mirror-imagery in Titles and Texts of the Middle Ages and English Renaissance,* trans. Gordon Collier (Cambridge: Cambridge University Press, 1982). See also Ritamary Bradley, "The Speculum Image in Medieval Mystical Writers," in *The Medieval Mystical Tradition in England,* ed. Marion Glasscoe (Woodbridge: Boydell and Brewer, 1984), pp. 9–27.

teaching to be found in the chapter ("breviter capiant et contineant aliquam sententiam").[7] What Love is doing coincides with this: by a process of argument and definition his title does indeed capture and contain the *sententia* of the source. The "lyf" is "blessed" because it surpasses the lives of all other "mere" saints: this recapitulates the main assertion of the opening passage of Love's *proheme* that "souereynly the wordes and the dedes written of oure lord Jesu crist" predominate amidst all other "ensaumple of vertues and good lyuyng of holy men writen in bookes" (p. 7).

But Love is not satisfied to halt at calling his work "the blessed lyf of Jesu crist." The term "mirrour" is applicable because the life in its supreme excellence and incarnational mystery may not be fully described, unlike the lives of other saints. The mirror metaphor, then, is used, somewhat paradoxically, to advertise, on one hand, the veracity of the work to the *Vita* and, on the other, its inevitable insufficiency. The work has an imaginative *modus agendi* of "maner of lickenes," which is necessary because the divine nature of Christ and other ghostly substances integral to the *Vita* cannot be represented unless by fleshly imaginations, which humans can refract through what they "kyndely knowe." The temporally-bound *kynde knowynge* which constrains the human imagination allows only for an insufficient notion of the divine to be implanted in the soul, with all the incompleteness of the mirror-image instead of the complete reality. A further imaginative insufficiency born of necessity involves the provisional sundering of the divinity from the humanity. In instructions prefacing the commencement of the Passion the readers are told to "depart in manere" (p. 216) the godhead from the manhood, but to do so only for the time being. Thus might they meditate on the Passion, even though, it is asserted, it would be false to declare that the manhood was ever at any time parted from the godhead. To sum up, Love's choice and *translatio* of vernacular title for the *Meditationes Vitae Christi* is his most overarching and concentrated *expositio sententie per aliam linguam* (to invoke the authoritative

---

[7]John of Genoa, *Catholicon*, s.v. *capitulum* (Mainz, 1460; repr. Westmead: Gregg, 1971), unfol. For the importance of this work in the Middle Ages see Nicholas Orme, *English Schools in the Middle Ages* (London: Methuen, 1973), p. 93.

contemporary definition of translation from the *Catholicon*).[8] For him, though the literal sense of the original title and its *matere* is "meditaciouns of cristes lyf" (p. 8), the *sentence* of the work is the *Mirrour of the Blessed Lyf of Jesu Christ*.

The repackaging of biblical *matere* embodied in the metaphorical reworking of Love's *nomen libri* would doubtless have infuriated the Wycliffites, for whom the only real mirror worth looking at was the "speculum voluntatis" of God, Holy Writ itself.[9] The Lollard Bible was fighting for the same audience as the *Mirrour,* but with a very different strategy. Whereas Love's readers are enabled by a licensing directive to meditate on the Sacred Humanity under the careful supervision of a priest-translator, the Lollard Bible readers are presented, in the General Prologue to the second version of the Wycliffite Bible, with a take-away home exegesis kit (complete with instructions for fourfold exegesis, Tyconian rules, figurative language, *caritas* and all), each and all of which attempt to empower vernacular readers as autonomous interpreters of Holy Writ.[10] Fourteen long chapters belabor such enabling precepts, yet modern attention generally focuses on the final chapter dealing with the business of the translation itself. We should not regard these chapters as just a rather long run-up to the wicket of Chapter 15. On the contrary, many of the Lollards' most important concerns and contentions are elaborated therein, especially their approach to teaching biblical reading and interpretation.

Though the translators flouted the ecclesiastical establishment, they were all the more dangerous for their impeccable exegetical orthodoxy,

---

[8]*Catholicon*, s.v. *glosa*, unfol.

[9]John Wycliffe, *De Veritate Sacrae Scripturae,* ed. Rudolf Buddensieg, 3 vols. (London: Trübner, 1905–07), 1: 377.

[10]For this prologue see *The Holy Bible, containing the Old and New Testaments, with the Apocryphal books, in the earliest English versions made from the Latin Vulgate by John Wycliffe and his Followers,* ed. Josiah Forshall and Frederic Madden, 4 vols. (Oxford: Oxford University Press, 1850), 1: 1–60. For a modern edition of the final chapter of this prologue see "Prologue to Wycliffite Bible, Chapter 15," in *Selections from English Wycliffite Writings,* ed. Anne Hudson (Cambridge: Cambridge University Press, 1978), pp. 67–72. Quotations from the final chapter are cited from Hudson.

particularly their insidious brandishing of the Augustinian doctrine of charity as a *modus agendi* and final cause of reading and translating the Bible and their equally Augustinian conception of the New Testament as readily comprehensible to all:

> Therfore cristen men and wymmen, olde and 3onge, shulden studie fast in the newe testament, for it is of ful autorite, and opyn to vndirstonding of simple men, as to the poyntis that be moost nedeful to saluacioun; and the same sentence is in the derkiste placis of holy writ, whiche sentence is in the opyn placis; and ech place of holy writ, bothe opyn and derk, techith mekenes and charite; and therfore he that kepith mekenes and charite hath the trewe vndirstondyng and perfectioun of al holi writ, as Austyn preuith in his sermoun of the preysing of charite. Therfore no simple man of wit be aferd vnmesurabli to studie in the text of holy writ. (p. 2)

This co-opting of Augustine as Spin-Doctor of the Church owes much to, and is buttressed by, Augustine's presence in Lyre's *Postillae,* for Lyre's quotations and expansions of the Saint furnish the General Prologue with key material.[11] These are the key contentions. Anything expressed darkly outside the New Testament is stated openly within it: "the same sentence is in the derkiste placis of holy writ, whiche sentence is in the opyn placis" (p. 2). Here the governing exegetical concept is that of the so-called *sententia litterae,* according to which the literal sense, as revealed in the "opyn placis," is the basis for elucidating the deeper understanding of the "derkiste placis" of the text.[12] This deeper understanding by its very nature

---

[11]This is acknowledged, for example, in Forshall and Madden: "Heere Lire rehersith the sentence of seint Austyn, and of Isidre in these reulis, and declarith hem opinly bi holy scripture and resoun, and countrith not Austin, but declareth him ful mychel to symple mennis witt; and addeth more bi scripture and resoun, that Austin touchith not" (p. 55).

[12]Hugh of St. Victor made a famous distinction that stratified three levels of textual meaning, whereby the "letter" (*littera*) involved linguistic construction, the "sense" (*sensus*) was the straightforward, open meaning, and the *sententia* was a deeper level of understanding requiring an effort of exposition or interpretation; see *Didascalicon* iii.8, ed. Charles H. Buttimer (Washington, D.C.: Catholic University of America Press, 1939), p. 58. By the time of Nicholas of Lyre, there is increased emphasis on the *sententia litterae,* "the profound meaning of the literal sense." For illustration of Nicholas of Lyre's development of exegetical

coalesces with *caritas,* because it is born of "charite." Thus, charity and biblical meaning dovetail with one another and are within the grasp of all. For the Lollards' Carthusian rivals, the compilers of the *Mirrour* and the *Speculum Devotorum,* there is a different version of reader-enablement based on textually stimulated thinking on the Sacred Humanity, which is intended to continue after reading. As meditative translations the *Mirrour* and the *Speculum Devotorum* aim to render not just edifying *matere* but to translate into the soul of the reader a portable and permanent *modus agendi* with which to establish a post-textual devotional relationship with Christ or, as the *Speculum Devotorum,* playing on the term "drawe" ("translate"), puts it:

> Thowgth hyt be schortly seyde here vndyr a compendyus manyr, ȝytt hyt may be drawe ful loonge in a soule þat can deuoutly thynke & dylygently beholde the werkys of oure lorde that be conteynyd therinne. (p. 146)

Translation and meditative exposition in writer and reader alike attempt to capture and ingenerate *sentence.* The Wycliffite Bible, on the other hand, claims a twin exegetico-spiritual foundation and directive of *translatio auctoritatis* and *translatio caritatis. Charite* puts originary force into vernacular culture and makes an exegete of the reader in the best Lyrean-Augustinian fashion, thereby challenging and expropriating the Latin ecclesiastical establishment's ownership and control of authoritative discourse. That *charite* could mean and do so much in English and do so with such potently Augustinian sanction was incendiary, to say the least.

By the time that Chapter 15 is reached, the emphasis is not on the empowerment of the self-starting charitable reader but on the valorization of the translators themselves. This is done on the basis of their scholarly and ethical credentials and their invocation of divine grace, each of which is held to inform the very performance of their translating. This final

---

tradition see the important article by M. B. Parkes, "Punctuation, or Pause and Effect," in *Medieval Eloquence: Studies in the Theory and Practice of Medieval Rhetoric,* ed. James J. Murphy (Berkeley and Los Angeles: University of California Press, 1978), pp. 127–42, esp. 131–32.

chapter self-exegetically justifies the genesis of the English Bible by parading all the best scholarly literary attitudes. The gathering and consultation of experts and commentaries, especially Lyre (the most prestigious and author-itative exegete of the literal sense), the attention to linguistic difficulties, the willingness to correct, the recourse to *originalia,* to *Hebraica Veritas* and the moral living and *charite* of the translators themselves (echoing and appro-priating the *accessus*-category of *vita auctoris*) all play their parts.[13] Only then will "þe Holi Spiryt, autour of wisdom and kunnyng and truþe, dresse him [the translator] in his werk and suffre him not for to erre."[14] The strategic bid for enhanced efficient causality through the intervention of divine grace is present in the implication that the translators are subject to being helped to full cognition by God: "God of his grete merci ʒeue to vs grace to lyue wel and to seie þe truþe."[15] This does not mean that the Lollard translators are mystically inspired, yet the grace sheds light on what the human mind is attempting to judge.[16]

Concomitant strategies concerning efficient causality, in a different form, solve decorously the problems of the self-doubting Carthusian of Sheen, who, it will be recalled, considered abandoning the completion of the *Speculum Devotorum* altogether. First, *auctoritas* and responsibility are piously offloaded onto his Prior, whom he consults with his qualms: "he ful charytably confortyde me to parforme hyt wyth sueche wordys as cam to hys mynde for the tyme" (p. 3). Care is taken to show the Prior's correct attitude to the production of devotional texts. The Prior does what he does "ful charytably," with a loving intention, thus blessing the book with the purity and authority of his own *entent,* which, by virtue of his office and his personal spirituality, raises the level of authority higher up the scale of

---

[13]See Hudson, "Prologue," passim. For discussion of the important concept of *originalia* (works of *auctores* in complete form) see Minnis, *Medieval Theory of Authorship,* pp. 153–59; and J. de Ghellinck, "'Originale' et 'Originalia'," *Bulletin du Cange* 14 (1939): 95–105.

[14]Hudson, "Prologue," p. 71.

[15]Hudson, "Prologue," p. 69.

[16]For a short summary of Augustinian attitudes towards such illumination see Frederick C. Copleston, *A History of Medieval Philosophy* (London: Methuen, 1972), pp. 36–37.

efficient causality than that which could be offered by the writer alone. The avowed instrumentality of the compiler is further underscored by his choice of the term "parforme" to describe his literary role. Revealingly, he later refers to himself three times at least as the "fyrste wrytare" of the meditations (pp. 5, 11, 21), that is, a mere *scriptor,* as Bonaventure put it—the lowest form of medieval literary role.[17] But by requiring that the prayers go in aid of the "*fyrste* wrytare" he is ensuring that they benefit him and do not go astray to any scribe who might copy his work in the future.

The compiler is also "sumwhat bore vp" by the advice of others and the merits of those who are intended to profit from the work:

> And so on the mercy of god trustynge to whom ys no thynge vnpossyble wyth drede of my vnkunnynge & vnworthynesse, also sumwhat bore vp be the conseyil of goostly fadrys & the merytys of hem that be þe mercy of god mowe be profytyd be my sympyl traveyle in sueche tymys as I mygth traueyle be my conscyence wythoute lettynge of othyr excersysys and othyr dyuerse occupacyonys & lettyngys that mygth falle in dyuerse wysys I thowgth be the grace of god to make an ende therof, & so att the laste oure lorde of hys mercy ȝaf me grace as I hope to parforme hyt. (pp. 3–4)

Written as part and parcel of actual monastic duties, the *Speculum Devotorum* displays an authorized and "real-life" *vita auctoris.* Again, as with the Wycliffites, it is necessary to have the "grace of god" to "parforme" the work (p. 3). There is also another intriguing aspect to the conception of the efficient causality of the *Speculum Devotorum.* Its fruitful future reception helps teleologically to pull it into being, for its readers' merits impart a finally causal efficiency of their own. So, the actual production of the text is not just a matter of authorial push but also readerly pull. Further justifications for carrying on with the work are provided by the exculpatory purity of *entent* of the compiler and by the celebrated precedent of four beneficially complementary treatments of Christ's life in four different but divinely ordained gospels (pp. 4–5). The superabundant *sentence* of the *Vita*

---

[17]For discussion of Bonaventure's definition see Minnis, *Medieval Theory of Authorship,* pp. 94–95.

cannot be contained in any one version, therefore this further version is permissible and even useful.[18] Perhaps, in the end, the Carthusian of Sheen does feel he can *quyte* Love at least a little, for he constructs his own title in a manner not dissimilar (p. 5), thereby positioning his work at the commanding and canonical heights of all human discourse. Though an enormous claim, it is no more than orthodox, correct, and credible.

In drawing together some of the threads of these attempted so-called clinching moments, it seems that all three texts aim to bestow vernacular autonomy and authority on themselves and their reception-lives. Each self-exegetical moment, however, stresses a different yet related aspect of textual production, mediation, or reception, invariably drawing on and rhetorically exploiting chosen materials from traditional academic literary theory to give it resonance. Such invocation and deployment of theory helps theory in its turn to keep its puissance by virtue of its being accorded a prominent profile in highly valued textual activities of considerable cultural power. Thus the Wycliffites emphasize their own application of the doctrine of *charite,* their access to grace and efficient causality, and their correct array of academic literary attitudes and procedures—all of which combine to make not just vernacular Bibles but also vernacular Bible readers. Through a theoretical sensibility the *Speculum Devotorum* justifies its genesis. Though its writer feels pressured by the *Mirrour* and the *Meditationes Vitae Christi,* he is able to resort inventionally to a version of grace and efficient causality refracted though the social relationships and transactions of monastic life, in which God, his first reader the "gostly syster" (p. 1), the rest of his readers, and his Prior all have their agency in the production and validation of the work. These agents of his text are also actants in his autobiographical paratext, his moralized *vita auctoris/compilatoris.* The compiler's literary transactions seem real, however affectedly conventional some of them may be. He uses the overlap between conventions of conduct and of author-itative discourse. His paratext is a zone of transaction and translation between the text and the outside world, between theory and praxis. Finally,

---

[18]For further discussion of this matter see Johnson, "Late-Medieval Theory and Practice of Translation," pp. 313–24; and Johnson, "Prologue and Practice," pp. 73–76.

Nicholas Love, wishing to embody and enforce the meditativeness, *auctoritas* and generic sovereignty of his work, exploits a theoretical category when he renders its *nomen libri* anew, a sign of conformity to pseudo-Bonaventurean priorities and the particular ecclesiastically driven vernacular exigencies of his day.

All three texts attempt to structure reader access to, and ingestion of, biblical *sentence*. As bids for cultural sites, they inter-relate and compete in varying ways. The Wycliffite Bible is an outright challenge to ecclesiastical authority. Its fight is not so much with the Latin Bible and *Latinitas* but with texts such as Love's *Mirrour*, which, with its anti-Lollard polemic and its added coda of a treatise and prayer on the Eucharist, seeks to control the same ground. The theory invoked by both books serves a vernacular directive, the biblical enablement/containment of those without Latin. Ironically, Love's enormously successful *Mirrour* probably prevented an allied text, the *Speculum Devotorum,* from getting much of a hold in late medieval codices. The two meditative Carthusian *Vitae Christi* were just too similar. Sometimes, however, a text aims to match or displace another text that is palpably dissimilar in genre or even in content—as is the case with the *Mirrour's* claim to outdo the different but related genre of saints' lives. John Walton's voguish verse Boethius overgoes Chaucer's prose *Boece,* matching its *sentence* by recourse to Nicholas Trevet's commentary and exceeding it in the field of eloquence by being rendered in lofty stanzaic form.[19] More

---

[19]See Boethius, *De Consolatione Philosophiae,* trans. John Walton Canon of Oseney, ed. Mark Science, EETS, o.s., 170 (London: Oxford University Press, 1927). For demonstrations of Walton's use of the commentary of Trevet and his use of exegetical methodology see A. J. Minnis, "Aspects of the Medieval French and English Traditions of the *De Consolatione Philosophiae,*" in *Boethius: His Life, Thought, and Influence,* ed. Margaret Gibson (Oxford: Blackwell, 1981), pp. 312–61, esp. 343–47, 350–51; Rita Copeland, "Rhetoric and Vernacular Translation in the Middle Ages," *Studies in the Age of Chaucer* 9, ed. Thomas J. Heffernan (Knoxville: New Chaucer Society, 1987), pp. 41–75, esp. 57–62, 66–75; Rita Copeland, *Rhetoric, Hermeneutics and Translation in the Middle Ages: Academic Traditions and Vernacular Texts* (Cambridge: Cambridge University Press, 1991), pp. 145–49; and I. R. Johnson, "Walton's Sapient Orpheus," in *The Medieval Boethius: Studies in the Vernacular Translations of De Consolatione Philosophiae,* ed. A. J. Minnis (Cambridge: D. S. Brewer, 1987), pp. 139–68, esp. 144–54, 165–68.

complexly, though, Walton reveals in his preface that he is competing not so much with another Boethius as with Chaucer's *Troilus* by disparaging its (or its narrator's) anti-Boethian unenlightenment.[20] Similarly, Osbern Bokenham, in his hagiographic *Legendys of Hooly Wummen,* serves up a complement to Chaucer's *Legend of* [merely] *Good* [pagan] *Women.*[21] Moreover, in what is conceivably a moralized *translatio* of the *Canterbury Tales,* he postures as a pilgrim-translator, journeying laboriously through devout textual duties as if he were visiting the shrines of the saints concerned. In Bokenham's version of pilgrimage-literature his tales display no Chaucerian variety, being reverentially similar and univocally rehearsed with pardon-seeking predictability by a sturdily *non*-fictional pilgrim-compiler.

We have, with Bokenham, further extraordinary transformation of literary theory, used to valorize not so much his sources as his own work, the theory being intertwined with autobiography and petition. Refracting one theoretical discourse through another, he produces an intriguing three-levelled *expositio* of the *littera, sensus,* and *sententia* of the Aristotelian Four Causes and applies them garrulously and autobiographically to his own literary activity (lines 1–240). He tells us under consideration of the formal cause (lines 107–22) how he gathered his sources when he went on a pilgrimage to Italy (and how the local wine-sellers fleece pilgrims). While expounding the final cause (lines 123–74) he relates his motivation for translating the Life of St. Margaret: she saved him from a tyrant and a nasty end in a Venetian fen. In the same prologue (esp. lines 1–28) he draws on the earlier tradition of prefatory *circumstantiae,* which he uses to gloss the Four Causes.[22] So, Aristotelian discourse is seen to confirm and

---

[20]Walton, *Boethius, Prefacio Translatoris,* stanza 8. See Johnson, "Walton's Sapient Orpheus," pp. 159–63; and Johnson, "*This Brigous Questioun:* Translating Free Will and Predestination in Walton's *Boethius* and Chaucer's *Troilus and Criseyde,*" *Carmïna Philosophiae* 3 (1994): 1–21, for discussion of Walton's competition with Chaucer.

[21]Osbern Bokenham, *Legendys of Hooly Wummen,* ed. Mary S. Serjeantson, EETS, o.s., 206 (London: Oxford University Press, 1938). For more detailed discussion of Bokenham's use of theoretical attitudes, see generally Johnson, "Tales of a True Translator."

[22]The tradition of making prologues and appraising texts according to a scheme of *circumstantiae* is most notably associated with Remigius of Auxerre and owes its origins to

elaborate the discourse of *circumstantiae*, which in turn encompasses and distils the Aristotelian. Furthermore, in that his paratext contains not only explication and valorization of his *matere* but also petitions and prayers for his own sake, it could be said that his "mainstream" hagiographic narrative is marginalized and becomes the threshold into a centralized text of prayer, thereby reversing the text/paratext relationship. Concomitantly, the women saints who are the ostensible *matere* become efficiently causal in the production of the work, for their aid is routinely invoked. It is in the paratext where Bokenham, his female "patrons," and his readers have their transactions with the saints (for succor, pardons, etc.); so his display of theory here may be seen as a form of decorum, bordering perhaps on reverential ritual.

To conclude, vernacularized theory, a palpable and flexible system of criteria, helps vernacular culture toward textual self-articulation and toward enhanced sophistication and reflectiveness in textual production and reception. It helps to bestow autonomy and value and foster forms of rivalry/complementarity, not only with regard to Latin culture but also with regard to textual inter-relationships and sitings within vernacular culture. Such theory can also, perhaps, be seen not just as empowerment of the vernacular but also as the export of ideological capital by the source-superculture on its own agenda. The directive for disseminating such vernacular texts as sermons, preachers' handbooks, devotional works, hagiography, and Lives of Christ such as Love's *Mirrour* comes frequently from above and outside. So, when Boethius is apparently "appropriated" by English culture, should we not say also that English culture has Boethius visited upon it and is accordingly "Boethianized," "Virgilianized,"

---

ancient rhetoricians' belief that anything subject to discussion could be examined by a series of questions: "who" (the author), "what" (the actual text), "why" (the objective of the text), "in what manner" (in what fashion the work was composed), "where" (the place it was written), "when" (the time of composition), and "whence/by what means" (the matter from which the work was composed). Not all headings would always be deployed, as is the case with Bokenham, who simplifies the schema down to "what" and "why." See Minnis, *Medieval Theory of Authorship*, pp. 16–17, 19; Copeland, *Rhetoric, Hermeneutics, and Translation*, pp. 66–73, 161–66; and Johnson, "Tales of a True Translator," passim.

"Bonaventureanized," "rebiblicized," even "latinized" from outside? The interaction of the priorities of source-culture and target-culture have a homologue in the dialectic between the rhetorical and hermeneutic aspects of translations as both reworkings and exegetical interpretations. When it comes to making texts, both hermeneutics and rhetoric, for all the ostensibly innocent coherence and neutrality of their learned provenance, have to negotiate "loaded" *sentence* as conditioned by the individual contingencies of particular texts. The various theoretical forms and turns these dealings assume in paratexts specify and valorize transactions whereby the translator packages his text for the outside world and whereby the outside world, in the form of the reader, passes over the threshold into the text and, as here, out again.

Translating Chrétien de Troyes: How Faithful?

William W. Kibler

Hilaire Belloc began his Taylor Lecture in 1931 by saying:

> The art of translation is a subsidiary art, and derivative. On this account it has never been granted the dignity of original work, and has suffered too much in the general judgment of letters. This natural under-estimation of its value has had the bad practical effect of lowering the standard demanded, and in some periods has almost destroyed the art altogether.[1]

But if translation is a subsidiary art, and a largely unrespected one, it is also a necessary art. This has long been the case in comparative literature and, with the demise of traditional philology in recent generations, is becoming more and more a necessity in medieval studies as well. Although on the one hand we regret that fewer and fewer people are capable of reading Old French texts like the romances of Chrétien de Troyes with full confidence in the original, on the other hand there is the salutory fact that because of the increasing availability of reliable and readable translations of Chrétien and so many other medieval writers, more people have become familiar with Chrétien's genius and the richness of the vernacular literature to which he contributed. In this sense, translation serves culture and furthers knowledge of the target language.[2]

Chrétien himself was a translator and surely would not have looked down on the process as so many scholars do today. He tells us in the

---

[1] Quoted by Justin O'Brien, "From French to English," in *On Translation*, ed. Reuben A. Brower (New York: Oxford University Press, 1966), p. 79.

[2] See Renato Poggioli, "The Added Artificer," in *On Translation*, ed. Brower, pp. 137–47.

famous prologue to *Cligés* that he "translated Ovid's *Commandments* and the *Art of Love* into French" ("l'Art d'Amor an romans mist," line 3) and produced, as well, translations of several tales from Ovid's *Metamorphoses*.[3] Translation in the Middle Ages was a respected, even revered, occupation,[4] and imitation was considered the highest form of flattery. Writers like Chrétien, or Chaucer several centuries later, honed their linguistic and poetic skills by producing translations of material they admired and wished to imitate and emulate.

Medieval translation, however, was a very different undertaking from modern academic translation. It is more akin to what we might call "adaptation," a free rendering of an earlier text that concentrates more on what it says than how it says it—more on *matière* or *san* (to use Chrétien's terms)[5] than on form. When Chrétien set out to translate a story from Ovid's *Metamorphoses,* as he apparently did in the case of Philomela, he sought to convey not so much the words or the Latin poetic form as the meaning, or import, or—as he would put it—the *san* of the original. He did not hesitate to add anachronistic touches to make the text more comprehensible and enjoyable to his courtly patrons, or even to include entire developments that were not in Ovid. Yet I venture to say he still considered his work a "translation" of the Latin original. Similarly, modern "literary" translators such as Ezra Pound, Stuart Merrill, or Kenneth

---

[3]Chrétien de Troyes, *Arthurian Romances,* trans. William W. Kibler (*Erec and Enide* trans. Carleton W. Carroll) (Harmondsworth: Penguin, 1991), p. 123.

[4]One way to judge the prestige accorded the art of translation is to note the many writers engaged in the practice and the number of important patrons, many of them royal, who commissioned translations into the vernacular. It is clear from his preface to *Cligés* that Chrétien, one of the greatest of all vernacular poets, began his career by doing translations of Ovid and, perhaps, other Latin writers; Jean de Meun, the author of the second part of the *Roman de la Rose*, was himself one of the most prolific translators of his day; and by the fifteenth century such writers as Laurent de Premierfait and Jean de Vignay could make their reputations exclusively as translators. Henry II Plantagenêt and his wife Eleanor of Aquitaine, Philippe IV, and Charles V were among the most important royal patrons of vernacular translators; Charles's brother Jean, duc de Berry, the legendary collector, commissioned a number of translations for his personal library.

[5]From the prologue to *Le Chevalier de la Charrete.*

Rexroth seek not so much to reproduce the exact words or images or poetic patterns of the originals they translate as to convey the mood, or feeling, or tone of the original.

However, academic translators[6]—and I consider all modern English translations of Chrétien "academic translations," from W. W. Comfort, through D. D. R. Owens, David Staines, and myself, to Dorothy Gilbert, Ruth Harwood Cline, and Burton Raffel[7]—seek as much to convey the *matière* (and sometimes, as in the case of the last three translators cited, the form) as they do the *san*. They seek above all to be *faithful* to the original. Now "faithful" is a tricky term indeed, for there are many levels of fidelity. Literary translators accuse the academics of pedantically following the text word for word, seeking fidelity at the expense of elegance and grace, thereby robbing the work of its beauty and appeal. Academic translators accuse the literary practitioners of betraying or, worse yet, deforming the text, producing a new work that is more the creation of the translator than of the original author. Yet these same literary translators would claim to be more *faithful* to the original, for having captured its *san*, than the poor, "slavish" academic translator.

Both literary *and* academic translators are quick to admit, however, that their task is essentially an impossible one, particularly in the case of a writer like Chrétien, who is in complete control of all the resources of his art and who writes in a language that no one today completely understands,

---

[6]The distinction between "literary" and "academic" translators, and the quarrel between them, forms the starting point for most of the essays in Roger Shattuck and William Arrowsmith, *The Craft & Context of Translation, A Critical Symposium* (Austin: University of Texas Press, 1961; repr. Garden City, N.Y.: Anchor, 1964).

[7]See: *Arthurian Romances*, trans. D. D. R. Owen (London: Dent, 1987); *The Complete Romances of Chrétien de Troyes*, trans. David Staines (Bloomington: Indiana University Press, 1990); *Arthurian Romances*, trans. Kibler; *Yvain: or, the Knight with the Lion*, trans. Ruth Harwood Cline (Athens: University of Georgia Press, 1975); *Perceval: or, The Story of the Grail*, trans. Ruth Harwood Cline (Athens: University of Georgia Press, 1983); *Perceval, The Story of the Grail*, trans. Nigel Bryant (Cambridge: Brewer, 1982); *Yvain, The Knight of the Lion*, trans. Burton Raffel (New Haven: Yale University Press, 1987); and *Erec and Enide*, trans. Dorothy Gilbert (Berkeley: University of California Press, 1992).

employing technical and cultural terminology and evoking concepts and institutions that are no longer familiar to a modern reader.

Translating Chrétien from Old French to modern English is a very different (and more difficult!) task from translating a modern novel from French to English. Not only are there the usual problems of lexical inequivalencies, syntactic and formal differences between the original and target languages, false friends, and the like, but everything is complicated by the *alterity* of Chrétien's text. In what follows, I would like to look at three kinds of alterity that the would-be translator of Chrétien must inevitably face: first, in the form; second, in questions of grammar, syntax, and style; and third, in problems of culture and civilization, i.e., the fact that the concepts that inform Chrétien's narratives and the words he uses to convey those concepts often have no immediately recognizable equivalents in the modern idiom.

Chrétien composed his romances in a poetic form—the octosyllabic rhymed couplet—that has no convenient English metrical equivalent. Moreover, this poetic form was the accepted and usual medium for fictional narratives in Chrétien's twelfth century, whereas modern fiction is always in prose. (By a certain irony, in the generation that immediately followed Chrétien, prose was developed in the vernacular precisely because it had connotations of veracity and historicity by contrast to the fictional verse medium.)

No one handled the Old French octosyllabic couplet better than Chrétien. This relatively short line with frequent rhyme could become monotonous in untalented hands, but Chrétien used it with great freedom and sensitivity—varying his rhythms; adapting his rhymes and couplets to the ebb and flow of his sentence, rather than forcing his syntax to adhere to a rigidly repeated pattern; using repetition, word-play, and enjambment; combining sounds harmoniously through the repetition of complementary vowels and consonants; and using expressive cadences to highlight significant words. The closest formal English equivalent to the octosyllable is the iambic tetrameter, with its nearly obligatory caesura after every second foot. This generally produces herky-jerky, sing-song meter in English, much too monotonous, in my opinion, for a poem of any length. And should the would-be translator seek to complicate his task with rhymes, he quickly discovers that rhymes came much easier to Chrétien in Old French, with its many homonyms, parallel verbal endings, and infinitives, than they do in modern English. Where Chrétien's verse is noted for its smoothness, naturalness, and rhythmic flow—its ability to convey the rhythms of speech—modern rhyme is perceived by its hearer or reader as virtually opposed to natural speech rhythms. And while Chrétien's verse was produced for the ear—that is, was intended to be read aloud—a modern translation of Arthurian romance is intended for the eye, for silent reading. In my view, rhyme is quite simply an impediment to both understanding and appreciation.

I would even go so far as to contend that prose is the form Chrétien himself would have chosen for his fictions had he been writing today. Since the impressive triumph of the Vulgate Cycle of Arthurian romances in the early thirteenth century, virtually no one has produced a successful Arthurian work in verse—with the notable exception of Tennyson, who was writing poetic "idylls," rather than narrative fiction, anyway. Poetic treatments by Matthew Arnold, Edwin Arlington Robinson, Charles Williams, and others have met with virtually no success and remain largely unknown, even to the "happy few." But there has been a spate of recent Arthurian narratives in English: T. H. White's *The Once and Future King*; John Steinbeck's *The Acts of King Arthur and his Noble Knights*; Marion Zimmer Bradley's *The Mists of Avalon*; and Mary Stewart's *Merlin Trilogy*, to name only a few of the more notable.[8] All of these have been written in prose. To move from theory to commercial practicality: it is a fact of our contemporary society—however much we may individually regret it—that poetry does not "sell." The bald truth is that the overwhelming majority of modern readers are put off by verse and prefer prose.

But if we are to renounce verse and all its trappings, how are we to proceed? Chrétien is a poet of the twelfth century, and no one is going to alter that fact. To remove all signs of alterity in vocabulary, diction,

---

[8]White, *The Once and Future King* (London: Collins, 1958); Steinbeck, *The Acts of King Arthur and his Noble Knights* (New York: Farrar, Straus and Giroux, 1976); Bradley, *The Mists of Avalon* (New York: Knopf, 1982); and Stewart, *Merlin Trilogy*, 3 vols. (London: Hodder and Stoughton, 1970–79).

content, and tone is to write a new work. This might be within the domain and interests of the self-designated "literary translator," but it is certainly not within the purview of academic translation as currently practiced. However, a translation that is wholly faithful to the words and forms of Chrétien will produce a text that is unpalatable and probably incomprehensible to the modern reader. What must be sacrificed, and what kept? Must we maintain the ellipses, the loose syntax, the shifting tenses, the frequently post-positioned noun subjects, and the ambiguous pronouns of the original? I think not, for it is my belief that all of these traits—which are perfectly acceptable stylistically as practiced by the medieval poet—produce English that is garbled, awkward, or grammatically incorrect.

Let us start with extreme cases, ellipses of the subject and direct object pronouns, and pronouns without clear antecedents. I do not believe that even the most ardent academic translator could contend that in such cases we should follow the original too closely:

> De li ocirre est si estoute
> que sovant se prant a la gole;
> mes ainz se confesse a li sole,
> si se repant et bat sa colpe. (*Charrete*, lines 4180–83)[9]
> [To kill herself is so determined / that repeatedly grabs herself by the throat; / but first confesses to herself alone / and repents and beats her mea culpa.]

> ses armes vermoilles sont,
> Et vos li donastes, ce dit. (*Graal*, lines 2814–15)
> [His arms are red / And you gave him, this he says.]

Similarly, Old French allowed for a much looser syntax in the case of relative pronouns than do either modern French or English:

---

[9]Editions of Chrétien cited: *Erec and Enide*, ed. and trans. Carleton W. Carroll (New York: Garland, 1987); *Lancelot, or, The Knight of the Cart (Le Chevalier de la Charrete)*, ed. and trans. William W. Kibler (New York: Garland, 1981); *The Knight with the Lion, or, Yvain (Le Chevalier au Lion)*, ed. and trans. William W. Kibler (New York: Garland, 1985); and *The Story of the Grail (Li Contes del Graal), or, Perceval*, ed. Rupert T. Pickens, trans. William W. Kibler (New York: Garland, 1990).

que quant li rois un boen anplastre
me feisoit sor mes plaies metre,
qui molt se volsist antremetre
que j'eüsse tost garison. (*Charrete*, lines 4036–39)
[when the king a good bandage / caused on my wounds to be put / who very
much wanted to undertake / that I have quick healing.]

The "translations" just provided have been as obtusely literal as possible,
preserving word order and reflecting omitted pronouns. Whereas in certain
grammatical contexts subject and object pronouns are regularly omitted in
the older language, they are *necessary* in modern English (or French).
Without some basic accommodation to the syntax and grammar of the
target language, a translation is not even a translation, but merely a jumble
of meaningless words.

Although it may appear that I have been belaboring the obvious here—
and to some extent I have—there is, I believe, a more important point to
be made, since pronoun omissions and unclear antecedents in Old French
can lead to real difficulties in translating and genuine differences of opinion
among translators, as the following passage from the combat between Yvain
and Esclados le Roux in Chrétien's *Le Chevalier au Lion* illustrates:

Mes andui sont de si fier cuer
que li uns por l'autre a nul fuer
de terre .i. pié ne guerpiroit,
se jusqu'a mort ne l'enpiroit. (*Yvain*, lines 851–54)

Who will yield to whom in the last two lines: the person striking the blow,
or the person struck? The masculine singular direct object pronoun *le* (*l'* in
the last line cited) could refer to either, and the subject is unexpressed.
D. D. R. Owen, Burton Raffel, and I assume from the apparent logic of
the phrase that the person struck would yield, and translate accordingly:
"But both were knights of such heart / And such courage that neither
would ever / Yield a foot of ground / Until mortally wounded" (Raffel,
lines 851–54).[10] David Staines and Ruth Harwood Cline, in contrast,

---

[10]OWEN: "Yet they are both so stout-hearted that neither on any account would yield a
foot of ground to the other without being mortally wounded" (p. 292). KIBLER: "But each

applying the Old French grammatical "principal" that when the subject is not expressed it generally remains that of the previous verb, have: "But both men are so stouthearted that neither would yield a foot of ground until he delivered a fatal blow" (Staines, p. 267).[11] Grammar (I think) favors Staines and Cline, logic (I believe) favors Kibler, Raffel, and Owen; it is, at least in the light of our current knowledge of Old French syntax, impossible to be certain which Chrétien intended.

The following passage illustrates two further Old French stylistic traits that I would like to argue need to be adjusted to the modern idiom: tense shifting and post-positioned subjects:

> Qant Lanceloz l'ot correcier,
> de la pes feire et adrecier
> au plus qu'il onques puet se painne
> tant qu'il l'a feite. Lors l'en mainne
> li rois la reïne veoir.
> Lors ne lessa mie cheoir
> la reïne ses ialz vers terre. (*Charrete*, lines 4455–61)
> [When Lancelot heard her become angry / as quickly as he can he strives / to make and establish peace / until he made it. Then takes him / the king the queen to see. / Then did not at all let fall / the queen her eyes toward ground.]

Although not so literal as my earlier "translations," this is still far too close to the original, and it is evident that at least the two post-positioned subjects in the last four lines need to be changed: "Then the king takes him to see the queen; then the queen did not at all let her eyes fall toward ground." However, with these lines we come to the first point where genuine differences of opinion regarding style and grammar begin to arise among translators of Chrétien, for not all would agree that a single, consistent narrative tense is necessary, because expected, in the modern language. It has become almost a point of honor for some modern

---

was so proud of heart that neither would yield a foot of ground on any account, unless he were wounded to the death" (p. 305).

[11]CLINE: "Both warriors were of such worth / that neither'd yield a foot of earth / until he'd struck a deadly blow." (lines 797–99).

translators, most notably those rendering Chrétien or other medieval texts into modern French, to seek to convey the "medieval flavor" of the original by respecting the verb tenses in the narrative, claiming thereby to heighten "the dramatic tension of the narrative."[12] Upon closer inspection, however, not one of these translators sticks consistently with the tense sequencing used by the Old French poet, for indeed such would place an impossible strain on modern syntax and grammar. D. D. R. Owen, the only English translator of Chrétien to take this stance, fudges by saying, "[I retain] Chrétien's frequent switches of tense between past and present, except where a change seemed too offensive for even the tolerant ear."[13] So, in effect, he follows Chrétien's tenses when this is convenient and sacrifices them to modern usage when it is not. Such practice, to my mind, is logically and stylistically indefensible and, moreover, serves to give a quaintness to the text that is unwarranted.

Chrétien wrote in a perfectly contemporary style, using a syntax that was, if anything, in advance of his day, and he employed a rich, precise, and up-to-date descriptive vocabulary that avoided archaisms and mannered expressions. To seek to give an archaic feel to Chrétien's text, whether by quaint tense-shifting or the use of a pseudo-archaic "Scriptural" syntax and vocabulary (as in W. W. Comfort's translation), is, I firmly believe, to betray the very spirit of the original.

But this does not mean that one must sacrifice everything to modernity. I believe that the translator of medieval romance, particularly Chrétien's, must avoid the temptation to abridge, to eliminate the synonymic repetitions and other passages that challenge modern notions of artistic unity and decorum. Where Old French authors employed an exuberant manner of expression, preferring to "circle in" on a subject by using several often nearly synonymous nouns, adjectives, or verbs, our modern languages tend to prefer concision or, as the French would have it, *le mot juste*. But Chrétien's romances were destined for oral performance—were heard, rather than read. Where written culture favors brevity and conciseness, orality

---

[12]D. D. R. Owen, *Arthurian Romances*, p. xxv.

[13]Ibid.

tends to prolixity—as any Congressional debate or scholarly gathering will amply illustrate. While excessive repetition can be just as disagreeable in modern English as frequent tense shifting, I believe that a judicious use of paired synonyms can convey the pace and stately flavor of the original without offending our modern ears. Witness the following passage from *Yvain*:

> "Ma dameisele, ou sont
> cil qui vos blasment et ancusent?
> Tot maintenant, s'il nel refusent,
> lor iert la bataille arramie."
> Et cele qui ne l'avoit mie
> encor veü ne regardé
> li dit. . . . (*Yvain*, lines 4398–4404)

Within half a dozen lines there are two paired terms, "blasment et ancusent" and "veü ne regardé." While it would be simple to economize one term in each expression, the repetition, to my ear at least, adds to the harmony of the passage: "'My lady, where are those who condemn and accuse you? I shall challenge them to immediate battle, if they do not refuse it.' And she, who had until this moment not seen or noticed him, said. . . ."[14]

Just as we must not remove all vestiges of medieval style and syntax, we should not eliminate the many terms that refer to specifically medieval customs, institutions, or objects. Are we to do away with brattices, corbels, baileys, barbicans, hauberks,[15] mangonels, quintains, ventails, and tunics because we no longer live in castles or dress in armor? Are we to call all large, strong, herbivorous domestic mammals just "horses," because the

---

[14]This point gave rise to the most sustained discussion in the question-and-answer period following the presentation of this paper at the 28th Annual Congress on Medieval Studies, May 6–9, 1993 (Kalamazoo). Where such synonymic repetitions are widely viewed as stylistically and rhythmically effective in English, they are sensed as awkward and inappropriate in modern French—due largely, no doubt, to the stylistic strictures propagated by the Académie française since the seventeenth century.

[15]Raffel, for example, avoids English *hauberk* in favor of "mail," "shirt-mail," "mail from his armor" (line 4525); Cline has the redundant "hauberk's mesh of shining mail" (line 816).

distinction between palfreys for riding, sumpter horses for carrying burdens, and war-horses (*destriers*) for battle is no longer familiar in our motorized society? Are we to forego the wonderfully imprecise, but poetic, canonical hours—prime, terce, sext, none, vespers—in favor of some form of precision time-keeping that would have been wholly foreign to the medieval mind-set? Must *none* become "three p.m.," or *bas vespres* be translated "six o'clock" if it is winter, but "9:00 p.m." (or later) if the action of the passage occurs during the summer months? I hope not. Nor should we seek to convert other medieval measures, such as ells for cloth, or sestiers for wine, or deniers for coins, into modern equivalents that would necessarily imply a kind of false precision wholly foreign to medieval society.

While I would thus argue that we should and must retain terms that refer to medieval cultural artifacts and customs that may no longer be familiar to all modern readers, there is another set of high-frequency terms about which the translator must take special care. These are the false friends that arise between Old French and modern French or English, which is not at all the same group as the well-known *faux amis* between modern French and English. The Old French *faux amis* would include much of the courtly and pre-courtly vocabulary studied by Glyn Burgess[16]—words such as *courtoisie*,[17] *bon*, *aventure*, *franc*, *riche*, *preux*, *beau*—words that are highly charged semantically in Old French but which have often lost their specifically "courtly" connotations in modern usage—as well as a number of other terms that were used in special ways in medieval texts that may not be evident to someone having only a passing acquaintance with the culture of the Middle Ages.[18] Let me illustrate with a few examples from Chrétien.

In a famous scene in the *Chevalier au Lion*, Yvain comes upon a lion engaged in mortal combat with an adversary:

---

[16]Glyn S. Burgess, *Contribution à l'étude du vocabulaire pré-courtois* (Geneva: Droz, 1970).

[17]Is it "courtesy"? "courtliness"? or "brave," "noble"?

[18]A brief discussion of the problems in translating three such terms—*prouesse*, *largesse*, and *debonaireté*—is found in the "Remarques sur la traduction" by François Mosès, preceding his French translation of *Lancelot du Lac: roman français du XIIIᵉ siècle* (Paris: Librairie générale française, 1991), pp. 33–36.

vit .i. lyon en un essart,
et .i. serpent qui le tenoit
par la coe, et si li ardoit
trestot les rains de flame ardant. (3352–55)
. . . .
et li serpenz est venimeus,
si li saut par la boche feus (3363–64)

What exactly is this adversary? Two recent prose translations give "serpent,"[19] which at first glance seems the perfect English equivalent, if only because its "outer skin" is identical in modern English and Old French. Two recent verse translators prefer "snake,"[20] which is slightly more adventuresome and is probably what the first two translators understood by "serpent": a scaly, limbless reptile. But if we look attentively at the passage (and at our only illumination of it), it seems evident to me at least that we are not dealing with a serpent or snake at all but with what we in the modern world would term a fire-breathing dragon. I would contend that the words "snake" or "serpent" conjure up for the modern reader an inaccurate image, because very different from that most likely intended by Chrétien. Although I cannot prove conclusively that Chrétien had in mind a dragon rather than a snake as he composed his description of the fatal combat, at least that is the way the thirteenth-century illustrator of the only illuminated manuscript of Chrétien's romances, Princeton University Garrett 125, depicted the scene. *Serpent*, in this context at least, is therefore a *faux ami*.

A second potential false friend is *Bretaigne*, found for example in the opening line of *Le Chevalier au Lion*, "Artus, li boens rois de Bretaingne." Modern usage distinguishes insular Britain (*Grande Bretagne*) from continental Brittany, or "Lesser" Britain, but Chrétien used the one form "Bretaigne" for both, leaving it to the translator to indicate which he meant. To translate this line "Arthur, good king of Brittany," as Burton Raffel does, is to be misled by a *faux ami* of the old language and restrict dramatically the geographical extent of Arthur's legendary kingdom.

---

[19] Owen, *Arthurian Romances*, p. 326; Staines, *Complete Romances*, p. 297.

[20] Cline, *Yvain*, p. 95; Raffel, *Yvain*, p. 101.

A third term that occurs frequently in medieval Arthurian romance and that I have only recently come to realize may be, in some contexts, a *faux ami*, is *pensif/pensive*. Morphologically related to *penser* ("to think"), it sometimes has the positive connotation of "pensive, musing, thoughtful" as in *Perceval* 4412–13, "je estoie si pansis / D'un panser qui mout me pleisoit" ["I had been musing on a most pleasing thought," Staines, p. 394]. However, in eight of the twelve occurrences of the word in *Yvain, Lancelot,* and *Perceval*, it is paired semantically with a word meaning "sad": "pensif et mat et morne" (*L* 3923); "mornes et pansis" (*P* 9170); "dolant et pansif" (*L* 5436); "pensis et dolanz" (*Y* 3642); "angoisseus et pansis" (*Y* 547); "pansis et destroiz" (*Y* 4654); "pansis et muz" (*P* 891); and "mout correciez et mout pansis" (*P* 7993). Consulting the recent English translations listed above in note 7, I found it rendered in these eight instances variously as "pensive" (5x), "downcast" (3x), "worried" (2x), "in mournful thought" (2x), "confused" (2x), "brooding," "troubled," "depressed," "indignant," "vexed," "anxious," "upset," "contemplati[ve]," "angry," "sad," "absorbed in thought," and "filled with care." This is obviously quite a range of feelings for this single word to convey, and is testimony, I think, to the hesitation of the translators before a term that was in flux during the period in question. Godefroy glosses *pensif/pensive* in only one way, "qui pense," which is obviously inadequate. Tobler-Lommatzsch is scarcely more helpful, with "gedankenvoll, nachdenklich, besorgt, bekümmert" [pensive, reflective, anxious, distressed].

As has been noted above in the discussion of style, Chrétien, like most of his contemporaries, favored paired synonyms or binomial expressions. It is possible, I believe, to use the evidence of such binomials here to help in our interpretation of *pensif* in such contexts. In all of the above instances, "sad" would seem to provide an accurate translation for *pensif*. Of course that leaves one with the problem of how to translate *morne, dolent, destroiz, muz,* and *angoisseus*! But it does help fathom other instances in which *pansis* is not paired:

Li rois Artus fu asis / Au chief d'une table pansis (*Graal*, lines 887–88)
Li chevaliers d'aucune perte / Estoit pansis (*Graal*, lines 4326–27)
li chevaliers pansis (*Lancelot*, line 541)
Yvains pansis chemine (*Yvain*, line 3345)

Our translators have rendered *pensis* in these instances as "pensively" (4x), "thinking" (2x), "deep in thought" (2x), "lost in thought" (2x), "absorbed in thought," "immersed in thought," "dejectedly," "worriedly," "contemplating," "brooding," and "musing." Never as "sad." Certainly in the first two examples, both from *Le Conte du Graal,* a good case can be made for "sad." In the first instance, Arthur and his queen have just been insulted by the Red Knight, and no one has made a move to avenge them. In the second example, Gawain is suggesting to Arthur that Perceval, contemplating the three drops of blood on the snow, may be *pensis* for some loss he has suffered, such as having had his ladylove stolen from him. "Sad" would seem to fit both contexts very nicely.

In the third example, Lancelot, having ridden in the cart and slept in the strange bed in which he was wounded by a lance hurled mysteriously from the ceiling, is looking—might we not say "sadly"?—out the castle window over the rolling meadows. In my final example, Yvain has just defeated the enemy of the Lady of Noroison and spent a night in her castle. Reluctantly, the next morning, he must leave: "bien l'en poist / que plus remenoir ne li loist" (lines 3343–44; "it pained him that he could remain there no longer," Kibler, p. 337). I now believe that the line quoted above, in which Yvain rides off, could be more accurately rendered "Yvain rode *sadly* away" rather than "deep in thought" (Kibler), "absorbed in his thoughts" (Staines), "pensively" (Cline), or "immersed in his thoughts" (Owen).

As the foregoing examples make clear, I hope, translating Chrétien can be a challenge as well as a pleasure, and every choice made by the translator affects in some way the eventual reception of the text. The secret to translating Chrétien effectively, it seems to me, is to follow one of the precepts that the great Champenois master himself most fervently advocated: *mesure.* One must produce a translation that, while faithful to the ideas, institutions, and mores of medieval society, nonetheless seeks to make those distant concepts comprehensible, accessible, and pleasurable to the modern reader. A translator of a romance by Chrétien needs more than excellent competence in both the source and target languages (in our case, Old French and modern English). He needs an appreciation and affinity that go beyond the purely textual, allowing him to understand the nuances of the artistry and the subtleties of the civilization. He must seek not only the proper word or expression to convey cultural concepts from a distant and largely unfamiliar past, but also settle on the tone and form that are most appropriate to recreate in the modern reader the excitement, the wonder, the suspense, and the romance of the original. The vocabulary, syntax, tone, and form must all be appropriate to the task; they *need* not—indeed, they *must* not and *cannot* be literally the same as the original, or we would be left with the kind of gibberish evidenced by my "translations" of the first several passages cited above. The translator must "invent" a form and tone in English that will come as close as possible to evoking the sort of response in the modern reading audience that he senses the medieval text might have produced in Chrétien's listening public. He should not be a slave to the formal model of the original, especially when the effect of such imitation is to call attention to the form at the expense of the *matiere et san* (*Lancelot*, line 26). The judicious use of a concrete vocabulary, coupled with a slightly formulaic and repetitive style, is, in my opinion, a much better and more authentic way to convey some of the alterity of the medieval romance than to dislocate modern syntax or tense sequencing, or to imprison the fluidity and grace of Chrétien's octosyllabic rhyming couplets within the bars of an over-rigid prosody.

On Translating Chrétien de Troyes

David Staines

My translations of the romances of Chrétien de Troyes originated in "The Tradition of King Arthur," an undergraduate course I first developed at Harvard University in 1974. That course followed the Arthurian story from early Welsh literature all the way down to twentieth-century English literature. When some students complained that Geoffrey of Monmouth and Wace were dull, I promised them that beauty and wit were waiting in the romances of Chrétien de Troyes. My promise was, for many of these students, unfulfilled, for they confessed that they found little beauty and less wit in W. W. Comfort's translations. Their disappointment led to my foolhardy plan and ultimate commitment to translate all of Chrétien's romances.

Fifteen years later, when my translations were completed and about to be published, the publisher invited me to add a prefatorial statement on the nature of my translations. My own experience as a translator bore out Richmond Lattimore's observation that "The translator, if he is human, will deal with most problems as he meets them. His principles will come out later, by way of self-explanation, or self-defence."[1] During my fifteen-year dedication to Chrétien, I found little distance or, indeed, incentive to formulate my own principles. The less said, I thought then, the better, and I turned for support to Paul Valéry, who offers so many cogent reflections on poetry and the difficulties inherent in translating it. In my prefatorial "Note on the Translation," I devoted five sentences to my understanding of the impossible but necessary task of translation:

---

[1]Richmond Lattimore, "Practical Notes on Translating Greek Poetry," in *On Translation*, ed. Reuben A. Brower (New York: Oxford University Press, 1966), p. 48.

"A true poet is strictly untranslatable," wrote Paul Valéry, poet and critic. And yet such an assertion of the impossibility of translating poetry—a humbling warning indeed—has been no deterrent, even to Valéry himself.

In these translations of the romances of Chrétien de Troyes, I have tried to capture in modern English prose the meaning and the emphases of the original French poems. I have deliberately avoided archaic words and phrases, for Chrétien's language did not employ archaisms, and I have also avoided contemporary colloquialisms, which seem inappropriate to his style. Although my prose cannot reproduce the rhyme or the rhythm of Chrétien's octosyllabic couplets, I hope these translations suggest something of the beauty and the wit of the original poetry.[2]

It was toward the end of his life that Valéry uttered most fully his affirmation of the impossibility of translating great poetry. In his lecture, "Allocution solennelle," delivered from the stage of the Théâtre Français on September 4, 1939, he proclaimed:

Whereas the painter, the sculptor, and the musician may reach a foreign public, may be understood far beyond the boundaries of their own country, create an international work, a poet is never profoundly, intimately, and completely understood and felt but by his own people: he is inseparable from the speech of his nation. But for him this speech is more living than for his fellows; he guesses at and uses its most special resources and neglected musical riches; he makes precious objects out of qualities of speech to which the majority are insensitive and which he reveals through his art. He pays back to his country in currency of gold what he had received in ordinary speech. But all this restricts him still more to the special fact of belonging to his country. You will observe, indeed, that the prose writer, the novelist, the philosopher, the moralist can be translated, and often are, without too much damage. But to the poet belongs the privilege and the inevitable disadvantage that his work cannot be translated either into prose or into a foreign language. A true poet is strictly untranslatable; with him form and thought are equally powerful; the virtue of the poem is one and indivisible. Our art, then, is made of the body and spirit of the French language, and this truth, so palpably felt, leads us to apprehend the true function of a poet, the very real importance of his role, both as I have defined it and in the preservation of the homeland.[3]

---

[2] *The Complete Romances of Chrétien de Troyes*, trans. David Staines (Bloomington: Indiana University Press, 1990), p. xxix.

[3] Paul Valéry, *The Art of Poetry*, trans. Denise Bernard-Folliot, ed. Jackson Mathews (New York: Pantheon, 1958), pp. 270–71.

Valéry's admission of the impossibility of translating poetry reflected his definition of poetry itself, an art, he proclaimed in the same speech, "whose productions are made of words and forms of speech: an art of language." As a consequence, he noted, "of all arts, poetry is the one most essentially and eternally linked to a people, who are the principal author of the language it uses."[4]

Two years after this lecture, Valéry wrote a preface to *Les Cantiques spirituels de St. Jean de la Croix,* a new reprint of the sixteenth-century Spanish poet's *Spiritual Canticles* in their 1641 French translation by Reverend Father Cyprian of the Nativity of the Virgin. His high praise for these translations emphasizes his affirmation of the impossibility of poetic translation and the simultaneous necessity of making such an attempt. Father Cyprian, Valéry observed, translated successfully:

> It is impossible to be more faithful—even though our reverend translator has modified the type of stanza. He had adopted our octosyllabics instead of following the variations of the original meter. He realized that prosody must suit the language, and unlike other translators (particularly in the sixteenth and nineteenth centuries), he has not attempted to impose on French what French does not itself impose on or propose to the French ear. This is really to *translate,* which is to reconstitute as nearly as possible the *effect* of a certain *cause*—here, a text in Spanish—by means of *another cause,* a text in French.
>
> In doing this, Father Cyprian has enriched our poetry, although in the most discreet (and until now almost imperceptible) way by a very slender collection, which is, however, of a most assured and pure quality.[5]

For Valéry, Father Cyprian was a translator and a poet, and, confronting the verse of St. John of the Cross, he saw the challenge: "the most exquisite poetic gifts had to be exercised under the most adverse conditions." Father Cyprian

> did not allow himself the joy of discovering within himself the unexpected beauties which the dialogue between the idea and the mind gives rise to. On the

---

[4]Valéry, *The Art of Poetry,* p. 270.
[5]Valéry, *The Art of Poetry,* p. 286.

contrary. . . . His originality is: to admit of none; and yet he makes a kind of masterpiece by producing poems whose substance is not his own and each word of which is prescribed by a given text.[6]

Father Cyprian was a poet, and Valéry regarded his translations as unique poems: translations where their author himself is non-existent, making himself the transparent purveyor of the world of St. John of the Cross.

Valéry's contemporary Ezra Pound, himself too a critic, a poet, and a translator, would not have approved of Father Cyprian's translations. He did not seek fidelity in translation:

In the long run the translator is in all probability impotent to do *all* of the work for the linguistically lazy reader. He can show where the treasure lies, he can guide the reader in choice of what tongue is to be studied, and he can very materially assist the hurried student who has a smattering of a language and the energy to read the original text alongside the metrical gloze.[7]

Pound calls a poetic translation an "interpretative translation . . . where the 'translater' is definitely making a new poem."[8] And Pound's own translations, whether from the Greek, the Anglo-Saxon, or the Chinese, reflect his commitment to a not necessarily faithful, definitely interpretative translation, for he sought not to learn carefully the languages he was translating but, rather, to interpret the world of his source in a new poem.

"Interpretative translation," the work of the true poet as both Pound and Valéry would agree, is a re-creation of the original work. The interpretative translator uses the work as the starting point for a re-creation, but observes no necessary or even desired fidelity to it. Close textual fidelity incurred Pound's wrath:

English translators have gone wide in two ways, first in trying to keep every adjective, when obviously many adjectives in the original have only melodic value,

---

[6]Valéry, *The Art of Poetry*, pp. 291–92.

[7]Ezra Pound, "Cavalcanti," in *Literary Essays of Ezra Pound*, ed. T. S. Eliot (Norfolk, Conn.: New Directions, 1954), p. 200.

[8]Pound, "Cavalcanti," p. 200.

secondly they have been deaved with syntax; have wasted time, involved their English, trying first to evolve a definite logical structure for the Greek and secondly to preserve it, *and all its grammatical relations*, in English. . . . certainly more sense and less syntax (good or bad) in translations . . . might be a relief.[9]

The only interpretative translator is the poet, although, as Octavio Paz recognizes, the quality of the interpretative translation is not necessarily high:

In theory, only poets should translate poetry; in practice, poets are rarely good translators. They almost invariably use the foreign poem as a point of departure toward their own. A good translator moves in the opposite direction: his intended destination is a poem analogous although not identical to the original poem. He moves away from the poem only to follow it more closely.[10]

Pound did not develop his concept of "interpretative translation," but such a development may be central to a proper understanding of scholarly translation, which is such a prominent dimension of twentieth-century translation practice. To borrow Pound's terminology, scholarly translation is non-interpretative translation. The interpretative translation is the labor of the poet, the interpretative translation being a new poem. The non-interpretative translation is the labor of the scholar, the non-interpretative translation being a prose rendering, a reproduction rather than a re-creation of the original work.

The primary aim of the non-interpretative translator is fidelity, not word-for-word fidelity, but a fidelity to the sense that is rooted in the words themselves. An interpretative translation, by its nature as a new poem, must eschew fidelity as a primary principle, for its primary aim is the new poem; that new work is a poem written by a poet, even though it is rooted in another text.

Chrétien de Troyes has not been the focus of interpretative translators. Ruth Harwood Cline laudably attempts to capture in modern English

---

[9]Ezra Pound, "Translators of Greek: Early Translators of Homer," in *Literary Essays of Ezra Pound*, ed. Eliot, p. 273.

[10]Octavio Paz, "Translation: Literature and Letters," trans. Irene del Corral, in *Theories of Translation: An Anthology of Essays from Dryden to Derrida*, ed. Rainer Schulte and John Biguenet (Chicago: University of Chicago Press, 1992), p. 158.

Chrétien's octosyllabic couplets. "The purpose of this verse translation," she writes,

> is to give English-speaking readers an impression of Chrétien de Troyes as a poet as well as a storyteller. . . . Chrétien de Troyes depended upon rhyme and meter to establish the swift pace of his romances. He used poetical images and metaphors, and frequently he employed the poetic device of rephrasing and repeating an important idea to fix it against the forward movement of the poem. These effects are lost in prose translations; worse, they seem prolix or redundant and become barriers against appreciating Chrétien's skill as a writer, which was very great.[11]

Since Cline herself is not a poet, her translations of *The Knight with the Lion, The Story of the Grail,* and *The Knight of the Cart* do not become poems in their own right, though, like interpretative translations, they often take the liberty of ignoring whole lines or longer passages to conform to the rigid octosyllabic couplets, which are out-of-place in contemporary English poetry.[12]

Dorothy Gilbert's translation of *Erec and Enide* proves less satisfying than Cline's translations. Gilbert defines her mode of translation:

> A verse translator works with a list of compelling priorities, one that demands constant reexamination. Meter must be absolutely right; rhythm must be appropriate, whether rapid, slow, smooth, or broken unexpectedly for a purpose. At times the rhythm may be like a glassy river with scarcely a ripple; at other times it will "work like a sea." Rhyme must be consistently effective, without too monotonous a chime.[13]

Fidelity, Gilbert notes, "is added to these considerations" and, therefore, is secondary to them.

---

[11]Chrétien de Troyes, *Yvain: or, The Knight with the Lion,* trans. Ruth Harwood Cline (Athens: University of Georgia Press, 1975), pp. xvi–xvii.

[12]See Cline's translations of *Yvain,* and *Perceval, or, The Story of the Grail* (New York: Pergamon, 1983), and *Lancelot, or, The Knight of the Cart* (Athens: University of Georgia Press, 1990).

[13]Chrétien de Troyes, *Erec and Enide,* trans. Dorothy Gilbert (Berkeley: University of California Press, 1992), p. 29.

Interpretative translations require translators who are true poets. When they are undertaken by such non-poets as Cline and Gilbert, the result is non-poetry, neither poetry of its own time nor a re-creation of its source's poetry. The non-poet belongs in the domain of the non-interpretative translation.

My initial choice of rendering Chrétien's poetry in prose reflected my own commitment to non-interpretative translation where fidelity to sense is the primary principle.

My second choice was the form of language: "I have deliberately avoided archaic words and phrases, for Chrétien's language did not employ archaisms, and I have also avoided contemporary colloquialisms, which seem inappropriate to his style."[14] In other words, non-interpretative translation demands a sensible and sensitive journey that avoids, on the one hand, archaisms, and, on the other, colloquialisms. Such a translation must speak *to* and *of* its time, while never violating the level of style of the original.

If Ezra Pound offers the concept of non-interpretative translation, another English critic, poet, and translator, John Dryden, presents the first detailed classification in English of the function and position of translators. As Rainer Schulte and John Biguenet point out in their anthology *Theories of Translation*:

> Already in his time, [Dryden] mapped the diverse streams of translational thinking, streams that forged the guidelines for the discussions of more recent times. Some of his formulations have become all too familiar to those who have launched themselves, successfully or unsuccessfully, into the practice of translation.[15]

For Dryden, there are three kinds of translation: metaphrase, "turning an author word by word, and line by line, from one language into another"; paraphrase, "translation with latitude, where the author is kept in view by the translator, so as never to be lost, but his words are not so strictly followed as his sense, and that too is admitted to be amplified, but not

---

[14] *The Complete Romances*, trans. Staines, p. xxix.

[15] *Theories of Translation*, ed. Schulte and Biguenet, p. 1.

altered"; and imitation, "where the translator (if now he has not lost that name) assumes the liberty not only to vary from the words and sense, but to forsake them both as he sees occasion; and taking only some general hints from the original, to run division on the ground-work, as he pleases."[16]

Whereas Dryden's "imitation" is a variation and extension of Pound's "interpretative translation," his first two categories, "metaphrase" and "paraphrase," are divisions of my non-interpretative translation. "Metaphrase," as Dryden cautioned, runs the risk of pedanticism: "Too faithfully is, indeed, pedantically: 'tis a faith like that which proceeds from superstition, blind and zealous," and he wisely concluded: "'Tis almost impossible to translate verbally, and well, at the same time."[17]

Dryden's "paraphrase" is the ideal non-interpretative translation. The middle ground between the literalism of "metaphrase" and the license of "imitation," to borrow Willis Barnstone's terminology,[18] "paraphrase" or "translation with latitude" honors the words of the original while strictly following their sense. And one observation Dryden makes about "imitation" is a further and necessary caution to non-interpretative translators:

> I take imitation of an author . . . to be an endeavour of a later poet to write like one who has written before him on the same subject; that is, not to translate his words, or to be confined to his sense, but only to set him as a pattern, and to write, as he supposes that author would have done, had he lived in our age, and in our country.[19]

Non-interpretative translators must imagine "what the author would have done, had he lived in our age, and in our country"; the distance between the translation's audience and the original audience demands such an imagining. These translators, if they are to be in any way part of their own

---

[16]John Dryden, "Preface to *Ovid's Epistles*," in *Of Dramatic Poesy and Other Critical Essays*, vol. 1, ed. George Watson (London: Dent, 1962), p. 268.

[17]Dryden, "Preface to *Ovid's Epistles*," pp. 268–69.

[18]Willis Barnstone, *The Poetics of Translation: History, Theory, Practice* (New Haven: Yale University Press, 1993), pp. 26–27.

[19]Dryden, "Preface to *Ovid's Epistles*," p. 270.

time, must reflect their own world as well as their original's world. What is demanded is to find the balance, to do justice to the original in the garment of the present time without the present detracting from the original by calling almost exclusive attention to itself. When attention focuses more on the present translation as a self-contained object, the translator has abandoned non-interpretative translation for the more self-centered world of interpretative translation.

Let me present an example of an original disappearing in a translator's self-absorbed exclusivity. From the opening of Book II of Ovid's *Ars Amatoria,* I quote Peter Green's fine translation:

> Why hurry, young man? Your ship's still in mid-passage,
>   and the harbour I seek is far away.
> Through my verses, it's true, you may have *acquired* a mistress,
>   but that's not enough. If my art
> Caught her, my art must keep her. To guard a conquest's
>   as tricky as making it. There was luck in the chase,
> but *this* task will call for skill.

In his essay "Metre, Fidelity, Sex: The Problems Confronting a Translator of Ovid's Love Poetry," Green quotes a negative reader for the press, who recommended the following more contemporary and supposedly better translation of the same lines:

> But what's your hurry, callow youth?
> You're far from court, and that's the truth.
> I won your dolly by my art:
> Her body's yours, but where's her heart?
> You can't rely on Lady Luck
> for more than just an easy fuck.[20]

This suggested translation forsakes Ovid and his world for a relentless commitment to the contemporary and the vulgar.

---

[20]Peter Green, "Metre, Fidelity, Sex: The Problems Confronting a Translator of Ovid's Love Poetry," in *The Translator's Art: Essays in Honour of Betty Radice*, ed. William Radice and Barbara Reynolds (Harmondsworth, Middlesex: Penguin, 1987), p. 104.

Closer to my subject are the opening three lines of Chrétien's *Erec and Enide*, which I quote from my own translation: "The Peasant has a proverb: 'What you scorn may be worth more than you think'."[21] Dorothy Gilbert, on the other hand, translates the same lines:

> The Peasant in his proverb says
> that a scorned object often is
> truly a prize and a windfall.[22]

The Peasant's proverbial saying, focusing on the scorner, becomes, in Gilbert's translation, an impersonal aphorism, and the word "windfall," replete with its contemporary connotations of materialism, stock markets, and recessions, calls attention to the translator and her time, not to Chrétien and his poem.

The path between the Scylla of archaisms and the Charybdis of colloquialisms is the route the non-interpretative translator must constantly seek. Any archaic phrasing or contemporary usage that jars the reader out of Chrétien's fictive world calls attention to itself and the translator, and this jarring is a violation of the primary role of the non-interpretative translator, namely to be the servant of the original poem and, as nearly as possible, the transparent purveyor of the original to his or her own audience and time. Transparency is the aim of the non-interpretative translator, the surrender or extinction of the self in the service of the original author. Transparency is not the aim of interpretative translators, who deliberately choose to call attention to their creation as their *own* work, who surrender not themselves but, to some degree, the original author. Non-interpretative translators want the original work to be reflected as fully and as clearly as possible: "A real translation is transparent; it does not cover the original, does not block its light, but allows the pure language, as though reinforced by its own medium, to shine upon the original all the more fully."[23]

---

[21] *The Complete Romances*, trans. Staines, p. 1.

[22] *Erec and Enide*, trans. Gilbert, p. 41.

[23] Walter Benjamin, "The Task of the Translator," trans. Harry Zohn, in *Illuminations*, ed. Hannah Arendt (New York: Schocken, 1969), p. 79.

Complementing the transparency of the non-interpretative translation is its necessary dependence upon earlier editions of its text, relevant textual and critical studies, and all the scholarly investigations that come to bear on that text. Such dependence gives the translator the maximum capability to enter the world of the text with all the knowledge currently available.

My acknowledgements to *The Complete Romances of Chrétien de Troyes* open with an admission:

> Like many teachers, I have introduced my students to the romances of Chrétien de Troyes through the translations of W. Wistar Comfort, which were first published in 1914 in the . . . Everyman Library. . . . My dissatisfaction with Comfort's *Arthurian Romances* does not diminish my respect for his unique achievement: at a time when comparatively little editorial and critical study of Chrétien had taken place, Comfort was indeed a pioneer.[24]

There are, of course, differences between Comfort's translations and my own, and one important difference is the immense scholarship now available to the translator of Chrétien. Whereas interpretative translators often eschew too much information about the original text, non-interpretative translators thrive on the growing body of knowledge, which diminishes the distance between the translator and the original text.

The unique dependence of non-interpretative translators on scholarly materials places them finally in a location different from that of interpretative translators. Scholarship provides maximum access to the world of the original text, and non-interpretative translators attempt to live in the world of their source whereas interpretative translators deliberately remain in their own private world, bringing their text into their world and not burdening themselves with the relentless need to stay as close to the original as possible. This burden of dependence is also the privilege of dependence, the privilege of dwelling in another world, in living with an author, and, finally, in coming to know that writer and his or her writing as closely as is humanly possible given the realities of spatial and temporal distances.

---

[24] *The Complete Romances*, trans. Staines, p. vii.

"A true poet is strictly untranslatable," affirmed Paul Valéry, yet he himself was a translator as well as a critic and a poet. Translation is a challenge: to undertake an impossible task, and to settle for an always unsatisfying product. For the non-interpretative translator, there is a unique reward if the challenge is accepted: to serve an author by extinguishing the self and seeking transparency results in an exclusive privilege, the privilege of living in another world, of living in another's world.

DATE DUE

			Printed in USA

HIGHSMITH #45230